GAME OF MY LIFE

NEW YORK

METS

GAME OF MY LIFE

NEW YORK

METS

MEMORABLE STORIES OF METS BASEBALL

MICHAEL GARRY

Foreword by Howie Rose

SPORTS
PUBLISHING

Sports Publishing books may be purchased in bulk at special discounts for sales promotion, corporate gifts, fund-raising, or educational purposes. Special editions can also be created to specifications. For details, contact the Special Sales Department, Sports Publishing, 307 West 36th Street, 11th Floor, New York, NY 10018 or sportspubbooks@skyhorsepublishing.com.

Sports Publishing® is a registered trademark of Skyhorse Publishing, Inc.®, a Delaware corporation.

Visit our website at www.sportspubbooks.com.

10 9 8 7 6 5 4 3 2 1

Library of Congress Cataloging-in-Publication Data is available on file.

Jacket design by Tom Lau
Cover photo credit AP Images

ISBN: 978-1-61321-761-0
Ebook ISBN: 978-1-61321-784-9

Printed in the United States of America

This book is dedicated to my wife, Maureen, and my son, Ethan, for their love and support,

And to my late parents, Frances and Sol,

And to my Aunt May, for always being there for me.

CONTENTS

ACKNOWLEDGMENTS

They say it takes a village to raise a child; it took at least that to write this book.

I am obliged to first thank Jon Springer, my erstwhile colleague at *Supermarket News*, and the author of the book and website *Mets by the Numbers* for recommending me to Skyhorse Publishing.

My second thanks goes to Julie Ganz, my editor at Skyhorse Publishing, for believing I could do this and for serving as a constant sounding board throughout the challenging process of trying to "meet the Mets."

I deeply appreciate the efforts of Harris Schoenfeld, the Mets' coordinator for marketing and communications, who set up phone interviews for me with Edgardo Alfonzo, Ed Kranepool, and Ed Charles (the three Eds). This happened early in my research and was a springboard for everything that followed.

I owe a special debt of gratitude to Doug Dickey, the Mets' coordinator for special projects, corporate sales, and partnerships, for giving me access to the players at the Mets 2014 Fantasy Camp. During two glorious January days there, I met with Ron Swoboda, Al Jackson, Felix Millan, John Stearns, Eric Hillman, Anthony Young, Turk Wendell, and Todd Pratt.

Another person whose early help proved crucial is Meg Aldrich, owner, Talk Communications. She provided me access to a Nesquik-sponsored wiffle ball event in September 2013 at Citi Field's parking lot that raised money for the Madison Square Boys & Girls Club. It was there that I met the honorary coaches, Edgardo Alfonzo and Bud Harrelson, and through Edgardo, Harris Schoenfeld.

The person who tipped me off about the wiffle ball opportunity, Greg Prince, was an enormously helpful resource. Greg, who during the baseball season provides daily inspiration with erudite, funny, and brilliantly written observations about the Mets on his blog "Faith and Fear in Flushing" (which he shares with his equally talented colleague, Jason Fry), recommended a variety of helpful avenues. In addition, the first volume of his history of Mets victories, *The Happiest Recap, First Base: 1962-1973*, was one of my best guides to the early Mets.

I would like to thank Lorraine Hamilton, the Mets' senior director for broadcasting & special events, for arranging my two-day field press pass for the 2014 spring training camp, and Jay Horwitz, the Mets' vice president of media relations, for signing the pass when I arrived at Tradition Field in Port St. Lucie, Fla. At spring training I spoke to Daniel Murphy, Jon Niese, Dillon Gee, Travis d'Arnaud, Tim Teufel, and Frank Viola. I was also able to converse with the Mets' great radio broadcaster Howie Rose, who generously shared memories of the game of his broadcasting life, Johan Santana's no-hitter. I am also honored that Howie wrote the foreword to this book. WFAN's Ed Coleman passed along to me that the game of his broadcasting life was the Todd Pratt walk-off-homer playoff game in 1999 vs. Arizona.

In a few cases, I was able to connect with former players simply by reaching out to them directly, and I am especially grateful to those individuals. Benny Agbayani was the first Met I interviewed after he graciously returned a phone message I left for him at work. Bobby J. Jones called me after receiving a US mail-delivered letter, which initially went to someone else in the Fresno, California, area named Bobby Jones; I'd like to thank the other Bobby Jones for passing along my letter to the pitcher.

In mailing letters to former and current Mets, I referred to Harvey Meiselman's 2014 Baseball Address List.

Jane Allen Quevedo, the co-author of Felix Millan's autobiography, *Tough Guy, Gentle Heart*, put me in touch with Felix, who spoke to me on the phone from Puerto Rico. I was able to meet Jane; her husband, Carlos; Felix; and his wife, Mercy, at Fantasy Camp. All four are wonderful people who added immeasurably to the book.

My dear friend Steve Aaronson, whom I've known since our chance meeting at MIT's Baker House dormitory in 1973, was my photographer and assistant at Fantasy Camp, and made that trip more fun, productive, and memorable than it would otherwise have been.

A special note of gratitude goes to attorney Alan Neigher, who generously provided valuable legal advice at the outset of this project.

Steve Jacobson, retired sports reporter and columnist for *Newsday*, and author of *Carrying Jackie's Torch*, graciously offered insights about Al Jackson, Ed Charles, Casey Stengel, and the early days of the Mets, which he covered first-hand.

The following people also contributed time and advice: Mark Rosenman (host of SportsTalkNY, WLIE, 540 am), Gary Perone, Nick Diunte, Chris Mack, Jordan Weiss, Paul Kocak, Gary Velez, Howard Pripas, Barry Horn (Dallas Morning News), and Fred Lief (Associated Press).

Much of my Mets-watching at Shea Stadium and Citi Field over the past 30 years has been done in the company of another dear friend, Ron Faber, and in more recent years, his son, Ben Faber. Thanks, guys, for the great company and the many Mets-focused discussions, debates, and trivia contests.

Projects of this type require considerable forbearance from one's family, and I have received more than my share from my wife, Maureen, and my son, Ethan, whose love and support never waver.

Finally, I'd like to thank the many Mets fans I have encountered in my life. These are people I had never met before but with whom I would easily strike up baseball conversations based on my Mets cap or their Mets T-shirt, whether at an airport or in a supermarket or sitting next to me at the ballpark. Sports, like music, is a kind of universal language, and loving a particular team opens up lines of communication like few other things in life.

And thanks to the Mets for making life interesting.

Michael Garry
August 2014

FOREWORD

I've learned something over the years about major league baseball players. Their recall about famous big league games that took place when they were kids is rather limited, and for a very good reason. They weren't watching! Time after time I have brought up a famous play from a classic game in conversation with a player, only to get a blank stare or a shrug of the shoulder in return. When I ask any of these players how it can possibly be that he can't recite chapter and verse about a seminal moment in a particular season, invariably the response is the same.

"How should I know? I was busy playing, not watching!"

When you think about it for a moment, it makes sense. Anyone blessed with the ability to play major league baseball had to spend morning, noon, and night honing those skills. Most Valuable Players could not have been couch potatoes. The rest of us, however, have a much different story to tell.

A great deal of my youth was spent sitting in the upper deck at Shea Stadium, watching some of the games described by the participants in this book. Ron Swoboda, for example, speaks about what most of us consider to be the defining moment of his major league career. His unforgettable catch in the 1969 World Series will always be his signature, but for me, a home run he hit three years earlier remains one of my favorite baseball memories.

On August 4, 1966, the Mets played the San Francisco Giants at Shea Stadium. Future Hall of Famer Juan Marichal pitched for the Giants against New York's Dennis Ribant. The Mets, in the fifth year of their existence, had never beaten Marichal, and this did not appear to be the day that streak would come to a close. San Francisco built a 3-0 lead entering the bottom of the sixth inning, and Marichal was working on a perfect game. With two out in the bottom of the inning, and Marichal still perfect, Mets manager Wes Westrum surprisingly allowed Ribant to hit for himself. Sure enough, Ribant hit a little 38 hopper through the middle for the Mets' first hit, but the inning ended with the Giants still ahead 3-0.

After they added two runs in the seventh to increase their lead to 5-0 with Marichal still in command, the game appeared to be over. However, the Mets chipped away, and trailed 6-4 going to the bottom of the ninth inning. When Ken Boyer homered to lead off against an out-of-gas Marichal to make it 6-5, the Giants went to the bullpen, and eventually, with one out and two runners aboard, Swoboda hit a pinch hit homer against Bill Henry and the Mets won the ballgame 8-6.

To this twelve-year-old seated in the upper deck, it was the greatest game ever played. The Mets hadn't beaten Marichal, but they sure did beat the Giants. Ron Swoboda became an instant idol, and all the way home I told myself that I would never forget the date. Every year on August 4th I think back to 1966 and recall with a smile how even though I hadn't played, and certainly had no clue about what was coming three years later when the Mets shocked the world and became World Champions, this was, even though I was not yet a teenager, the Game of My Life.

I sincerely hope you enjoy reading about the magical moments in the careers of so many Mets favorites who were not seated in the upper deck, and certainly weren't playing the role of couch potato when they took part in the games of their lives.

Howie Rose
December, 2014

INTRODUCTION

In every major league baseball game, there is usually at least one moment of unexpected beauty—an over-the-shoulder catch, a towering home run into the upper deck, a knee-buckling curveball strikeout—that leaves an indelible impression on fans in the stands or those watching on TV or even listening on the radio.

Amid the balls and strikes, routine grounders, and between-inning fanfare, it's what we take away with us and what makes us look forward to the next game. Ultimately, beyond the wins and losses, those moments are why we love baseball.

For big league players, the power of those moments is even more pronounced. More than the money, more than the glory, it's why they play this very hard game. It's what they live for. And for most players, there is one moment or group of moments that stands out from the rest, and makes them smile and reflect—in short, the game of their life.

This book is about 25 big league ballplayers—an active roster's worth—who have played for the New York Mets, and the game of each player's life. The players and their stories span the 52-year-old history of New York's National

League franchise, which was created to replace the Brooklyn Dodgers and the New York Giants after they abandoned New York City for California (unthinkable!) after the 1957 season. Every position on the diamond is represented.

The chapters are presented chronologically, starting with "Little" Al Jackson, the best pitcher on the original 1962 Mets team, and ending with catcher Travis d'Arnaud, one of the building blocks (we hope) of the Mets' future.

The games of their life are as diverse and unique as the players themselves, from Ron Swoboda's diving World Series catch to Edgardo Alfonzo's historic six-for-six, to David Wright's Shea Stadium-quaking playoff excitement.

As befits a team with the checkered history of the Mets, not every player's most unforgettable game was in a winning cause. Al Jackson, Ed Kranepool, Anthony Young, and Travis d'Arnaud played the game of their life in contests that the Mets lost. With others—Bud Harrelson and Daniel Murphy, for example—it was the victory that made the game special rather than anything the player did. Many of these games, of course, took place during the playoffs or World Series. Other players hold their first game in the big leagues very close to their heart.

Each chapter breaks out the player's most memorable game and puts it in the context of his overall career and life, since no unforgettable moment or game happens in a vacuum.

Most of the chapters are based on interviews I conducted with each player—on the phone, at the Mets 2014 Fantasy Camp, at their 2014 spring training workouts, or in one case (Bud Harrelson) at Citi Field. In each of these interviews, the player identified the game he considers the game of his life. In some cases these interviews were supplemented by third-party sources, such as newspaper accounts and online data, all of which are listed at the end of the book.

In a handful of instances, I wrote about players I was not able to interview directly by using third-party material. These are individuals who starred in games that are widely regarded as iconic and central to the Mets' story—the games of our lives—as well as closely linked to the players themselves, i.e., Mike Piazza and the first post-9/11 game; Mookie Wilson and the "Bill Buckner" World Series game; and Johan Santana and the Mets' first and, as of this writing, only no-hitter. I also have a chapter on David Wright based on his public comments citing the 2006 playoffs, and particularly game seven of the National League Championship Series, as his peak Mets experience so far.

Two of the Mets' greatest pitchers—Dwight Gooden and Tom Seaver—do not have their own chapters. I had a few meetings with "Doc" and numerous email exchanges with his agent, but it turned out that his favorite memory as a player was throwing a no-hitter for the Yankees while his father was hospitalized and severely ill; it was the last game his father saw him pitch. This, though, is a Mets book.

Seaver, known as Tom Terrific and "The Franchise" and the Mets' sole Hall-of-Fame player, declined through Karen Seaver, his niece and the business manager at Seaver Vineyards, in Calistoga, California, where he makes Cabernet Sauvignon. She wrote me in an email that Seaver wasn't available to interview while he was working on treating his Lyme disease.

I interviewed the Mets' great home run hitter Darryl Strawberry in 2011 at a Bronx supermarket about nutrition and childhood autism (a cause he has taken on). Last year, at an autograph signing event, I asked him about the game of his life as a Met. He replied that there were so many big games it was hard to isolate one.

Though these players don't have individual chapters, they are referenced in the book. Seaver, for example, is a big part of the Ron Swoboda chapter, since he threw the pitch that Swoboda so magnificently caught in Game Four of the 1969 World Series. "I never realized before that a man's whole life could be encompassed in a single play, in a single game, in a single day," Seaver once said about that game.

Finally, on a personal note, I would like to say that this book was undoubtedly the "project of my life" to date as a journalist, full of wonderful interactions with Mets players that I never expected to have. A lifelong Mets fan who saw them play in the Polo Grounds, I have rooted for all of the players in this book, but my appreciation for them as athletes and people deepened considerably as I interviewed them and investigated their careers and lives.

I hope you enjoy this book.

Let's Go Mets!

Michael Garry

August 2014

Chapter 1

AL JACKSON

Pitcher, 1962-1965, 1968-1969
Throws/Bats: Left

The Game: August 14, 1962 vs. Philadelphia Phillies,
at the Polo Grounds

METS STATS	
GAMES:	184
COMPLETE GAMES:	41
SHUTOUTS:	10
INNINGS PITCHED:	980.2
WINS:	43
LOSSES:	80
ERA:	4.26
WALKS:	304
STRIKEOUTS:	561
WHIP:	1.363
WAR:	3.1

The Run-up

As a bona fide member of the Mets' inaugural team of 1962, Alvin Jackson—known affectionately as "Little Al," though at 5-feet-10 and 169 pounds, he wasn't that small—notched a number of pitching firsts, to wit:

- The team's first shutout (also his first win), vs. the Phillies at the Polo Grounds in the first game of a doubleheader on April 29, 1962. By the time Jackson left the Mets for good in 1969, he had 10 shutouts, tied for sixth in team history with Ron Darling, whom he coached in the minor leagues.
- The first one-hitter (there have been 38 in team history), against the Houston Colt .45s (now Astros), the Mets' 1962 expansion partners, at the Polo Grounds on June 22, 1962. Light-hitting second baseman Joey Amalfitano secured the only safety for Houston, a single with one out in the first. The Mets won 2-0, Jackson's second shutout.
- The first victory and shutout at Shea Stadium, which Jackson found a welcome change from the dilapidated Polo Grounds, on April 19, 1964. The Mets defeated the Pirates 6-0.

Jackson, from Waco, Texas, cut his teeth in the Pittsburgh Pirates organization, which signed him as an amateur free agent in 1955. He performed admirably in the Bucs' minor league system, winning 55 games while losing 34, with a sterling 2.58 ERA from 1958 to 1961. But the Pirates only brought him up to the majors for three games in 1959 and two in 1961, skipping their 1960 championship season altogether.

It was in the minors with Pittsburgh where Jackson found his identity as a pitcher. Early in his career, he tried to throw hard, but that resulted in a preponderance of walks. "I was very wild, very wild," Jackson, still trim at 78, told me in his raspy drawl at the Mets 2014 Fantasy Camp. A coach wisely advised him to eschew power pitching and start throwing a two-seam sinker, which would cause batters to hit the ball on the ground. He perfected the pitch during spring training one year, trying to induce grounders from each hitter.

Jackson's first chance to play regularly in the big leagues came in 1962, at age 26, when the Mets selected him 11th in the expansion draft as the team's first left-handed pitcher. He started the third game of the franchise's existence. As one of the younger Mets on a team built around aged stars, he worked closely with "the Old Perfessor," manager Casey Stengel, on the nuances of the game.

Despite his reputation for double-talk and whimsical riffs, "Casey was sharp," said Jackson. Stengel once schooled him on how a left-handed pitcher can use the momentum generated by his pitching motion to quickly field a bunt up the third-base line and throw a runner out at third. "When you cross over, you're on your way to the third base line," he said. "I would take three steps and I'm over there and I'd throw to third. I worked at it."

Stengel was very receptive to black and Hispanic players, said Steve Jacobson, a longtime reporter and columnist for *Newsday* who covered the Mets' first spring training camp in 1962 and is the author of *Carrying Jackie's Torch*. Stengel's acceptance undoubtedly helped the black and Hispanic players on that inaugural Mets squad—Jackson, Charlie Neal, Clarence "Choo Choo" Coleman, Felix Mantilla, Joe Christopher, Elio Chacon, and Sherman "Roadblock" Jones—who had come into professional baseball in the years directly following Jackie Robinson's integration of the game in 1947, and faced some of the same struggles Robinson did.

Jackson encountered racial prejudice at the hotel where the Mets resided in St. Petersburg, Florida, during their first spring training. "The manager of the hotel phoned Jackson in his room and said, 'We'd appreciate it if you didn't use the dining room,'" Jacobson said. "So the Mets had their own team dining room. It looked ecumenical, but it was the only place black players could go."

Despite his 8-20 record, Jackson was one of the Mets' few bright spots during their dismal debut season, in which they lost 120 games, the most defeats suffered by a major league team since 1900.

In order to obtain those eight wins—20% of the Mets' total of 40—Jackson had to be dominant, or close to it. Seven of his wins were complete games, including four shutouts, the only ones the Mets had in 1962 (and all, curiously, taking place in the first game of a doubleheader). His ERA in his eight victories was 1.16. Overall, he led the team in ERA (4.40) and tied for the lead in strikeouts with 118.

One of his shutouts in '62 was a 1-0 triumph over pitching great Bob Gibson and the St. Louis Cardinals. Jackson would duplicate the feat at the end of the 1964 season, almost preventing the Redbirds from reaching the postseason. Those were the only two times the Mets defeated Gibson between 1962 and 1966. A shutout, Jackson said, was "the only way you could beat him."

Two of Jackson's losses in 1962 featured untimely mistakes by first baseman "Marvelous Marv" Throneberry, the epitome of early Mets ineptitude. Throneberry was particularly unreliable in his defensive play—he made 18 errors that year—as well as in his base running. (His hitting that season was more serviceable, with 16 home runs, 49 RBI, a .244 average, .306 on-base percentage, and .426 slugging percentage in 116 games.)

In the first game of a Father's Day doubleheader on June 17, 1962, Jackson allowed the Cubs to score four times in the first. The Mets unexpectedly responded in the bottom of the frame with four runs of their own. But it could have been six were it not for Throneberry, who hit what ordinarily would have been a triple, except that he missed stepping on first and second base and was called out on appeal. The next batter, Charlie Neal, had to settle for a solo homer rather than a two-run shot. Sure enough, the Mets lost by one run, 8-7, as Throneberry struck out with the tying run on first to end the game.

A Throneberry snafu would also prove lethal in another Mets loss, which Jackson calls the game of his life.

The Game

In recent years, managers have placed a great deal—some would say an inordinate amount—of emphasis on how many pitches a pitcher throws during a game. Hurlers who hit the 100-pitch mark are watched closely and usually don't remain much beyond 110 or 115 pitches. This attention to pitch count has emerged as a consequence of the alarming increase in arm injuries and the proliferation of Tommy John surgeries.

In the 1960s, however, there was little if any concern shown to the number of pitches a starter would throw, as long as he was getting outs. In one famous 1963 contest, Juan Marichal of the Giants and Warren Spahn of the Braves dueled through 16 scoreless innings until Willie Mays cracked a homer off Spahn in the bottom of the 16th. Marichal threw a total of 227 pitches, Spahn 201.

Al Jackson turned in his own marathon performance on August 14, 1962, at the Polo Grounds, a Tuesday afternoon affair attended by just 5,351. He held the Phillies to just one run through 14 innings, only to give up two scores in the 15th after an error at first base by Marvelous Marv, and lose 3-1. The 15-inning outing by Jackson set a Mets single-game longevity record tied three years later by Rod Gardner. It's unlikely to be threatened under current pitch-count protocols.

Jackson threw 215 pitches in the four-hour-and-35-minute contest, according to an account the next day in the *New York Times*. He held 57 Philadelphia batters to six hits, giving up just two singles in the first nine innings. He also walked five while striking out six.

In eight of the 15 innings, including the 10th, 13th, and 14th, he set down the side in order; and between the sixth and 11th innings, he retired fourteen Phils in a row.

For just about any other team, this would have been more than enough to win, but not for the '62 Mets.

Why did Jackson stay in the game for 15 innings? Simple: that's what he wanted to do, despite manager Stengel's wishes. "Casey tried to take me out—I wouldn't come out," he said.

Jackson subscribed to the school of thought that each game he started was his to finish, as long as he was getting batters out. "That's the way I was taught," he said. "That was the only way I was going to be."

Al Jackson

Steve Aaronson

Jackson said that he was also driven by a desire to earn a win—especially on a team so inclined to lose—rather than settle for a no-decision. "I think then, more so than now, you had a great desire to win." A no-decision was a "waste," he added. "It doesn't do you any good. You want to win. And whatever it takes. And I'm the guy to do it, since I started it."

Fortunately, despite throwing 215 pitches, Jackson didn't suffer any physical repercussions. He finished the year going at least eight innings in five of his final eight games. "I was just blessed, I guess," he said. "I never had arm trouble."

Jackson's mound opponent that day was Dallas Green, who would manage the Mets three decades later. Green lasted into the 11th inning himself, giving up one run on a string of sevens—seven hits, seven walks, and seven strikeouts.

Needless to day, the '62 Mets were not a high-scoring bunch, finishing next to last in the league with 3.8 runs per game. The Mets' sole run in this game came in the third. Second baseman "Hot Rod" Kanehl singled to left and advanced to second on a wild pitch. He crossed home plate after a single to right by Richie Ashburn, the Mets' best hitter, who finished the year with a .306 average.

The Phillies tied the score in the fifth. Jackson issued a walk to shortstop Ruben Amaro, who moved over to second on a sacrifice bunt by Green. Tony Taylor's single to left chased Amaro home, knotting the score at one.

The Mets had ample scoring opportunities throughout the game, but they hit into six double plays, stranding 14 base runners. Six DPs are the most in club history in an extra-inning game (five is the team record for nine innings), and one shy of the major league mark set by the Giants in a game against the Astros in 1969.

Still, Jackson soldiered on. But the 15th inning proved to be his undoing, thanks to Throneberry. Phillies center fielder Tony Gonzalez slapped a ground ball down the first base line that zipped under Marv's mitt and between his legs into right field. By the time back-up catcher Chris Cannizzaro, who came in to play right field in the 14th, could retrieve the ball, Gonzalez was on second. The next batter, Bob Oldis, singled to right, sending Gonzalez to third.

Jackson walked Amaro intentionally, and then Mel Roach, who had entered the game in the 11th, ripped a single to left that scored Gonzalez and Oldis. Jackson retired the next three hitters, but the damage had been done.

In the bottom of the 15th, reliever Jack Baldschun walked Joe Christopher but otherwise made quick work of the Mets to end the game and pick up the win. Jackson's valiant effort, all 15 innings of it, was for naught.

A curious footnote regarding Throneberry's error in the 15th: historical records differ as to how it was made. Robert Teague of the *Times*, presumably providing an eyewitness account in his game-day story, clearly describes "a ground ball from Tony Gonzalez down the first-base line," which "Marvelous Marv stooped and scooped—and missed." However, both Retrosheet.org and BaseballReference.com—two respected compilers of box scores—say the ball was hit to third base, and Marv's error was missing the throw from Sammy Drake, who came into the game in the bottom of the ninth as a pinch runner and took over at third in the 10th.

Jackson himself described Throneberry's inning-opening miscue this way:

"A ball is hit to my first baseman."

"Marv?" I asked.

"Yes. I'm going over to cover first base. And it goes right through his legs. And I lost the game."

Notwithstanding the loss, Jackson evinced considerable pride in his ability to persevere through 15 innings.

The Aftermath

The Mets improved marginally in 1963 to 51-111, still a vast 60 games under .500, but Jackson's record took a decided turn for the better. He finished the year 13-17, accounting for more than one-fourth of the team's 51 wins. No Mets pitcher would win more games in a season for another three years.

In 1964, Jackson regressed a bit to 11-16 with a 4.26 ERA, though he went 7-5 with a 3.68 ERA in home games at the new Shea Stadium. One of his road victories was the 1-0 shutout against Bob Gibson in the last weekend of the season. The Cardinals, still in the thick of the '64 pennant race, imagined the Mets would be easy prey, but Jackson allowed them just five scattered hits. The Mets won the next day as well, but the Cards finally prevailed in the last game, with Gibson coming out of the bullpen to nail down their first pennant since 1946.

After his shutout, Jackson was asked to report to the in-stadium studio for an interview with announcer Harry Caray about his impressive pitching performance. But to get there, he had to pass through the Cardinals clubhouse, where he was subjected to withering ridicule. "They chewed my ass out so bad," said Jackson. Incredulous that visiting players had to run the gauntlet just to be interviewed, he asked them, "What kind of ballpark you got here?"

Jackson labored through another last-place season with the Mets in '65, going 8-20 again, with a 4.34 ERA. He still tossed three complete-game shutouts and finished with a career-best 1.354 WHIP (walks and hits per inning pitched). He received little run support from the Mets hitters, who scored two runs or less in 15 of his 31 starts.

Before the '66 campaign, the Mets, seeking a reliable third baseman, decided to trade Jackson and Charley Smith to the Cardinals for former NL MVP Ken Boyer. Jackson had his best season in the majors for the Cardinals in 1966, with a 13-15 record and a sparkling 2.51 ERA, sixth best in the National League. In 1967, he went a respectable 9-4, mostly in relief, yet the Cardinals chose not to use him in their triumph over the Red Sox in the World Series, which lasted seven games.

Jackson maintained an abiding respect for Gibson, his fierce mound opponent with whom he joined forces on the Cardinals. To Jackson, Gibson seemed to operate differently from mere mortals. In 1967, after being injured and missing most of the second half of the season, Gibson returned in September and pitched five innings against the Phillies. In preparation for the game, he "just played catch with a guy who worked for the front office," Jackson said. "That's all he did. And then he won three games in the World Series, finished all of them."

Gibson had a reputation as a mean, relentless competitor. I asked Jackson if that was true. "Oh my God, yeah. Yes, indeed. He was dog eat dog."

The day after the '67 World Series ended, the Cardinals sent Jackson back to the Mets as payment for reliever Jack Lamabe. Though the Mets improved in '68 under Jackson's old Mets teammate Gil Hodges, Jackson's record was only 3-7 in his second go-around, yet he posted his best ERA as a Met, 3.69.

In '69, after he got off to a dreadful start, the Mets shipped Jackson to Cincinnati, and he didn't get to experience the championship celebrated in New York that October. He finished his career that season with the Reds.

Sadly, Jackson never played in the postseason for the Pirates, Mets, or Cardinals, despite being associated with each team during a championship season.

But after retiring as a player, Jackson reinvented himself as a coach, and has worked effectively in that role for nearly four decades. Except for two two-year stints with the Red Sox and Orioles, he has spent that time with the Mets, including one year as the manager of the Kingsport Mets in the Rookie League. He served as the Mets bullpen coach for the 1999 Wild-Card Team and the 2000 National League Champions, with whom he finally got a chance to experience the World Series.

Now in his late 70s, he continues to work with Mets players in Florida as a pitching consultant. "I don't even know how to stop," he said.

Jackson greatly influenced generations of Mets pitchers. The Mets' right-handed pitcher Ron Darling, a stalwart of the '86 champions and the '88 pennant winners, credits his development in AAA Tidewater to Jackson's rigorous coaching. Besides showing Darling how to throw the split-finger fastball, Jackson "taught me how to be a professional," Darling wrote in *The Complete Game*, a book about his experiences in baseball. "He got me to recognize that baseball might have been a game before, but now it was also my job."

Jackson recalled working with Darling on his command, instructing him to throw 30 pitches to one spot. It was not enough to succeed in such an exercise, he said, but to understand your method. "Then, when you need it, you know how to do it."

Chapter 2

ED KRANEPOOL

First base, Outfield, 1962-1979
Throws/Bats: Left

The Game: May 31, 1964 vs. San Francisco Giants, at
Shea Stadium, second game of doubleheader

METS STATS	
GAMES:	1,853
AT-BATS:	5,436
HITS:	1,418
HOME RUNS:	118
AVERAGE:	.251
ON-BASE %:	.316
SLUGGING %:	.377
RUNS:	536
RBI:	614
STOLEN BASES:	15
FIELDING %:	.993
WAR:	4.4

The Run-up

As a player, Ed Kranepool—Steady Eddie—was, above all else, durable.

His career lasted the longest of any player in Mets history—18 seasons, from his call-up in September 1962 as a 17-year-old (still the youngest Met ever), through the 1979 campaign.

He holds the Mets career record for most games (1,853) and is second to David Wright in several categories, including hits, with 1,418. For these achievements, he was elected to the Mets Hall of Fame in 1990.

And on May 31, 1964, "The Krane" played in the longest doubleheader, in terms of innings played (32) and time elapsed (nine hours, 52 minutes), in baseball history. The San Francisco Giants won the first game 5-3 in a brisk two hours and 29 minutes, but in the second contest Willie Mays and company required 23 innings, over seven hours and 23 minutes, to dispose of the Mets, 8-6. The nightcap stands as the longest game, time-wise, ever played in the National League.

"It was a long, long day—the longest day of my life," Kranepool told me in a phone interview.

As if that weren't enough, the previous day the 19-year-old Kranepool played in all 18 innings of a doubleheader in Syracuse, New York, for the Mets' Buffalo Bisons AAA team, before getting the call to rejoin the Mets.

During his first few years in the bigs and also in 1970, Kranepool was demoted to the minor leagues when he struggled at the plate. To his credit, he always found his way back to the majors in short order. "You have to be resilient to be able to come back," he said. "You never give up, you believe in yourself and that's the whole key."

That resilience helped him survive the back-to-back doubleheaders, which added up to a grand total of 50 innings—the equivalent of 5 1/2 nine-inning games. "They wouldn't ask a player to play 50 innings today," Kranepool said. "His agent would be calling and saying, 'What, are you crazy?'"

Born November 8, 1944, Kranepool grew up without his father, who perished in combat during World War II. Jim Sciafa, his neighbor and first little league coach, became "like my stepfather," he said. "He took me under his wing. I was very close to him until a couple of years ago when he passed away." As a young player, he also formed a close bond with the Mets' inaugural manager, Casey Stengel.

"A great guy to play with, he loved the young players," Kranepool said of the skipper. "For whatever reason—I think it started with the Yankees, he developed a lot of young players there—he took an interest in us, wanted to make us better."

Stengel would work with his players before the game, talk to them all the time, and impart his decades of baseball wisdom, said Kranepool. "And you know what? I really loved him."

Kranepool spent his childhood in the New York City borough of the Bronx rooting for the nearby Yankees, for whom he hoped to play. (He would later wear No. 7 for his idol, Mickey Mantle). But the Queens-based Mets, seeking young, local talent, aggressively courted him after scouting his exploits at James Monroe High School, where he was compared to alumnus Hank Greenberg. Aided by a $75,000 bonus, they won him over and signed him as an amateur free agent in June 1962. Mets executive Johnny Murphy and scout Bubber Jonnard "treated me great and they wouldn't leave my house until I signed," he said.

Because he started so young, Kranepool was only 34 when he retired from the game after the 1979 season. He almost became a Mets executive as part of a group vying to purchase the team in late 1979, but that opportunity disappeared when another entity, headed by Fred Wilpon and Nelson Doubleday, made the winning bid.

Rather than seeking work as a scout or a coach, he entered the "real world" of business, having already worked as a stockbroker and restaurant owner in the offseason during his playing career. Beginning with such ventures as point-of-purchase display manufacturing and sports marketing, he ultimately found a home with a New York-based credit-card processing firm, IRN Payment Systems, where he has worked in sales for more than 25 years.

Kranepool took part in many of the Mets' most iconic contests during the franchise's first two decades, but he considers the 23-inning affair—arduous as it was, and despite being on the losing side—the game of his life.

The Game

He wasn't supposed to play more than five innings in the second game of the doubleheader on May 31, 1964, never mind 23. But this was the '64 Mets, still in the hapless, cellar-dwelling phase of their early existence.

"[Manager] Casey [Stengel] came to me and said, 'I'd like you to start the game. I know you're tired, but give me five innings,'" Kranepool said. "By the fifth inning I think he used up most of his players. There was no alternative so I said, what's the difference, five innings or nine innings? Not knowing it was going to go 23 innings."

By the time the last pitch was thrown, with a scattering of fans remaining, it was well after 11 pm. Kranepool cracked to reporters that if the game had lasted 40 more minutes, it would have started in May and ended in June. "They got a kick out of that," he said. Thankfully, Stengel gave him the next day off, Kranepool said, so he didn't have to play in an exhibition game in Norfolk, Virginia.

What made the nine hours and 52 minutes of baseball even harder to endure for the 6-foot-3, 205-pound Kranepool was that the between-game meal consisted of only a cup of soup and Saltine crackers—certainly a far cry from the lavish spreads current players enjoy. "That's all [general manager] George Weiss allowed in the clubhouse," said Kranepool. "Maybe you also had a couple of chocolate bars." Today's players, he added, "are babied, they're coddled."

In the first game of the doubleheader, Kranepool went one for four, lacing a single to right field in the second inning off the Giants' ace right-hander Juan Marichal and scoring on a three-run homer by Jim Hickman.

He fared better in the nightcap, though—at least during the first nine innings—knocking an RBI triple to center field off starter Bob Bolin in

Ed Kranepool

AP Photo/Harry Harris

the sixth inning, a double to left in the seventh, and an infield single in the ninth—a home run short of a cycle. But—having already played 36 innings in two days—he went zero for five the rest of the game, including two strikeouts and a double-play grounder, and finished three for 10, not bad for 23 innings.

"If I could've had a sandwich in between games, I might've hit a home run," he said. "I don't remember what I did in the next five at-bats, but certainly it was all downhill. Physically, I was wiped out."

The 23-inning game included a stout comeback by the Mets, which was started by Kranepool. After trailing 6-1 after three innings, they scored two in the sixth on his RBI triple and Charley Smith's single, which drove home Kranepool. In the seventh, Joe Christopher, who had four hits in the game (as did Smith) belted a three-run homer, tying the game at six.

There it stayed until the 23rd as Larry Bearnarth, who pitched seven innings, and Galen Cisco (nine innings) held the Giants in check. (Nine days later, Bearnarth would set a Mets record that still stands for longest relief appearance—10 innings—in a win at Shea against the Cubs.)

Finally, in the 23rd, the Giants broke through. Cisco gave up a triple to Jim Davenport, and intentionally walked Cap Peterson. Pinch hitter Del Crandall smacked a double to drive in Davenport, and, for an insurance run, Alou delivered Peterson with a single. The Mets went down meekly in the bottom of the 23rd with two K's and a fly ball to right by Amado Samuel, the last hitter of the longest day in baseball history.

"It probably wouldn't have ended if they didn't have a guy in the bullpen, [back-up catcher] Del Crandall, who hadn't played," said Kranepool. "I'd still be playing."

By the end, the general exhaustion on both sides had consumed the starting players as well as most of the subs. "It was just an endurance test at that point. On and on and on. And you hate to say it—you want to win, of course—but I'm glad the game ended.

"It was a long day. One of those days you want to forget," added Kranepool ironically about the day on which he played the game of his life. "Those days would make for a long season."

The Aftermath

Having survived a 32-inning doubleheader, Kranepool would face another marathon affair nearly four years later, on April 15, 1968, when the Mets lost to the Houston Astros 1-0 in a 24-inning night game at the Astrodome. Lasting six hours and six minutes (an hour and 17 minutes less than the 23-inning game), the pitchers' duel ended at 1:37 am CT. It remains the longest shutout ever in innings played.

Kranepool, playing first base, went 2 for 8 with a walk and two sacrifices. In contrast to the 1964 ordeal, he played in only one game that day, and just one the day before.

Nevertheless, the 24-inning marathon also left a lasting mark on the national pastime, thanks to Kranepool.

The practice among stadium ground crews in those days was to sweep the infield once per game, in the fifth inning. For extra-inning games, especially those lasting 15+ innings, one sweep would hardly suffice, leaving the infield with bumps and crevices that could affect the direction of a ground ball or the footwork of the fielders.

The infield dirt at the Astrodome was prone to accumulating "a lot of clumps," said Kranepool, who noticed that by the end of the 24-inning contest "balls were taking all kinds of crazy hops."

He addressed the infield-sweeping matter with Mets general manager Johnny Murphy, who took it up with Major League Baseball's rules committee. "I told him, we're out on the field in extra innings, why can't the ground crew come out? It's a five-minute procedure," Kranepool said.

The rule was changed so that the infield would be swept every five innings, allowing extra-inning games to be played with a smooth playing surface. "I got the rules changed in baseball," said Kranepool, one of the few players to ever do so.

Kranepool would participate in one more 20+ inning game—a 4-3 loss to the Cardinals at Shea on September 11, 1974, that lasted 25 innings over seven hours and four minutes (19 minutes shorter than the 23-inning game). It's the longest game (by innings) ever played in the National League, tied with a Chicago-Milwaukee 25-inning American League contest played in 1984.

Fortunately for Kranepool, he only had to pinch hit in the game, leading off in the bottom of the 12th; he grounded out to first. "I'm glad I wasn't part of that one," he said.

Though he didn't get a pinch hit in that game, Kranepool served the Mets admirably as a pinch hitter from 1974 through 1978, his prime hitting years, batting .396 in that role. In '74, he set the major league single-season record for batting average by a pinch hitter—.486 (17 for 35) while compiling a .614 slugging percentage. Kranepool had endured years of mixed reviews from Mets fans, but during this period Shea Stadium patrons greeted his at-bats with shouts of "Ed-die! Ed-die! Ed-die!" In his career, he produced 90 pinch hits, still a Mets record, including five home runs.

The irony of Kranepool's success as a pinch hitter was that it was driven by his resentment at not playing full-time. "When I pinch hit, I was really trying to show up the manager as an incentive for myself to do well, instead of brooding and not taking it seriously. And if I got a hit every time I went up to pinch hit, then there would be a reason for him to play me."

The 25-inning game, with a Cardinals team that included past Met Ron Hunt and future Mets Joe Torre and Keith Hernandez, finally ended after Bake "Shake 'n Bake" McBride scored the go-ahead run thanks to two Mets errors (they committed four in all). Following an infield single, McBride was leaning the wrong way at first base and would have been picked off—except that relief pitcher Hank Webb threw the ball in the dirt near first (while balking) and it scooted away from first baseman John Milner into short right field. McBride took off and didn't stop running. Milner retrieved the ball and fired it home to catcher Ron Hodges, who had McBride dead to rights but dropped the ball, allowing him to score.

In the bottom of the 25th, Mets pinch hitter Brock Pemberton singled, but Milner struck out to end the game, at 3:13 am ET.

If Kranepool had played first base instead of Milner, would he have snagged the ball in the dirt that Milner missed? Though not considered a defensive standout, Kranepool was a reliable first baseman, with a lifetime fielding average at that position of .994, slightly better than Milner's .991. In 1971, he led National League first basemen with a .998 fielding average, which is tied for the best fielding percentage by a Met. "I had good hands," he said.

Throughout his career, Kranepool also found himself patrolling the outfield (left or right) where he wasn't as adept, with a lifetime fielding average of .975. But he found the outfield less physically grueling than first base. "Balls aren't taking bad hops, throws aren't going in the dirt and hitting you in the ankles and the rear end," he said. And if playing the outfield meant he could get four at-bats rather than sitting on the bench, he was all for it.

Kranepool retired after the 1979 season, before the Mets played their next three extreme-extra-inning games, two of which they won. The first one, a 16-13 Mets victory in Atlanta on July 4, 1985, ended after 19 innings at 4 am ET, when a scheduled fireworks show commenced. It was the Mets' first win in a game lasting 19 innings or longer. More recently, they played two 20-inning games—a 2-1 win vs. the Cardinals in St. Louis in 2010 and a 2-1 loss to the Marlins at Citi Field in 2013. They still haven't won a hyper-extra-inning game at home.

Apart from his marathon games, Kranepool played a vital role in many other historic Mets contests of shorter duration.

During the 1969 championship season, while platooning with mid-season pickup Donn Clendenon at first base, Kranepool delivered several key hits, including eight game-winning RBI. He considers his biggest hit that year a game-winning single off Ferguson Jenkins on July 8 that capped a three-run ninth-inning comeback against the division-leading Cubs; he had hit a solo home run earlier in the game. This victory, the Mets' sixth straight win, was considered a turning point in their season, marking when they truly came of age as contenders. The next night they would win again as Tom Seaver pitched his near-perfect game against the Cubs.

"And now you felt that something special was going to happen," Kranepool said. "We didn't miraculously win the World Series or the playoffs. We deserved to be there. We were the best ball club from June on; we won a lot of ballgames. We beat every club we had to. It wasn't like '73 when we finished first, two games over .500. We were a good ball club."

Kranepool played in all three games of the '69 Championship Series against the Atlanta Braves, hitting .250 with an RBI. He played only in Game Three of the World Series against the Baltimore Orioles, but made it count with a homer in the eighth inning off Dave Leonhard, capping a 5-0 win for the Mets.

"That's the culmination of your career, getting to a World Series and participating," he said. Gil Hodges's platoon system, he added, worked to perfection. "The lefties won the playoffs, [and] the righties won the World Series."

But Kranepool didn't like being in a platoon. "Nobody wanted to platoon. I was a regular player earlier on. I was coming into my peak and I wanted to play every day, but the manager dictates the lineup and you can't do anything about it. Platooning is just the easiest way for a manager to take care of the writers, to keep them off his back."

He questions the conventional wisdom behind the platoon system—that left-handed batters like him fare better against right-handed pitchers (and right-handed batters hit better against southpaws). He believes the odds are stacked in favor of that result because left-handed batters, for example, aren't given enough opportunities to face left-handed pitchers.

"When you play in the minor leagues, either you can hit or you can't hit," he said. "So if you hit .300 or better in the minor leagues, you played against everybody, righties and lefties. There's no platooning. You should bring them up and let them play [against everybody.]"

Kranepool's next playoff platoon opportunity came in the 1973 National League Championship Series against the Cincinnati Reds, when he made his only start in the fifth and deciding game, a 7-2 Mets win; he drove in two runs with a single in the first inning.

"[Manager] Yogi [Berra] finally woke up in the fifth game and put me in. I always did well against [pitcher Jack] Billingham and I got a base hit."

Kranepool would only pinch hit in the World Series against the Oakland Athletics, batting three times without a hit. He remains disappointed that the Mets lost the series in seven games, after taking a three-games-to-two lead. He is of the school that believes Berra erred in starting Tom Seaver in game six on short rest instead of employing the well-rested George Stone and saving Seaver for Game Seven.

A veteran of marathon baseball games, Kranepool understood the value of rest.

Chapter 3

ED CHARLES

Third Base, 1967-1969
Throws/Bats: Right

The Game: October 12, 1969 vs. Baltimore Orioles, at Memorial Stadium, Game Two, World Series

METS STATS	
GAMES:	279
AT-BATS:	861
HITS:	214
HOME RUNS:	21
AVERAGE:	.249
ON-BASE %:	.309
SLUGGING %:	.368
RUNS:	94
RBI:	102
STOLEN BASES:	13
FIELDING %:	.949
WAR:	5.2

The Run-up

In *42*, the 2013 film about the breaking of the color barrier in Major League Baseball, a 12-year-old black boy is in several scenes, marveling that a black man, Jackie Robinson, is actually getting to play baseball with whites in the Jim Crow South.

In one scene, Robinson, portrayed in the film by Chadwick Boseman, makes his professional debut on March 17, 1946, at City Island Ball Park in Daytona Beach, Florida, with the Montreal Royals (the Brooklyn Dodgers' AAA farm team). The boy, played by Dusan Brown, is there to see him. "Please God, show them that Jackie can do it," he prays.

At the end of the film, text on the screen informs the viewer that the boy, Ed Charles, "grew up to become a major league baseball player. He won the World Series in 1969 with the Miracle Mets."

Charles, who turned 80 shortly after the film's premier in April 2013, also appears in the special features section of the CD release. In an interview with the filmmakers at the Jackie Robinson Rotunda, inside the front entrance to Citi Field, he talks about Robinson's importance to him and to history; the interview takes place near a large blue sculpture of Robinson's uniform number, 42, a number that is retired by every team in Major League Baseball.

One of nine children, Charles did in fact first encounter Robinson as a 12-year-old in March 1946. He would run home from school to watch him practice with the Royals at Kelly Field, part of a recreation complex located across the street from Charles's home in a segregated part of Daytona Beach. "I was so shy back in those days I just stood there looking at him like he was God or something. Like this is not happening."

The serendipity of Robinson appearing before him at an impressionable age made a profound and lasting impression on Charles, not only inspiring him to pursue his dream of a baseball career but to stick with it despite countless obstacles along the way.

Charles would persevere through an extended, racism-filled apprenticeship in the minor leagues, toil on a mediocre Kansas City Athletics team, and join a Mets team still enduring many growing pains. But it would all pay off in the end, with Charles going out on top, a card-carrying member of the Mets' 1969 championship ensemble.

In the fifth and deciding game of the '69 World Series, after Cleon Jones made the final catch and kneeled on one knee, the unbridled joy of the Mets and their fans was captured in an iconic photo of Charles, catcher Jerry Grote, and pitcher Jerry Koosman converging on the pitcher's mound. As Grote embraces Koosman, holding him aloft, an ebullient Charles is leaping right beside them, a radiant smile across his face.

Charles is familiar with the photo. "Naturally, I'm just overjoyed," he said. "We won the World Series. When you're a kid, you dream about it. To actually have it happen to you? I mean, it's indescribable. That's what was going through my mind. I used to dream about playing in a World Series. Here comes Jackie Robinson opening the doors for a guy like me. And now my dream is realized."

Players like Charles, who was drafted by the Boston Braves in 1952 and played nearly a decade in the minor leagues—often in the deep South—contributed in a less glamorous but still essential way to the process of bringing acceptance of black players to professional baseball. Playing in such Southern minor league cities as Fort Lauderdale, Florida; Corpus Christi, Texas; Jacksonville, Florida; and Louisville, Kentucky, Charles faced the same kind of withering racism that Robinson had to endure.

"We considered ourselves Jackie's disciples," said Charles. "Baseball would not have been successful in this experiment if we hadn't opened things up in the South."

Charles emulated Robinson's playing style, striving to be an all-around player who could get on base, steal, and play good defense. And like Robinson, he had to refrain from fighting back against racist tormentors so that he wouldn't be kicked off the team. Outside the ball field, Charles was subjected to Jim Crow racial segregation laws that forced him to eat on the team bus rather than in a restaurant, relieve himself in a shrub rather than in a bathroom, and find lodging with black families rather than stay in the team's hotel, among other indignities. "That was standard procedure in those days for the players of color," he said.

Charles was deeply vexed at the length of time he had to spend in the minor leagues before getting a shot at the majors. He attributed the delay to a "quota system" in the 1950s that limited the number of blacks that could be on a big league squad. His performance on the field—his overall minor league average was .291—should have justified a promotion, he felt.

As a third baseman, Charles had his path to the Braves blocked by the presence of future Hall of Famer Eddie Mathews at that position, but he also played shortstop and second base. In 1958, when he played 75 games at second while hitting over .300 for the Braves' AAA affiliate in Wichita, Kansas, he thought his time had come, but the Braves instead promoted a weak-hitting white infielder named Joe Koppe.

Charles returned to third after that, hoping the Braves would trade him. "They should have traded me rather than holding onto me," he said. "They didn't take into consideration my worth."

A trade finally came after the 1961 season. Milwaukee sent Charles, Joe Azcue, and Manny Jimenez to the Kansas City (now Oakland) Athletics in exchange for Bob Shaw and Lou Klimchock (who both subsequently played briefly for the Mets).

He made his big league debut with the A's in 1962, the year the Mets came into being. "I was like Jackie—a 29-year-old rookie," he said. He excelled that year, and was regarded as one of the best players on a struggling A's team during their time in Kansas City.

Charles played for the A's, owned by the mercurial Charlie Finley, through the early part of the 1967 season, when he was traded to the Mets for Larry Elliot and $50,000. He was 34.

Charles enjoyed his best year in New York in 1968, under new manager Gil Hodges, batting .276 and leading the club with 15 home runs in what was called the "year of the pitcher" in baseball.

As the team's oldest player, Charles helped steady a team filled with young talent. "I was [Hodges's] unofficial commander on the field," he said.

It was with the Mets that Charles, known as "The Poet" in Kansas City, acquired the nickname that Mets fans associate with him— "The Glider." "We were playing a game at Shea on a Sunday afternoon and [Jerry] Koosman was pitching," Charles recalled. "A guy hit a bullet down to me at third and I just scooped it up and threw the guy out. Koos got so excited he ran over there and said, 'That was one hell of a play!' And I looked at him like he was crazy. Then he said, 'You don't approach fielding like the average infielder—you sort of glide at the ball. That's it—you're The Glider from now on!'"

In 1969, sharing third base responsibilities with Wayne Garrett in manager Hodges's platoon system, Charles played in just 61 games for the Mets, hitting .209. But he credits the platoon, which Hodges also used at first base (Clendenon/Kranepool), second base (Weis/Boswell) and right field (Swoboda/Shamsky), for propelling the Mets past the Cubs and onto World Series glory that year.

One of Charles's most important hits came on a seminal day in Mets history, on September 24, 1969, when the team clinched first place in the new National League East for its first championship of any kind. In the first inning of the game, against the Cardinals at Shea Stadium, he slammed a two-run homer (his last in the big leagues) off future Hall of Famer Steve Carlton. Donn Clendenon also homered in the first, as well as the fifth, and the Mets went on to win 6-0 behind Gary Gentry's four-hitter. "To participate in the winning of the first [division] championship in Mets history, that was special," said Charles.

The Game

But the game of his life would come 18 days later, on October 12, in Game Two of the '69 World Series against the Orioles at Baltimore's Memorial Stadium. Winning Game Two was essential for the Mets, who lost the previous game and didn't want to go down two games to none against the heavily favored Orioles.

The Mets took a 1-0 lead in the top of the fourth on a homer to deep right field by Clendenon off left-hander Dave McNally. Charles doubled down the left-field line in the top of the seventh but was stranded at second base.

Meanwhile, Koosman was pitching masterfully, no-hitting the Orioles through six innings. But in the bottom of the seventh, he gave up a single to Paul Blair, who stole second, and another single to Brooks Robinson that scored Blair and tied the game at 1-1.

In the top of the ninth, after Clendenon struck out and Swoboda grounded out, Charles came to the plate. Despite his seventh-inning double, he was still feeling "a little teed off at myself" because he hadn't performed better in Game One against left-hander Mike Cuellar, who held him hitless.

Under the platoon system, the Mets played right-handed batters like Charles in Games One, Two, Four, and Five of the World Series, after playing their left-handed hitters in the three-game Championship Series sweep against the Braves.

Having sat out the Championship Series, Charles had felt a little "rusty" in Game One. But, he said, in Game Two, "I was beginning to find myself at the plate."

In the ninth inning that translated into arguably the biggest hit of his career—a clean single to left.

He tried to steal second, and ended up on third after a base hit to left by catcher Jerry Grote; then he scored the go-ahead run on another single to left by light-hitting second baseman Al Weis, who would hit a game-tying homer against McNally in the Mets' Game Five series-clinching victory. "Our Savior!" said Charles with a chuckle.

Charles's single in the ninth "was a very important hit for us in a very important game," he said. "Because we couldn't go two down to that team." It would be his final hit of the series.

Still nimble at age 36, he was able to make it all the way to third on Grote's single to left as a result of getting a good jump in his steal attempt. "It wasn't a hit and run," he said. "I felt like I read the pitcher pretty good and got a good jump. I was on my own."

Ed Charles, celebrating after the final out of the
1969 World Series.

After Weis's go-ahead hit, Koosman was left in the game to bat for himself, and grounded out. In the bottom of the ninth, he got two quick outs—a short fly ball from Don Buford and a groundout from Blair. But then he walked both Frank Robinson, who was replaced by pinch runner Merv Rettenmund, and Boog Powell, putting runners on first and second.

Hodges decided to bring in the Mets' primary relief pitcher that year, Ron Taylor, to face Brooks Robinson. "That was the right time for him to take out Jerry," said Charles, who had unbounded admiration for the man who would pitch the series clincher. "Jerry, you can say, was one of our clutch pitchers. If we have one game that we had to win, a lot of players would tell you they'd rather have Koosman than Seaver on the mound."

Charles set himself at third base. On a 1-2 pitch, Robinson pulled a grounder down the third base line. Charles snagged it and, seeing he would not be able to beat Rettenmund to third, fired it to first baseman Clendenon, who scooped it for the third out and the Mets' critical 2-1 Game Two victory.

"I framed the ball like I was supposed to do," Charles said. "It wasn't going to get by me. It was a medium drive, with an in-between hop. The most difficult thing is an in-between kind of hop."

Normally, with runners on first and second, Charles would have stepped on third for the force. "But as I made my move to third, I could see from my peripheral view that Rettenmund was coming down and he would probably beat me to the bag," he said. "So I just went to first because I knew that Brooks Robinson was a slow runner. I knew how much time I had."

Charles had contributed in Game Two with both his bat and his glove. And now the Mets were going home. "You always feel good in your own ballpark," he said. Good indeed, as the Mets took the next three at Shea and became a champion for the ages.

The Aftermath

Four days after the series clincher, the tumultuous celebration in New York City included a ticker-tape parade for the Mets in lower Manhattan, as well as a rally in midtown at Bryant Park, where Charles read one of his poems, "An Athlete's Prayer." He had taken up poetry in 1961 toward the end of his stay in the minor leagues as an outlet for his frustrations. "When I wanted to do something to ease the pressures, I just started writing," he said. He composed "An Athlete's Prayer" to express his gratitude for finally making it to the major leagues. It reads, in part:

Author of my talents, only you have I praised,
To Thee only shall my hands be raised.
For when I'm burdened with the weight of my team,
To my rescue You come, it will always seem.
For outstanding is my play on any given day
When You intervene and help lead the way.
Grateful to You I'll always be
For exploiting my talents for the world to see.

Charles pursued several paths after his retirement as a player. He first tried his hand at some business ventures, including a foray into music promotion at Buddha Records, followed by an attempt at a startup that marketed baseball novelties. Though the latter didn't succeed, it did lead to another serendipitous encounter with his idol in 1972.

"Yeah, that was something," Charles said. "I was trying to get a little novelty business started. At the time Jackie was trying to get a construction business off the ground. We both had appointments at the Small Business Administration in Manhattan. Jackie's appointment was after mine.

"When we were wrapping up my appointment, they said, 'Guess who's coming in next?' I said, who? 'Jackie Robinson.' I said Jackie Robinson! I got to meet him and thank him! So they said 'okay.'

"I can just picture this. As I approached Jackie, I was like that twelve-year-old kid, very nervous. I started telling him that he was my idol for so long and that I looked up to him and I tried to emulate him to a point.

"I told him I just want to thank you for enduring what you had to go through to open the door up for blacks, stuff like that. He was very gracious. He said 'I really appreciate that. You're the first black player to personally approach me and thank me like that.'"

Charles didn't want to leave it there, so he arranged to meet Robinson at his office in Englewood Cliffs, New Jersey, a few weeks later. At this second meeting "I had him all to myself," he said. "I was sitting there with a man whom I had idolized since I first saw him in Daytona Beach. I'm just running my mouth like crazy. We talked about everything—baseball, social issues, everything. And I tell you, I felt like I was on cloud nine. Having him be that close."

A few weeks after that meeting, on October 24, 1972, Jack Roosevelt Robinson, who had suffered from diabetes, died of a heart attack at the age of 53. "And I really literally cried when I got the news over the radio," Charles said. "It was like a thunderbolt hit me."

He was encouraged to write down how he felt about Robinson. The poem reads in part:

Yes, he made his mark for all to see
As he struggled determinedly for dignity.
And the world is grateful for the legacy
That he left for all humanity.

Charles would return to baseball as a scout for the Mets for several years, signing pitcher Neil Allen. (Allen performed well for the Mets as a reliever and was eventually traded with pitching prospect Rick Ownbey to the Cardinals for Keith Hernandez, who became the linchpin for the Mets' only other World Championship team in 1986.) He also coached their rookie team in Kingsport, Tennessee for three years.

Charles has remained in touch with the Mets, attending their Fantasy Camp in January and participating in events like Mike Piazza's induction into the Mets Hall of Fame in September 2013.

For the last thirteen years of his working life, until his retirement at age sixty-seven, Charles worked as a counselor for the New York City Department of Juvenile Justice at a home for juvenile delinquents in the Bronx. He tried to help troubled kids growing up in impoverished conditions not unlike his own in Daytona Beach. He applied the knowledge he acquired while living in Kansas City and pursuing a degree in the administration of justice. "I worked with kids with a lot of problems," he said. "I enjoyed working with the kids."

Charles wouldn't tell them about his playing days, but they usually found out about it anyway.

"Then they would say, 'Mr. Charles, what are you doing here?' I would say, well, I'm here because you're here. If you weren't here, I wouldn't be here."

A fitting tribute to the man he tried to emulate, who once said, "A life is not important except in the impact it has on other lives."

Chapter 4

RON SWOBODA

Outfielder, 1965-1970
Throws/Bats: Right

The Game: October 15, 1969 vs. Baltimore Orioles, at Shea Stadium, Game Four, World Series

METS STATS	
GAMES:	737
AT-BATS:	2,212
HITS:	536
HOME RUNS:	69
AVERAGE:	.242
ON-BASE %:	.319
SLUGGING %:	.387
RUNS:	246
RBI:	304
STOLEN BASES:	20
FIELDING %:	.971
WAR:	7.0

The Run-up

At Citi Field, the Mets' home since 2009, a navy-blue metal silhouette of a fielder making a headlong catch hovers over the entrance to the right field stands, juxtaposed behind block orange letters spelling out RIGHT FIELD.

The fielder's body is parallel to the ground—left arm outstretched, glove wide open, legs splayed—as he hurtles through space to make a game-saving catch.

The name Ron Swoboda is nowhere in sight, but it is Swoboda's catch on October 15, 1969, in Game Four of the World Series—better known as "The Catch"—that is permanently depicted above the right field gate at Citi Field.

"I did not know that was part of the construction of the ballpark," Swoboda told me during an interview outside the dining area at Mets Fantasy Camp in 2014. "Somebody I knew in New York emailed me and said, 'I think this is you.' I looked at it and of course I know what the silhouette looks like. It's my silhouette."

The New York Mets are famous for, among other things, a handful of spectacular outfield defensive plays in the postseason. On the other side of Citi Field, above the entrance to the left field stands, rests another navy-blue metal silhouette, this one of the over-the-fence, tip-of-the-webbing catch made by Endy Chavez in the 2006 National League Championship Series. And, of course, Swoboda's teammate, centerfielder Tommy Agee, made two eye-popping catches in Game Three of the '69 series (the day before Swoboda's grab) that prevented five runs from scoring.

The Game

The Mets, huge underdogs to the Baltimore Orioles going into the series, held a two-games-to-one lead and were ahead, 1-0, in the top of the ninth of Game Four. The Mets had scored their run on a second-inning solo homer by power-hitting first baseman Donn Clendenon, who would be named series MVP.

By the ninth inning, the late afternoon shadows covered the infield from the front edge of the pitcher's mound to home plate. The Orioles had their slugger Frank Robinson at third base representing the tying run, and their big first baseman Boog Powell on first as the go-ahead run. The Mets' ace, Tom Seaver, was still on the mound, having held the Birds in check all day and trying to rebound from his Game One loss.

But Seaver looked a little tired at this point. As Sandy Koufax would say the next day in a TV appearance with Mickey Mantle on NBC prior to Game Five, "I think he stopped pitching and started throwing the ball." Frank Robinson also may not have been at his best. When Robinson laced a line drive off Seaver in the ninth inning, Koufax thought he would try for second, but he didn't, possibly hampered by his in-step. Powell's subsequent single advanced him to third.

Third baseman Brooks Robinson, whom Swoboda had idolized as a kid growing up in suburban Baltimore, was now at the plate, with just one out. "When he came up to the Orioles, we loved him," he said. "We thought he was the coolest."

Before Seaver could pitch to Robinson, Mets manager Gil Hodges marched to the mound, exchanged a few words with Seaver while catcher Jerry Grote and Clendenon stood by, and returned to the dugout. Relief pitchers Tug McGraw and Ron Taylor were warming up in the bullpen.

On TV, Seaver's wife, Nancy, was caught on camera sitting in the stands, protected against the autumn chill in a light brown jacket and matching round hat, her short blond hair shaped like a crescent moon beside her face. She genuflected briefly toward her husband.

And around the country, Moratorium Day was taking place as Americans gathered in rallies and demonstrations to express their views on the Vietnam War.

At Shea, Frank Robinson could score on a fly ball to the outfield. But Brooks Robinson had not yet propelled a ball past the infield in this game.

Ron Swoboda

Steve Aaronson

The outfielders—Swoboda in right, Tommy Agee in center, and Cleon Jones in left—were playing straightaway.

Swoboda had been peeved at himself for allowing a catchable fly ball hit by Don Buford off Seaver in the first at-bat of the first game to go over his head and out of the ballpark for a home run. He really owed Seaver, and had been stewing about the miscue in the Mets dugout until teammate Ed Kranepool urged him to "shut up and get the next one."

Here was the next one. Robinson swung at Seaver's first pitch and sliced a sinking line drive to right-center field, looking for all the world like an RBI base hit that might give the O's the lead. Powell headed for second. A right-handed fielder, Swoboda took a few long strides and launched off his right leg as if sprung from a diving board. His body horizontal, glove reaching out, legs splayed, he snared the ball backhanded in the webbing, inches above the grass, and hit the ground sliding, his feet pointing up.

His hat flew off as his torso started turning toward the infield. He suddenly planted his left foot, and, leaning on his right knee, shot up and heaved the ball toward home plate. "I was fortunately facing in the right direction," he said.

The throw was not able to stop Frank Robinson from tagging up from third. The Mets appealed to the third-base umpire that Robinson had left third base too soon, but to no avail. The score was tied. "It's probably one of the best-looking sacrifice flies you've ever seen in your life," said Swoboda, who made all three outfield putouts in that half inning, including a deep fly to right-center field to retire the side.

Though Robinson scored, the Shea crowd roared at Swoboda's heroics. For all the adulation the catch inspired, Swoboda put it in perspective by referring me to a Mets highlight film released after the series; in one clip, as everyone is applauding the catch, someone asks, "Who was that?"

Had Swoboda, in his desperate lunge, failed to come up with the ball, it would have rolled to the fence; Boog Powell, though a slow runner, would have probably scored all the way from first and given the Orioles the lead. "Brooks said he would've gotten a triple easily, and he was slow," said

Ron Swoboda, making iconic catch in Game Four of the 1969 World Series.

AP Photo

Silhouette of Ron Swoboda making World Series catch, at Clti Field's right-field entrance.

Michael Garry

Swoboda. The O's would have been in a solid position to tie the series and force a return to Baltimore.

But for the third time in two days (counting Agee's two catches) the Mets—magically, amazingly, stunningly—stopped the Orioles and their formidable hitters from scoring on surefire blasts to the outfield.

In the bottom of the ninth, Swoboda's two-out single moved Jones to third, giving the Mets a chance to win. (Swoboda went three for four at the plate that day, with singles to center, left, and right.) But Art Shamsky grounded out, and the game went into extra innings. In the 10th, though, after Seaver got out of trouble in the top of the frame, the Mets pushed the winning run across on backup catcher J.C. Martin's controversial bunt play.

After Jerry Grote doubled, and was replaced by pinch runner Rod Gaspar, Martin bunted, and relief pitcher Pete Richert ran in to pick up the ball and throw to first. But his throw hit Martin in the wrist and the ball trickled away, allowing Gaspar to score the winning run. Some say Martin's path to first illegally obstructed Richert's peg.

As Gaspar came charging home, Seaver, watching from the dugout, saw his baseball life flash in front of him, according to *The Last Icon: Tom Seaver and His Times*, by Steven Travers. As stated in the book, "The perfect game I pitched when I was 12 years old, the grand slam home run I'd hit for the Alaska Goldpanners, the first game I'd won as a member of the New York Mets, the imperfect game I'd pitched against the Chicago Cubs, one after another, every minor miracle building toward that one magic day. I never realized before that a man's whole life could be encompassed in a single play, in a single game, in a single day."

The victory gave the Mets a three-games-to-one lead in the series, which they closed out the next day. Swoboda helped in the clincher with a double in the bottom of the eighth that just eluded Buford—his nemesis from game one—and drove Cleon Jones home with the go-ahead run. Swoboda later came home to complete the 5-3 final score. He batted .400 in the series with that sole RBI.

More than any hitting accomplishment, it's the World Series catch that has endowed Swoboda with a touch of baseball immortality. "Every time I see Brooks Robinson, I thank him for not hitting it right to me," Swoboda said.

The Aftermath—and what made it all possible

After retiring from baseball in 1973 (he also played briefly for the Montreal Expos and three seasons for the Yankees), Swoboda leveraged his communication skills by working as a TV sportscaster in New York. He later moved to New Orleans, where he has continued his broadcasting career over the past three decades.

But broadcasting is not the only thing that has kept him occupied. Swoboda is an inquisitive and articulate man with an acerbic wit and wide-ranging interests, including music, history, poetry and writing.

In 1968 and 1969 he participated in a USO tour of Vietnam to support U.S. troops. "They did seem to appreciate the fact that you came over there," he said. "We got helicopters that flew all over the damn place. We went everywhere, from dinner with [General] Creighton Abrams to little out-of-the-way places where they wouldn't even leave the helicopter on the ground. The helicopter took off and I'm like, 'Why did you do that?'"

It was because of his openness to experience and eagerness to learn that Swoboda became a better player—and an outfielder capable of making one of the great catches in World Series history.

Early in his career, he picked up the nickname "Rocky" for his choppy outfield play, though he possessed a strong throwing arm. Swoboda takes issue with the "conventional wisdom" that he was a lackluster fielder. "My feeling about conventional wisdom is that it's conventional but not wise," he said.

When Gil Hodges became the Mets manager in 1968, he would insert Rod Gaspar as a defensive replacement for Swoboda in the late innings. "That really drove me crazy," he said. Swoboda worked assiduously on his fielding to persuade Hodges that this substitution was no longer necessary.

"For some reason, I guess at that point in my evolution, I got off on the wrong foot with Gil and it never really got right and that was my fault," Swoboda said. "He wasn't hard to play for; he just wanted you to play. Shut up and play."

Like many outfielders, Swoboda struggled with line drives, particularly those hit directly at him. To become more adept, he had third base coach Eddie Yost hit him "thousands of balls" with a fungo bat from about 150 feet in front of home plate. That helped him get much better at reading the ball off the bat—making the instantaneous assessment of a ball's distance, arc, and speed.

"The whole point was to hit line drives and ground balls—left, right, over your head, in front of you," he said. "Balls in that difficult, nuanced zone. You're working on your footwork. You build a certain confidence in your hands."

He also learned a technique tailored to his particular tendency as a fielder to veer right when a ball was hit to him. "I'm not ambidextrous," he said. "I'm dominant right and my first move was clockwise."

In working with Yost, Swoboda realized that he would react better to a batted ball if he drew an invisible vertical line way to the left; the ball had to be on the left side of that line before he would turn that way. For anything in the air to the right of the line, he turned to his right—"what I call my strong side"—which made him very sure about his first few steps. Brooks Robinson's line drive was hit decidedly to his strong side.

Of course, it wasn't a foolproof system because sometimes a ball would hook away from his initial direction. For those circumstances, Swoboda practiced a "recovery move," in which he quickly rotated around, "like a skater," to pursue the ball.

Swoboda also studied the moves of established outfielders. By observing the great St. Louis Cardinal centerfielder Curt Flood, he learned how to execute a "crossover" step in going from left to right, or right to left, moves he had struggled to make. He noticed Flood (also known for challenging Major League Baseball's Reserve Clause) did this by moving his feet *after shifting his weight.* "You commit your weight in one direction and your feet have to follow your weight—that's how it works. So I sort of figured that out and that's what I practiced. It helped you get a better jump on every ball."

By building his knowledge and confidence, Swoboda countered a fielder's worst enemy: uncertainty. "When you get unsure, that's when you fuck 'em up," he said. "You go, 'this way, no, this way.' If you do that, you're dead."

Sometimes a line drive hit right at him would appear to start low "and the next thing you know you're not tall enough for that play." At those times, he would employ his "hunker" move—"don't move anywhere, you might be wrong."

By the time Brooks Robinson hit his vicious line drive to right-center field in October 1969, Swoboda had practiced enough with Yost to convince Hodges he could remain in the game in the ninth inning. His outfield moves had become ingrained.

"On that particular play, I was in a white space, you know what I mean? White space. I just saw it and went. [Bullpen coach] Joe Pignatano told me one time, 'Don't think, you'll only hurt the team.' Well, I didn't think. I took off after it."

In approaching a fly ball, outfielders sometimes take a "deep" or "banana" angle—a slightly curved route—rather than a linear path, in order to ready themselves for the throw into the infield. However, the Robinson ball was struck so hard that it could not be reached on a fly that way. "I took the best angle I thought I could take to intersect the ball."

Even so, after committing to make the catch, Swoboda feared he wouldn't get to it in time. "I thought I was in trouble." But there was no turning back. "Yeah. Just kept going hard."

I asked Swoboda if, at an earlier time in his career, he would have chosen the safer option, to play the ball on a bounce.

"I don't know," he said. "I might have." Certainly with the all-or-nothing move he made, "it was a lot easier to screw up than to catch the ball."

Yankees legend Mickey Mantle, who knew something about playing the outfield, called Swoboda's catch "the best play I've ever seen in my life" during his Game Five pregame TV appearance with Koufax. "It was one of those plays where he didn't catch the ball and then dive; he had to dive the length of his body, or a little farther, to catch the ball.

"Sandy and I both thought that's the only spot in that play where he could have caught that ball. If he tried to run back and cut it off on the first bounce, we don't think he could have caught it; it would have went all the way to the wall, and Boog Powell would have scored."

As celebrated as his World Series catch became, Swoboda thinks he made a better catch earlier in 1969 in a game against the Cubs at Wrigley Field. Ernie Banks, the great Cub shortstop and first baseman, hit a foul ball deep into the right field seats, tipping off Swoboda that the right-handed Banks was trying to hit toward right field. "There is a certain point when the pitch gets deep into the strike zone and he can't hit it anywhere else but [right field], between [me] and the right field line."

By committing himself to fielding a ball he expected to be hit toward the right field line, Swoboda was prepared when Banks actually hit it there, breaking almost before the ball was struck. He dove and made the catch, rolling into Wrigley's brick wall. Then he jumped to his feet and fired the ball to first, doubling up the runner who had gone to second in a hit-and-run play.

"That's a better play [than the World Series catch] because I got two outs," he said. "I never made a better play than that."

Chapter 5

BUD HARRELSON

Shortstop, 1965-1977
Throws/Bats: Right/Switch

The Game: October 16, 1969 vs. Baltimore Orioles,
at Shea Stadium, Game Five, World Series

METS STATS	
GAMES:	1,322
AT-BATS:	4,390
HITS:	1,029
HOME RUNS:	6
AVERAGE:	.234
ON-BASE %:	.324
SLUGGING %:	.287
RUNS:	490
RBI:	242
STOLEN BASES:	115
FIELDING %:	.970
WAR:	18.6

The Run-up

When Bud Harrelson first played shortstop for the Mets in 1965—a year the team lost 112 games, second only to the 120 they dropped in their inaugural 1962 season—he would run toward left field on routine fly balls headed to the left fielder, just in case his fielding services were needed.

By 1969, the fortunes of the Mets had changed, but Harrelson was still not taking any chances.

On October 16, 1969, in the ninth inning of Game Five of the World Series, the final batter for the Baltimore Orioles, Davey Johnson, hit a fly ball to left field.

"I was running out there because in the early days of the Mets I had to catch a lot of outfield things as well," he said to much laughter at a symposium on the 50th anniversary of the Mets, held at Hofstra University in 2012. "And then [Cleon Jones] caught it and he kneeled, and when he did that I said, 'I'm gonna get a ring! I'm gonna get a World Series ring! Who woulda thunk?'"

Not many. The Mets shocked the world when they beat the overwhelmingly favored Baltimore Orioles, who had won 109 games during the regular season in 1969, tied for the fifth-highest total in baseball history with the '61 Yankees. Of course, the Mets weren't slouches either with their 100-win season, in which they won 39 out of their final 50 contests. But still, *the Mets?* The lovable losers who, leading up to 1969, had finished in the cellar in five of their first seven seasons, and next-to-last in the other two?

Yet Jones's catch clinched the improbable series victory and ended a game that Harrelson calls the game of his life.

Born in Northern California on D-Day (June 6, 1944), Harrelson was a diminutive but tough kid who despite his slight build made his high school football, baseball, and basketball teams. He played a year of college ball for San Francisco State before the Mets signed him in 1963, on the day after he turned 19, for about $10,000.

Early on, it was clear that Harrelson was the quintessential slap-hitting shortstop whose primary purpose was defense, not offense. On that basis he worked his way up the minors, mixing in service in the National Guard (which extended to his first few years with the Mets). He made it to the AAA level in 1965 in Buffalo, and the next year in Jacksonville, Florida, where he became a switch hitter and met future teammate Tom Seaver.

Harrelson made his debut with the Mets as a September call-up in 1965 and played in 19 games, managing only four hits in 37 at-bats, a microscopic .108 average. He more than doubled that average playing for Jacksonville in 1966 and was brought up on August 12, "my sister's birthday," he told me in the parking lot at Citi Field in September 2013, during a Nesquik-sponsored wiffle ball event to raise money for the Madison Square Boys & Girls Club. "Then I stayed for good."

When Seaver joined the Mets in 1967 he asked to room with Harrelson on road trips since "I was the only one he knew," Harrelson said. They remained roommates until Seaver was traded in mid-1977, also Harrelson's final year with the Mets. In 1967, Harrelson became the Mets' regular shortstop, taking over from his mentor Roy McMillan.

Harrelson's defense at shortstop was shaky in the minors, but it became his strong suit with the Mets, making him a favorite among the team's pitchers. "Whether I hit or not, the pitchers wanted me in the game," he said. His lifetime fielding average as a shortstop with the Mets was a superior .970, while his 13.6 defensive WAR (wins above replacement) is the best for any player in Mets history.

He played his position especially well when Seaver was on the mound. "Tom threw the ball where the catcher was calling for it," he told me. "He was consistent. If it was supposed to be inside, it was inside. So I could anticipate where it would be hit and get good jumps."

"We simply don't win two pennants without him," Seaver has said.

Harrelson brought his batting average up to .254 in 1967, but it dropped down to .219 in '68. That year, Gil Hodges became the manager of the Mets and changed the culture of the team to one that did not tolerate losing. The '69 Mets still revere Hodges for the influence he had on the team.

Hodges was a strong and decisive leader, said Harrelson. "When Gil evaluated players, he wanted no one else's input. He wanted to make his own assessments." Hodges decided the best course for the Mets was a platoon system, whereby he swapped right-handed and left-handed hitters at first base, second base, third base, and right field.

Harrelson prepared for the '69 season by lifting weights and quitting smoking. It showed as he raised his average to .248 while playing lockdown defense at shortstop. Everyone on the team raised their game, and the Mets overtook the Cubs in the pennant race, the Braves in the playoffs, and the Orioles in the Word Series.

"In '69, the teams that we were playing were making the mistakes the Mets made all the time," Harrelson said at Hofstra. "And we took advantage of that. If you look at the history of '69, we won 42 one-run ballgames; forty-two percent of our games were won by one run. So we were a different team in '69 than we were in '68 and before that."

In one of those games, on May 28, Harrelson lashed a game-winning single to break a scoreless tie in the bottom of the 11th, which started an 11-game winning streak. On September 23, his walk-off single in the bottom of the 11th against starter Bob Gibson broke a 2-2 tie and ensured the Mets at least a tie of first place in the National League East, which they would clinch the next night.

In the Mets' three-game sweep of the Braves in the National League Championship Series, Harrelson had only two hits, but made them count—a go-ahead triple that brought home two runs in Game One, and a double that drove in a run in Game Two.

During both the NLCS and World Series of 1969, he showed off his great glove, making only one error in 44 chances.

"Bud Harrelson was the anchor of the Miracle Mets of '69," said Mets TV play-by-play man Gary Cohen, during SNY's June 2012 broadcast announcing the Mets All-Time Team. "He was such a huge part of such important Mets teams." Harrelson was Cohen's favorite player growing up in Queens, New York—"my guy, always and forever."

The Game

The Mets wanted to win Game Five of the '69 World Series so they could wrap up the series at Shea Stadium, and avoid having to return to Baltimore for a Game Six.

They had Jerry Koosman on the mound, the winner of Game Two, and a pitcher who seemed to perform at his highest level in big games.

Harrelson had not batted particularly well in the series, stroking three singles in 13 trips in the first four games (he also had three walks). He went 0 for 4 in Game Five, but that did not reduce the magnitude of the game for him. "It wasn't about me," he said.

The Mets fell behind in Game Five by three runs in the third inning as Koosman gave up two home runs—a two-run shot by the pitcher, Dave McNally, and a solo blast by Frank Robinson. Koosman entered the dugout after the inning vowing the Birds would score no more.

In the fifth, McNally threw a ball in the dirt that the batter Cleon Jones believed had hit his foot, but home plate umpire Lou DiMuro disagreed. The ball was retrieved and tossed from the game, into the Mets dugout.

Hodges emerged with the ball and pointed out to DiMuro that it had a shoe polish smudge. The evidence suggested a hit-by-pitch and Jones was awarded first base, though some have wondered whether the ball Hodges brought out was different from the one McNally pitched. "A God-fearing, churchgoing, honorable man such as Gil wouldn't lie about such a thing, would he?" Harrelson wrote in his book, *Turning Two*. In any event, Donn Clendenon then drilled a two-run homer—his third round-tripper of the series—well over the fence in left field to bring the Mets within one.

Al Weis, another diminutive infielder (a second baseman), who had hit only two homers all year and had never done so at Shea Stadium, clouted one off McNally to lead off the seventh, which tied the score at three.

Koosman was true to his word and did not allow any further runs by the Orioles (while giving up only one hit) after the third. Meanwhile, the Mets continued scoring on an RBI double by Ron Swoboda off reliever Eddie

Watt; Swoboda ran home with the Mets' fifth run as the Orioles made two errors on Jerry Grote's line drive to first base.

In the ninth, Koosman walked Frank Robinson to start the inning, but Boog Powell hit into a force play, Weis tossing to Harrelson at second base. Brooks Robinson flew out to right and then Davey Johnson, who would manage the Mets to their second World Championship 17 years later, lifted a high fly to left. As Harrelson ran out, Jones settled under it and made the catch, famously kneeling on one knee, as if genuflecting to the baseball gods.

When Cleon Jones appeared on SNY's June 2012 broadcast announcing the Mets All-Time Team—he was selected at left field—he entered the stage and got down on one knee. "Davey swears that's the hardest ball he's ever hit in his life," Jones said on the show. "It must have been a supreme being standing over the ballpark and knocking it down to me."

Harrelson described the scene of bedlam that ensued after Johnson made the final out. In what had become a familiar scene at Shea Stadium in 1969, fans started pouring onto the field "like water rushing over the top of the dugouts," he told me. "They tore up the field and I ran right off."

In *Turning Two*, Harrelson wrote that "the horde of humanity poured down from the stands and overran Shea Stadium like bulls in Pamplona, trampling anything in their path." He clutched his glove with one hand and his cap in the other, and raced to the dugout "as if I were going for a triple." The joy he felt at that moment—a moment of triumph he never equaled again as a player—"was like nothing I had ever experienced."

In the clubhouse after the game, Mets broadcaster Lindsey Nelson interviewed many of the principals on the Mets and in the team's management as well as Major League Baseball executives.

"It was a team effort today as it has been all year," said Harrelson in a serious tone. "Once or twice, one individual would stand out, but overall I think today was an example of our game, of a team effort, and fighting back, never quitting. Just a great year, a great team, and I'm glad to be here."

Said Hodges: "It's been a great year, and thank God it's over now."

Bud Harrelson

AP Photo/Harry Harris

"This is the happiest day of my life," said Johnny Murphy, the Mets general manager.

"We knew we could beat Baltimore," said Tommy Agee. "And when they were talking so much, they gave us that much of an incentive to win. They were talking so much they forgot to play."

"Well, Lindsay, this is the same ball club that didn't belong on the same field with the Baltimore Orioles," said Cleon Jones. "But we beat 'em."

Said Seaver: "We never put our heads between our legs, we always fought. And it's the greatest feeling in the world."

The Aftermath

Harrelson went on to have several more productive seasons with the Mets, making the All-Star game in 1970 and 1971. He set a since-surpassed major league record with 54 consecutive errorless games at shortstop in 1970, and won a Gold Glove the following year. He gained considerable street cred for his dustup with Pete Rose in game three of the 1973 playoffs, after the much heftier Rose made a belligerent slide into Harrelson at second base trying to break up a double play. Harrelson went on to have his best postseason batting average in the Mets '73 World Series loss to the Oakland A's, hitting .250.

In 1986, he and Rusty Staub became the first two players to be inducted into the Mets Hall of Fame. Harrelson is seventh among the Mets all-time hits leaders with 1,029, just ahead of sluggers Mike Piazza and Darryl Strawberry.

Though he finished his playing career with the Phillies and the Texas Rangers, Harrelson resumed his association with the Mets as a minor league manager and then as third base coach from 1985 through the start of the 1990 season, when he replaced Davey Johnson as manager. His tenure as manager was short-lived, however, as the Mets collapsed in the second half of the '91 season and he was fired with a week to go.

Over the past 15 years, Harrelson has devoted himself to running the Long Island Ducks of the independent Atlantic League, as co-owner, coach, and senior vice president.

The ring Harrelson received for being a world champion in 1969 would not be his last. He would get another as third base coach of the Mets' 1986 World Championship squad. He is the only individual to play a role in both of the Mets two titles. When I spoke to him at Citi Field, he was wearing the '86 ring.

Chapter 6

FELIX MILLAN

Second base, 1973-1977
Throws/Bats: Right

The Game: September 18, 1973 vs. Pittsburgh Pirates,
at Three Rivers Stadium

METS STATS	
GAMES:	681
AT-BATS:	2,677
HITS:	743
HOME RUNS:	8
AVERAGE:	.278
ON-BASE %:	.326
SLUGGING %:	.337
RUNS:	308
RBI:	182
STOLEN BASES:	11
FIELDING AVERAGE:	.979
WAR:	8.1

The Run-up

Most professional athletes aspire to master the conventional techniques required for success in their sport. Hitters, for example, learn to keep their eyes trained on a pitch all the way to contact with their bat.

A few players, though, can successfully depart from convention in some way, devising their own signature style that separates them from their peers.

When Felix "The Cat" Millan, a right-handed hitter and second baseman for the Mets in the 1970s, came up to bat, he crouched low, near the plate, his left elbow almost even with his cheekbone, and, most tellingly, "choked up," gripping the handle of the bat about six inches from the knob, almost halfway up.

Most players, of course, hold the bat with their hands adjacent to the knob and if they do choke up in certain circumstances—a lost art in baseball—it's only by an inch or two. Millan's technique was more pronounced than that of just about anyone else in the history of the game. It allowed him to consistently make contact and become a consummate spray hitter.

Millan, a native of Puerto Rico and one of the early big leaguers from that island, originally signed with the Kansas City Athletics in 1964 but was acquired the following year by the Braves (still based in Milwaukee).

In the minor leagues, and throughout his life, Millan's wife of more than 50 years, Mercy, was his bulwark against self-doubt. She dissuaded him from quitting in 1966 and 1967 when he shuttled back and forth between the Braves and their minor league teams. "Before we got married he said, 'that's my dream, to become a major league baseball player,'" she told me. "He always kept telling me that. So once he said, 'we're going to go home,' because they started to bring him up and down, up and down. I said, no, you go home, I'm staying. Because you always told me it was your dream, and you want to follow your dream. We're going to make it."

Mercy convinced him, Millan said, "that you'll regret it later if you quit now."

Millan made his first big league appearance with the Braves (now in Atlanta) in 1966 at age 22. He played second base and employed his unorthodox stance for them through 1972, making the All-Star team three times. He came to the Mets in 1973, becoming an integral part of the "Ya Gotta Believe" squad that eked out a first place finish in the National League East, beat the highly favored Cincinnati Reds in the playoffs, and almost prevailed over the dynastic Oakland Athletics in the World Series, finally succumbing in seven games.

Millan remained a fixture at second base for the Mets—and one of their best ever at that position—until August of the 1977 season; an on-field fight with Pittsburgh catcher Ed Ott resulted in an injury that caused him to miss the remainder of the season. The following year, he decided to leave the big leagues and move to Japan, where he played for three years. His career ended at age thirty-seven in the Mexican League.

Millan's style of dramatically choking up on the bat was conceived as a way to remedy a hitting slump he experienced in 1965, while playing in the Northwest League for the Yakima Braves, the Braves' single A affiliate. "I was hitting about .210," he recalled. His manager, Hub Kittle, asked him to choke up so that he could "push the ball and move the runners." He practiced with Kittle almost every afternoon. "I ended up hitting .320," he said. "If I hit .320 this way, I'm going to keep doing it."

Choking up allowed Millan to wait longer for his pitch, with greater bat control, and consistently make contact on the fat part of the bat. It also helped him to hit the ball where it was pitched, a skill that made him a proficient practitioner of the hit-and-run play, as well as very difficult to strike out.

The pitch that could have proved difficult for a player who shortened his bat length was one on the outside part of the plate, which would be hard to reach. Millan met that challenge by standing very close to the plate. But such proximity made him more vulnerable to being hit by a pitch, and he racked up high numbers in that category, getting plunked a league-leading 12 times in 1975.

Felix Millan, choking up on the bat.

AP Photo

Players standing very near the plate can also have trouble hitting pitches thrown inside, close to their body. But Millan had the ability to "inside out" the inside pitch—a style later made famous by the Yankees' Derek Jeter—and drive it to right field.

Hitting in the second spot in the lineup in front of home-run threats throughout his career, and not possessing home-run power himself, Millan would more often see pitches in the strike zone than outside or inside. Pitchers did not want to walk him and have to face the next hitter—Henry Aaron in Atlanta; Cleon Jones, Dave Kingman, or Rusty Staub with the Mets—with a runner on base. "They threw me a lot of fastballs," he said. "I was lucky or blessed. They wanted me to hit the ball."

And Millan tried to oblige. Holding the bat like a hatchet, he relished contact with the horsehide. As a consequence, he didn't work out many walks. But he didn't strike out much, either. For his career, he fanned in just 4.2% of his at bats, the 26th lowest percentage in baseball history. With the Mets, he led the National League in most at-bats per strikeout in three consecutive seasons (1973-1975) and finished second in 1976. In 1974, he struck out only 14 times in 518 at-bats—or once every 37 at-bats—a Mets single-season record. "I was always trying to make contact, moving the runners or getting on base for the guys behind me," he said.

His ability to put the ball in play also led to many sacrifice hits; he led the National League in that category with 24 in 1974. Making contact also helped him avoid downturns. "I was blessed because I didn't get into too many slumps because I made contact or bunted."

Millan, who came from humble beginnings in the Puerto Rican countryside, made the most of his hitting talents over 12 major league seasons, accepting that he would never be a home run hitter. "Guys who hit home runs, they say, drive Cadillacs. Guys who don't hit home runs drive Chevys, Fords. But I was very happy to help my club any way I could."

He also helped by serving as an excellent defender at second base. While his best defensive years were with Atlanta, where he won two Gold Gloves, with the Mets he led Senior-Circuit second basemen in outs made (527) and games played (162) in 1975. He also finished second in putouts at his position (410) in 1973. He and shortstop Bud Harrelson formed a dynamic double-play combination.

Millan welcomed his move from Atlanta to the Mets after the 1972 season, when he and pitcher George Stone were exchanged for pitchers Danny Frisella and Gary Gentry—a trade that turned out to be much to the Mets' advantage. "When Eddie Mathews told me you've been traded to the Mets, I said, well, I'm going home, because there are so many Puerto Ricans and Latinos," Millan recalled. Much to his delight, he was often invited to the homes of Puerto Rican fans for rice and beans, his favorite native meal.

In 1973, Millan's first year with the Mets, he was named by New York sports writers the team's most valuable player for leading in games played (153), at-bats (638), runs scored (82), and batting average (.290) while establishing a franchise record with 185 hits (since surpassed). His consistency was vital for a team riddled with injuries to key players in the topsy-turvy 1973 season.

Despite having more losses than wins for most of the year, the Mets engaged in a furious race for the division crown in the mediocre National League East, winning 27 of their last 39 games and finally prevailing on the last day of the season. Their unprepossessing final record of 82 wins and 79 losses gave them a winning percentage of .509, the lowest for any pennant or division winner in major league history.

But having made it into the playoffs, the Mets, behind their formidable pitching staff of Tom Seaver, Jerry Koosman, and Jon Matlack, proved to be no fluke, getting past the vaunted Big Red Machine, before succumbing to the A's.

There were several turning points in the 1973 season. One occurred on July 9 when the Mets were 34-46, in sixth place in the six-team division, 12.5 games out of first. Team chairman M. Donald Grant held a pep talk with the players, highlighted by screwball-throwing relief pitcher Tug McGraw spontaneously blurting out, "Ya Gotta Believe!" (He had to reassure Grant later that he was not making fun of him.)

"Ya Gotta Believe" became a catchphrase McGraw would repeat throughout the rest of the season, infusing himself with the confidence to perform brilliantly on the mound. It also became the rallying cry for the team and lodged itself in Mets and baseball history as a symbol of perseverance and positive thinking. (Another enduring line from that season, courtesy of the Mets' ever-quotable manager Yogi Berra: "It ain't over till it's over.")

"We had that meeting and we started playing the way we were supposed to be playing," said Millan. "Everybody started saying, 'You gotta believe!'"

Millan recalls the late McGraw with fondness. "Tug McGraw was a big part of that season," he said. "He was always happy, joking around. He kept everybody loose." McGraw's enthusiasm sparked a great camaraderie on the team, with "everybody pulling for each other, everybody close to each other," he said. "If you were on the bench, it didn't matter. They were pulling for the guys playing on the field. The most fun I had playing, I had playing with the New York Mets."

The Game

Mired in sixth (and last) place in the Eastern Division on August 30, the Mets climbed to fourth, at 73-76, within 2.5 games of first, by September 16, a Sunday.

Millan was a solid contributor throughout the September stretch drive, delivering 34 base hits, including a 10-game hitting streak, all of them multi-hit games.

The week of September 17 offered the Mets an opportunity to make a move on the first-place Pirates, with whom they had a five-game series, the first two at Pittsburgh's Three Rivers Stadium and the next three at Shea. This was a potent Pirates team with the likes of Willie Stargell, Al Oliver, Manny Sanguillen, and an emerging Dave Parker (Roberto Clemente, one of Millan's heroes, had passed away the prior December). "The Pirates always had a good team," said Millan. Apart from '73, the Pirates and the Phillies won every NL East title between 1970 and 1980.

The Mets lost the first game on September 17, 10-3, dropping to 3.5 games behind the Pirates; it was an off night for Tom Seaver, who would go on to win one of his three Cy Young awards that year. But the next evening the Mets would bounce back in what Millan called the game of his life with the team.

Heading into the final frame, it looked as though the Mets would lose again. They had scored in the top of the third off Pittsburgh starter Bob Moose (who no-hit the Mets in 1969) on a run-scoring single to center by Rusty Staub. But then the Pirates jumped to a 4-1 lead in the bottom of the third against Jon Matlack, after a two-run single by Richie Zisk and a two-run double by Sanguillen.

That score held until the ninth inning. Bud Harrelson led off for the Mets with a foul out to left, off reliever Ramon Hernandez, who had replaced Moose in the seventh. But then pinch hitter Jim Beauchamp singled to left and Wayne Garrett doubled, advancing Beauchamp to third.

Up came Millan, batting second. His infield single had chased Moose from the game in the seventh. But he saved his best for now, tripling to center, which scored Beauchamp and Garrett and put the Mets within one at 4-3.

The Mets weren't done. Staub walked and Pirates manager Danny Murtaugh replaced Hernandez with Dave Giusti. But Giusti was entirely ineffectual. Pinch hitter Ron Hodges drove in Millan, who scored the tying run. Cleon Jones walked, and Don Hahn singled in Staub and Ted Martinez (running for Hodges). The Mets now led 6-4. Murtaugh replaced Giusti with the third reliever of the inning, Bob Johnson, who was able to retire the next two batters.

Tug McGraw had pitched a strong seventh and eighth but was removed for pinch hitter Hodges. At this critical moment in the bottom of the ninth, manager Berra surprisingly brought in neophyte Bob Apodaca to make his major league debut. He promptly walked two Pirates, and Berra replaced him with Buzz Capra, who kept things interesting by allowing one run to score and walking two more batters (one intentionally) before finally securing the third out.

Felix Millan

Steve Aaronson

The Mets had come back from a three-run ninth-inning deficit and held on to win. They were back to 2.5 games behind Pittsburgh. Millan had set the comeback in motion with his two-run triple. "That was a big hit," he said. "It was a very good comeback, and I'm happy I was part of it."

Facing lefty reliever Hernandez, also a native of Puerto Rico, was a fortuitous turn for Millan. With a lifetime ERA of 3.03 over nine seasons in the big leagues, including six with the Pirates, Hernandez knew his way around the strike zone. But Millan was familiar with him from Puerto Rico and Atlanta, where they were teammates in 1967.

"He was my good buddy from Puerto Rico," Millan said. He was a great guy. I always had a good relationship with him. He was a junk ball pitcher. Good curve ball and screw ball."

The triple was off a slow curve ball, Millan recalled. "I knew he [wouldn't] throw me a fastball. He would throw me a curve and I was waiting for that."

The comeback victory set the Mets on a winning path as they took the next six games, all at home, including three more against the Pirates, two against the Cardinals, and one against the Expos.

The Aftermath

The second game at Shea against Pittsburgh two days later would leave an indelible memory known as the "ball off the wall." Millan had two essential hits in this contest, a pitching duel between Jerry Koosman and Jim Rooker, who each pitched eight innings and gave up two runs.

Each team tallied once in the ninth and the score remained tied at three until the memorable 13th. With Mets swingman Ray Sadecki on the mound, Stargell struck out and Richie Zisk singled to left. After Sanguillen hit a fly to right for the second out, Dave Augustine, a minor league call-up, drove a 2-1 pitch to left that looked as if it might be his first major league home run. But it hit the top of the left-field wall and somehow bounced back into the glove of Cleon Jones, who fired it to Garrett at short, who relayed it to the plate where catcher Hodges tagged Zisk in a home-plate collision for the third out.

In the bottom of the inning, a still-functioning Hodges singled to knock in the winning run, putting the "ball off the wall" game in the annals of Mets miracles.

"Cleon was a good left fielder," said Millan. "We were lucky enough that the ball hit the top of the fence and came to him. That was a great play by Cleon."

With their final win against the Pirates on September 21, an easy 10-2 affair, the Mets vaulted past them into first place, a position they would not relinquish for the rest of the season.

But, with the Cardinals and the Pirates still on their heels, the Mets wouldn't nail down the division title until the last game of the season, a 6-4 win on October 1 over the Cubs in an overcast Chicago, with McGraw relieving Seaver and earning a three-out, one-hit save. Millan got two hits and scored the fifth run.

In the National League Division Series against the heavily favored Reds, Millan hit a robust .316 with two RBI and six runs scored as the Mets prevailed, three games to two.

In game three of the series, which the Mets won handily, 9-2, Mets shortstop Bud Harrelson and Reds left fielder Pete Rose engaged in their famous contretemps at second base after Rose, as he was wont to do, slid ferociously into Harrelson in an effort to break up a double play. It didn't work, as Harrelson got the ball over to first baseman John Milner (who had made the initial peg to Harrelson) in time to complete the twin killing.

In the ensuing brawl between Rose and Harrelson, which elicited the participation of players from both teams, Millan found himself on the side-lines. "When the ball was hit to first, the second baseman runs behind first in case you had a bad throw from short. I was going toward the [infield] fence, and when I turned around, everyone was fighting on the field."

Well before the fight, in the second inning, Millan had been part of a five-run rally in which he singled home a run and later scored on Staub's three-run homer.

In the deciding fifth game, with the score tied at two in the bottom of the fifth, Millan bunted Garrett over to third and was safe at first on a fielder's choice. They both scored as part of a four-run inning that iced the game, Millan came home on a pinch-hit single—a Baltimore chop, high above home plate—by Willie Mays, playing in his final season. Millan also singled and scored in the first.

One of Millan's most vexing moments as a Met occurred in Game One of the '73 World Series against the A's at the Oakland-Alameda County Coliseum. In the third inning, with two outs, pitcher Ken Holtzman doubled. The next batter, Bert Campaneris, hit a routine grounder to Millan that slipped beneath his glove and legs into right field, scoring Holtzman. Campaneris then stole second and scored on Joe Rudi's single.

Those two runs would be all the A's would score—and all they would need—as the Mets countered with only one run in the top of the fourth.

Millan, a two-time Gold Glover who had made only nine errors all year, attributed the snafu to the difference in the dirt in the Oakland ballpark compared to that at Shea. "I was waiting for the bounce and the bounce never came," he said. "If you don't know the field, you will make an error. I made an error—I didn't want to make it, but things happen."

Berra, for whom Millan has great affection, stood up for him in the media onslaught after the game. "When they asked him about my error, he said, 'I hope they hit 27 more that way because I know he's not going to miss it,'" Millan recalled. "I loved playing for Yogi. He was a good manager, a good person. A class-A person."

Millan was able to put the miscue behind him. "Some guys say, 'I hope they don't hit it again this way. I say, hit it again. This time I'm not going to miss it." In the remainder of the series, Millan was errorless, though he hit only .188 overall in the series.

Despite losing game one, the Mets still had a good shot at taking the series, which they led three games to two heading to Oakland. But they lost the next two games, and thus the series, to the A's.

Millan continued performing solidly for the Mets over the next four years, but his Mets career came to an unfortunate end in Pittsburgh as a result of the confrontation with Pirates catcher Ott. Somewhat paralleling the Harrelson-Rose incident, Ott slid hard into Millan to break up a double play, prompting Millan to hit Ott with the ball in his fist; Ott picked him up and slammed him, wrestling style, onto the turf. Millan suffered a grievous injury to his shoulder that ended his season. But he eventually forgave Ott and has been in touch with him in recent years.

"You know those things happen in baseball," Millan said. "I messed up right there [and as a result] I was injured."

"Felix was sorry as soon as it happened," said Jane Allen Quevedo, who helped Millan write his 2014 autobiography *Tough Guy, Gentle Heart*. "He's not a person who holds a grudge."

Millan rebounded nicely in Japan, batting .306 over three seasons with the Yokohama Taiyo Whales, to whom the Mets sold his contract. He led the Central League in hitting in 1979 with a .346 average and received the Best Nine Award, given to the best player at each position. The invitation to play with the Whales had come from their third baseman, Clete Boyer, with whom Millan had played in Atlanta.

Since retiring as a player, Millan has coached infielders for the Mets, worked as the organization's Latin American minor league coordinator, served as a roving instructor for Major League Baseball, and assisted at the Roberto Clemente Sports City in Puerto Rico, where he resides. He also participates regularly at the Mets Fantasy Camp in Florida, where he also has a home, and backs a little league in New York City.

Does he teach young players who are not power hitters his trademark batting stance? "I tell them, but not too many kids like the stance," he said. "They want to hit the ball hard. But I say, look, if you're fast, and you make contact, this will be good for you."

Chapter 7

JOHN STEARNS

Catcher, 1975-1984
Throws/Bats: Right

The Game: May 22, 1982 vs. Houston Astros, at the Astrodome

METS STATS	
GAMES:	809
AT-BATS:	2,679
HITS:	695
HOME RUNS:	46
AVERAGE:	.259
ON-BASE %:	.341
SLUGGING %:	.375
FIELDING %:	.985
RUNS:	334
RBI:	312
STOLEN BASES:	91
FIELDING %:	.984
WAR:	19.5

The Run-up

The Mets have been unusually blessed throughout their history at the catcher position. In their two championship seasons, the team was anchored by exceptional catchers—Jerry Grote in 1969 and Gary Carter in 1986. The World Series team in 2000 boasted the catcher who finished his career with the most home runs at that position in history, Mike Piazza. Another backstop of note: Todd Hundley, who shares the single-season team record for home runs (41) with Carlos Beltran.

Then there is perhaps the most hard-nosed catcher the Mets ever had— John Stearns, whose on-field exploits inspired *Sports Illustrated* to pronounce him the "Bad Dude."

In truth, "bad" is the wrong adjective for Stearns, who, as any attendee at Mets Fantasy Camp will attest, is a gentleman. Stearns himself has never been enamored of the nickname. "I wish the 'bad dude' thing had never happened," he said in an interview at Fantasy Camp.

Perhaps "tough dude" would have been a better fit, for Stearns, who excelled at both football and baseball at the University of Colorado, was a force to be reckoned with behind the plate. The Pirates' Dave Parker discovered as much at Pittsburgh's Three Rivers Stadium on June 30, 1978.

With the Mets leading 6-3 in the bottom of the ninth and one out, Parker, the Pirates' 6-foot-5, 230-pound right fielder, drilled a triple to left field, driving in two runs and bringing the Bucs within one.

The next batter, left fielder Bill Robinson, lifted a medium fly ball to Mets right fielder Joel Youngblood, who caught it for the second out. Though Youngblood had a great arm, the ball was hit far enough for Parker to tag up and attempt to score the tying run.

"Youngblood threw me a one-hopper just to the right of the plate," recalled Stearns. "I was able to catch it and dive on top of the plate on my knees. When I looked up, Parker was about six feet away, bearing down on me."

Stearns had time to bring the ball up for the tag and brace himself. Parker barreled into him, banging his cheek against the back of Stearns's head and knocking him about 20 feet back. As both men lay on the ground, Parker with a broken cheekbone, the umpire signaled that he was out. It was a game-ending double play and the Mets won 6-5.

The key to the play, Stearns said, was that he received the ball with enough time to protect himself and make the tag. "If I had been trying to catch that ball when Parker got to me, he would've killed me. I was lucky."

Two other catchers Parker had collided with at home plate earlier that season were not as fortunate, winding up on the disabled list.

In 2014, Major League Baseball implemented an experimental rule governing plays at the plate to prevent such "egregious" collisions. Among its provisions, the catcher is not allowed to block the runner's path to the plate before he has possession of the ball. That proviso may have prevented, or at least mitigated, the Stearns-Parker confrontation.

Not that Stearns, the former college safety, was shy about those sorts of encounters. "When I played football, I liked contact," he said. "I wanted to be the hitter."

The next year, Stearn's pugnacious style was in fine form on April 11 at Shea in a game against the Montreal Expos. This time, with one out in the top of the ninth and the score tied at two, it was future Met Gary Carter trying to score after a wild throw to first by Mets pitcher Pete Falcone. Mets right fielder Elliot Maddox retrieved the ball and made an accurate peg that nailed Carter at the plate despite a collision with Stearns. But Carter wasn't finished.

"He tried to flop on top of me and hold me down so the other guy on base [Lance Parrish] could move up," Stearns said. "So I flipped him up and took a swipe at him."

Both dugouts and bullpens emptied and both Stearns and Carter were ejected from the game, which the Expos ultimately won 3-2 in 11 innings.

Stearns was also famous for his rushes from the dugout, once to tackle an inebriated fan who jumped onto the field, and once to slam Expos pitcher Bill Gullickson to the ground after he threw a ball close to the head of Met Mike Jorgenson, who had been beaned the previous year. Then there was his legendary takedown in Atlanta-Fulton County Stadium of Braves mascot Chief Noc-A-Homa, who would taunt visiting players by running past their dugout before every game. Tired of this routine, Stearns sprinted after the Chief and "dragged him down," Stearns told the *New York Post*, adding, "It was just a fun thing, but Joe Torre was our manager and he didn't like it."

Stearns's football talent was such that the Buffalo Bills drafted him as a defensive back in the 17th round of the 1973 NFL draft. But he made baseball his career after the Phillies selected him as the second overall pick in the 1973 Major League Baseball draft. He played only one game for the Phillies in 1974 as a September call-up before being dealt to the Mets, along with outfielder Del Unser and pitcher Mac Scarce, for popular reliever Tug McGraw and outfielders Don Hahn and Dave Schneck.

Stearns played sparingly in both 1975 and 1976, backing up veteran Jerry Grote, but with a strong finish in '76 he became the Mets' full-time catcher the following year. Unfortunately, 1977 was the start of a precipitous seven-year downturn for the Mets that encompassed most of his career, as the team finished sixth in the National League East (last place) five times and fifth twice. Beginning in 1980, Stearns was also hampered by injuries that curtailed his playing time.

Still, on mediocre Mets squads, Stearns's all-around play stood out and he made the All-Star team four times. He is tenth on the Mets career WAR (wins above replacement) list with 19.5 and fourth in defensive WAR with 7.9.

As a catcher, Stearns possessed a strong and accurate arm, which enabled him to throw out 37.1% of the 795 runners attempting to steal a base in his career. That percentage puts him at 65th on the all-time list of catchers with at least 250 stolen bases attempted against them, six places behind Jerry Grote, considered a defensive standout. Only 34 catchers in baseball history have a lifetime caught-stealing percentage of 40% or greater.

Stearns grades his percentage better than average. In his coaching of catchers, he expects them to throw out at least 30% of runners. "If they are not throwing out 30 [percent], we need them to get better."

The Game

For all his prowess behind the plate, Stearns's fondest baseball memory centers on his hitting performance on May 22, 1982, in a game against the Houston Astros at the Astrodome. That day, he went four for five, including a single, double, and triple off the starting pitcher. And it wasn't just any starting pitcher. It was Nolan Ryan, the former Met who had thrown his fifth no-hitter (he would have two more) the previous September on his way to a career total of 5,714 strikeouts (the most ever) and 324 wins.

Stearns managed some hits off Ryan in the past, but nothing like this. "I had a good day in the Astrodome," Stearns said. "That was the game that stands out"—especially because the Mets won, he added.

Ryan pitched eight innings and left the game trailing three to one. Stearns notched his fourth hit, a run-scoring single in the top of the ninth, off Astros reliever Dave Smith, giving the Mets a 5-1 advantage.

The lead was erased, however, in the bottom of the ninth, due to a grand slam by Astros right fielder Terry Puhl. The score remained tied at five until the top of the 12th, when Stearns worked out a walk off reliever Randy Moffitt, stole second, advanced to a third on a fly ball to center field, and scored the go-ahead run on an error by catcher Alan Ashby. In the bottom of the 12th, Mets reliever Neil Allen retired the side, giving the Mets a 6-5 win.

The prototypical catcher is a slow runner and not, therefore, inclined to steal bases. But Stearns belied that stereotype. His 12th-inning stolen base, which set up the game-winning run, was one of 17 he stole in 1982. In 1978, he stole 25 bases, setting a National League record for catchers that Jason Kendall of the Pirates surpassed by one in 1998. For his career, he swiped 91 bags and was thrown out 51 times.

How did Stearns approach his at-bats against the Ryan Express and his 98-mile-per-hour heater? "Well, if I sat on a fastball I could get the bat around on it. I had to be looking for it," he said. "With Nolan, I'm going to go up there looking to hit his fastball. If he gets his breaking ball over and uses it early in the count, then he's going to get me."

John Stearns

AP Photo/Lennox McLendon

Fortunately for Stearns that day, Ryan threw him what he was looking for. "I got two or three pretty good pitches," he said.

The significance of getting two extra-base hits and a single off one of the most dominant pitchers in baseball history was not lost on Stearns. "Nolan Ryan had the best stuff of any pitcher I ever faced in my life, from little league all the way to my retirement," he said. "People don't realize he had a great breaking ball. His curveball dropped off the table. It was similar to Bert Blyleven's curveball, one of the best curveballs in the business. People never recognize that from him because he was the hardest thrower in the game."

The main criticism leveled at Ryan was that he lacked control, especially early in his career with the Mets but at other times as well. "No doubt, before he was 25, he was wild," said Stearns. "But he came along later, throwing strikes, off-speed pitches, fastballs in and out, mixing it up. Obviously a Hall of Famer."

Stearns acknowledged that there was a fear element with Ryan. "Absolutely, you were nervous facing Ryan because he's throwing harder than the rest of the pitchers. If a guy's throwing 98, that's a fast one. It's a little [nerve-wracking] facing a guy like that."

The Aftermath

His great hitting day in Houston contributed to Stearns's final batting average in 1982 of .293, the best of his career. From 1980 to 1982—his last three seasons with significant playing time—he hit for a reasonable average, with marks of .285 and .271 in '80 and '81, compared to between .243 and .264 the previous four years. But the improvement in average came at the expense of power; after belting 12,15, and 9 homers from '77 to '79, he hit 0, 1, and 4 the next three years, albeit in many fewer games.

Due to injuries, Stearns lost a great deal of playing time in 1980 and 1982, participating in just 91 and 98 games. (He played in 80 games in the strike-shortened 1981 season.) The next two years, he was limited to just four and eight games.

His first major injury was a broken finger caused by a foul tip in July 1980, causing him to miss the rest of the season. In 1982, he began suffering from an elbow ailment that ultimately ended his career.

"I tried for three years to come back, but I couldn't," he said. "It was a Tommy John surgery thing and back then I didn't get the right diagnosis by the doctors in New York and I didn't get that surgery right away. I ended up just trying to rehab it. But I was done."

Stearns left the Mets as a free agent after the '84 season. He made unsuccessful comeback attempts with the Reds and the Texas Rangers, and finally called it quits in 1986.

He concluded his career with close to 2,700 at-bats, a figure he felt should have been closer to 7,500: "I'm disappointed in that. But other than that, I'm grateful to have had the opportunity to play in New York."

With his passion for the game still intact, Stearns has worked as a scout, coach, manager, and announcer for almost thirty years. On the major league level, he served as the Yankees bullpen coach in 1989, and worked for the Mets as an advance scout in 1999, bench coach in 2000, third base coach in 2001, and again as a scout in 2002. He remained in the Mets organization through 2005 as a manager of their AA and AAA teams and as a roving catching instructor.

He moved on to manage the Washington Nationals' AAA and A teams and then the AAA squad of the Seattle Mariners for whom he was also catching coordinator. He was set to return to the big leagues in 2014 as the Mariners' third-base coach, but decided to step down while going through a difficult recovery from hiatal hernia surgery.

While serving as the Mets' bench coach in game one of the 2000 National League Championship Series against the Cardinals, Stearns reacted to Mike Piazza's run-scoring double by shouting into a TV microphone, "The monster is out of the cage!"

Stearns was no doubt seeing a reflection of his old self.

Chapter 8

TIM TEUFEL

Second Base, 1986-1991
Throws/Bats: Right

The Game: June 10, 1986 vs. Philadelphia Phillies, at Shea Stadium

METS STATS	
GAMES:	463
AT-BATS:	1,279
HITS:	328
HOME RUNS:	35
AVERAGE:	.256
ON-BASE %:	.336
SLUGGING %:	.411
RUNS:	182
RBI:	164
STOLEN BASES:	6
FIELDING %:	.976
WAR:	7.4

The Run-up

Like the Mets '70s-era second baseman Felix Millan, who choked up a good six inches on the bat handle, Tim Teufel had an unusual batting style, known as the "Teufel Shuffle."

Many batters, while standing in the batter's box, wave their raised bat around, or point it at the pitcher, or pound it on the plate; they do this to center themselves and lock in on the impending pitch. The right-handed Teufel waved his bat a bit, but mostly he rotated his hips and buttocks in a rhythmic back-and-forth motion, like a belly dancer at the bat. This routine kept his hips flexible and allowed them to move in tandem with his swing.

Teufel grew up in tony Greenwich, Connecticut, though his family was not wealthy, and attended Clemson University in South Carolina. He was drafted by the Minnesota Twins in the second round of the 1980 draft. After a stellar season at AAA in 1983, the Twins called him up that September and he played for the team through 1985, demonstrating some power with 14 homers in '84 and 10 in '85.

He came to the Mets in 1986 to provide a right-handed complement to Wally Backman at second base and bat mostly against left-handed pitchers—though he had hit much better than usual against right-handers in 1985. The Mets acquired Teufel, who had asked the Twins to trade him, and minor leaguer Pat Crosby in exchange for Bill Latham, Joe Klink, and Billy Beane, future Oakland A's general manager of *Moneyball* fame.

Though mild-mannered, Teufel got caught up in the '86 Mets' rowdy culture when he was arrested with Ron Darling, Bob Ojeda, and Rick Aguilera after a bar fight in Houston with off-duty police officers moonlighting as bouncers. The players had been celebrating the birth of Teufel's son, Shawn, who would become a pitcher in the Mets minor league system in 2014.

Teufel batted .247 and hit just four homers in 279 at-bats in '86, but one was a particularly memorable grand slam.

The Game

The '86 Mets are famous for their come-from-behind victories in the postseason against the Houston Astros and the Boston Red Sox. But they were also quite adept at late-inning and extra-inning comebacks during the regular season.

Among their 108 regular-season victories, the Mets had eight "walk-off" victories at Shea Stadium, including four in extra innings. They won an additional nine games in extra innings on the road.

One of the most dramatic walk-off wins of the year took place on June 10, 1986, a Tuesday night, against the Phillies at Shea Stadium, with 27,472 fans in attendance. Teufel, pinch-hitting for Backman in the bottom of the 11th of a 4-4 tie, launched a game-winning grand slam off right-hander Tom Hume. It was one of seven pinch-hit homers Teufel hit during his career, and at the time just the eighth pinch-hit grand slam in baseball history.

"Personally, that was my most memorable moment other than the World Series," he said during an on-field interview in 2014 at spring training in Port St. Lucie, Florida. "Just because it was extra innings and won the game. Kind of a dramatic way to end a game."

The third-place Phillies, at 26 wins and 27 losses, were not a major threat to the first-place Mets, who were already dominating the league at 37-16, especially after Philadelphia's star third baseman Mike Schmidt was scratched from the lineup due to a strained left calf muscle.

The game started with Backman playing second base and batting second against Phillies right-hander Charles Hudson. The Phillies scored a run in the third inning and again in the fourth off Mets starter Bob Ojeda. Gary Carter singled home the Mets first run in the bottom half of the fourth, and put the Mets ahead with a two-run homer in the sixth.

The Phillies regained the lead with a run in the seventh and one in the eighth, but Carter drilled his second homer of the day in the bottom of the eighth, knotting the score at four. Neither team scored in the ninth.

Left-handed Phillies reliever Randy Lerch came into the game in the 10th, retiring the side in order. But in the 11th, Lerch allowed a leadoff

Tim Teufel

AP Photo/ G. Paul Burnett

single to Ray Knight—a weak grounder that took a bad hop past fill-in third baseman Rich Schu. On a hit-and-run play, Rafael Santana grounded out, moving Knight to second.

Phillies manager John Felske then decided to have Lerch intentionally walk right-handed pinch-hitter Barry Lyons to avoid the righty-lefty matchup, even though Lyons had been hitless in his only eight at-bats in the big leagues, and face Lenny Dykstra, a vastly superior, if left-handed, batter. Lerch walked Dykstra as well (not intentionally) to load the bases.

Using his own lefty-righty strategy, Mets skipper Davey Johnson brought in the right-handed Teufel—who had been struggling in clutch situations and batting just .234—to pinch-hit for Backman against the lefty Lerch. But Felske countered by bringing in right-handed sinkerball thrower Tom Hume, sporting a ghastly 6.60 ERA, to face Teufel, who had proved in 1985 that he was more than capable of handling right-handed pitching.

Felske also positioned right fielder Glenn Wilson behind second base to improve the chances of throwing out the winning run at the plate (assuming Teufel didn't hit the ball to right). The other two outfielders played shallow.

But all of Felske's maneuvers fell short, as Teufel blasted Hume's third pitch over the left-field fence for his second homer of the year and his first career grand slam (he would hit two more), ending the almost four-hour contest with an 8-4 Mets triumph. Reliever Roger McDowell, the Mets' fourth pitcher of the game, got the win.

Through 2014, the Mets had seven walk-off grand slams in team history (Teufel's was the fourth). Apart from Teufel, only one other player, Ike Davis, delivered a walk-off grand slam as a pinch-hitter—at Citi Field, on April 5, 2014, against the Reds.

"You come up in those situations, you just need a [hit]," said Teufel. "It wasn't like I was trying to hit a home run. It was just a drive that took off. It was a cut fastball and I just caught it right."

Teufel employed a somewhat different strategy as a pinch hitter than he did as a member of the starting lineup. "I'm looking to get the job done early," he said. "I'm not in there taking pitches. You try to get your timing a little quicker.

"With all that being said, it was just one of those times that I was able to get a pitch that was up a little bit and do something with it."

As much as the fans celebrated his grand slam, Teufel especially enjoyed watching his teammates' reaction. "You're more into your teammates than anything," he said. "They were waiting at home plate, which was kind of cool. I got to jump into the pile."

The Aftermath

Teufel played in two games in the '86 National League Championship Series against the Astros, managing just one hit. But he fared better in the World Series against the Red Sox, batting .444 in nine at-bats over three games, including a homer in the eighth inning of game five, which the Mets lost, 4-2.

In Game One of the World Series, Teufel let a ball go through his legs at second base, enabling the Red Sox's only run to score as Boston won 1-0. He faced the media with aplomb after the game, answering every question.

Teufel's error was oddly similar in effect to the miscue committed by second baseman Felix Millan—his comrade in unusual batting stances—in the first game of the 1973 World Series against the Oakland A's, which led to both of Oakland's runs in a 2-1 victory. The difference, of course, was that the Mets lost the '73 series in seven games, but went on to win the '86 series in seven, taking Teufel off the hook.

In 1987, as the Mets fell off their '86 perch, Teufel had his best year offensively while playing in 97 games under the platoon with Backman. He matched his career highs in home runs (14) and RBI (61) set with the Twins, and achieved career bests in average (.308), on-base percentage (.398), and slugging (.545).

In Teufel's final four seasons with the Mets ('87-'91), his batting average declined, but he reached double-digits in home runs with 10 and 12 in 1990 and '91, respectively. His good eye at the plate earned him walks and kept his on-base percentage over .300.

In 1989, after the Mets traded Backman and promoted touted prospect Gregg Jefferies to full-time second baseman, Teufel started only 30 games at second base, and filled in at first base. The '89 season also featured a mound brawl between Teufel and reliever Ron Dibble after Dibble drilled Teufel in the back with a 100-mile-per-hour fastball.

During the 1991 season the Mets traded Teufel to the San Diego Padres for shortstop Gary Templeton (who retired after one season). He finished his career in San Diego in 1993.

Teufel considers playing ten years in the major leagues an accomplishment for a player who, unlike most big leaguers, wasn't a superstar in high school. "I didn't get any scholarships whatsoever out of high school," he told SNY in 2014. "So I ended up just going down to Florida to play more baseball and go after my dream, not knowing what was going to happen. The development took a little bit longer for me. To come out of that scenario and be recognized was a feat in itself."

After retiring as a player, Teufel remained in San Diego and worked as an investment banker, spending quality time with his wife, son, and three daughters. He rejoined the Mets organization as a scout in 1998, but that ultimately wasn't enough. "When that dreaded itch comes, you want to get back on the field," he told SNY. "And that's when I notified the Mets that I want to get out of scouting and go onto the field. That's when the journey began."

Beginning as a minor-league infield coordinator, he became manager of the Mets' short-season single-A Brooklyn Cyclones in 2003 and went on to manage the single-A St. Lucie Mets in 2004, 2005, 2008, and 2009, as well as the Mets' single-A Savannah team in 2007. He followed that with managerial jobs with the Mets' AA Binghamton, New York, team in 2010 and AAA Buffalo club in 2011, as well as a stint as manager in the Venezuelan League.

Teufel has had some off-the-field issues in recent years. Notably, like Mets owner Fred Wilpon, Hall-of-Fame pitcher Sandy Koufax, writer Elie

Wiesel, and actor John Malkovich, among many others known and unknown, he was ensnared in the Madoff Ponzi scheme. In 2011, he was named in a "clawback" suit for $1.2 million in "fictitious profits" filed by trustee Irving Picard on behalf of victims in the scheme.

But on the ball field, all is well. Beginning in 2012 and continuing through the 2014 season, Teufel patrolled the left side of the diamond as third-base coach for the Mets, and worked on defense with Mets infielders like Daniel Murphy, Ruben Tejada, Wilmer Flores, and Dilson Herrera. "We want these guys to get better, we want them to be successful, and then we're all successful," he said in the SNY interview.

He also hosts an annual charity event—the Tim Teufel Celebrity Golf Tournament—in Greenwich, Connecticut, where it all began.

Chapter 9

WALLY BACKMAN

Second Base, 1980-1988
Throws/Bats: Right/Switch

The Game: October 15, 1986 vs. Houston Astros, at the Astrodome, Game Six, National Championship Series

METS STATS	
GAMES:	765
AT-BATS:	2,704
HITS:	670
HOME RUNS:	7
AVERAGE:	.283
ON-BASE %:	.353
SLUGGING %:	.344
RUNS:	359
RBI:	165
STOLEN BASES:	106
FIELDING %:	.978
WAR:	11.6

The Run-up

Mike Scott was looming, like the grim reaper.

The Mets knew that if they had to face The Houston Astros' indomitable right-handed pitcher in the seventh and deciding game of the 1986 National League Championship Series, they would most likely lose—and not move on to play in the World Series. Their 108-win regular season—the best in team history—would be for naught.

But they could avoid that nightmare by simply winning game six and clinching the series. It turned out to be anything but simple.

The 1986 Mets would, of course, get past the Astros and then the Boston Red Sox to win their second World Series. How they did that made for one of the most epic postseasons in baseball history.

On a team full of colorful characters, renowned for their swagger and competitive drive, second baseman Wally Backman fit right in. A scrappy, speedy 5-foot-9, 160 pounds, the Oregon native played with a preternatural intensity that continues to define him as a minor league manager.

A first-round pick in the 1977 draft, Backman, a switch hitter, joined the Mets in 1980 and became the starting second baseman in 1984. But after he struggled against left-handed pitching, the club traded for Tim Teufel in 1986. Beginning that year, they platooned at second base, with Teufel primarily hitting against left-handed pitchers, Backman right-handers.

"I have to be honest, I did not like platooning," Backman said in an interview at Fantasy Camp. "And I know Teuf didn't like platooning. But as we look back at it—and we're very good friends still, today—if you combined our statistics together, there's some amazing numbers for a second baseman back then. It created competition and I think it brought me and Teuf in '86 up to a top level." Backman has used the platoon system himself as manager of the Mets AAA team, the Las Vegas 51s.

The Backman/Teufel combination did indeed produce some impressive numbers in 1986: 666 at-bats, 193 hits, .290 batting average, 102 runs scored, and 38 doubles. Their power numbers were low—five homers and

58 RBI—but homers and RBI weren't their responsibility on a team with Darryl Strawberry, Gary Carter, and Keith Hernandez.

The '86 Mets, whose boisterous attitude incurred the wrath of their opponents, were a juggernaut that won the National League East by 21.5 games, by far the best margin of victory in team history. Backman usually batted second in the order, behind Lenny Dykstra, who platooned in center field with Mookie Wilson. The number one and two batters were the table setters, tasked with getting on base so that the three, four, and five hitters could drive them in. That happened often with the '86 Mets at the outset of games.

"If we got on base, we were going to score," said Backman, who once had five hits in a game for the Mets. "I can't tell you how many times in the first inning—it would be a great stat to find out—we were ahead, out of 108 games, with one of us getting on base and scoring a run. But it was a lot."

As per BaseballReference.com, it appears that Backman is correct; the team had an above-average tendency to score quickly, often more than one run.

In fact, of the 108 games the '86 Mets won, they scored at least one run in the first inning 41 times, or 38% of their wins. In addition, the team scored more than one run in the first inning in 23 of their victories (21%), including six times when they led off the game with four runs (the most they scored in the first).

Backman started in 62 of the Mets' 108 regular season triumphs, and in those games, the Mets scored in the first inning 29 times, or 47%. So Backman, who hit a career-best .320 that year, with an on-base percentage of .376, gave them a better chance to score in the first.

The Mets also scored in the first in 11 of their 54 losses (20%). In total, the '86 Mets scored 103 runs in the first inning, or an average of .636 runs in the initial frame. Compared to MLB teams playing between 2007 and 2013, that percentage would rank in the top 10 every year but one (2007, when it would rank 11th).

In the '86 postseason, the Mets won eight of 13 games, and scored in the first only once. That was in Game Three of the World Series in Boston, when they beat the Red Sox 7-1, scoring four runs in their first at-bats.

The '86 NLCS between the Mets and the Astros—both born when the National League expanded in 1962—was the stuff of high drama. The club's catalytic leadoff tandem of Dykstra and Backman came to the rescue on more than one occasion.

The Mets entered the NLCS having won seven of their 12 regular season games against the Astros. In Game One of the NLCS, the Mets' 1985 Cy Young winner Dwight Gooden faced off against the eventual winner of the NLCS MVP Award and the 1986 Cy Young Award, Mike Scott, fresh off his division-clinching no-hitter against the San Francisco Giants. Scott's 18-10 season featured a 2.22 ERA and 306 strikeouts, both tops in the NL. (He would never approach those stats again in his career.)

The Mets had faced Scott only once during the regular season, a 5-4 Astros win in which he gave up three earned runs in 8 1/3 innings, striking out seven. In this higher-stakes contest, Scott and his bewitching split-finger fastball held the Mets scoreless on five hits and struck out 14 over nine innings. The Astros managed just one run off Gooden, good enough for a 1-0 Houston victory.

The Mets bounced back in Game Two behind Bob Ojeda for a 5-1 victory over Nolan Ryan. Backman singled and scored in the two-run fourth, and singled in a run and scored in the three-run fifth.

Backman's pinch-hit single in the bottom of the ninth in game three at Shea set the stage for Dykstra's electrifying two-run, walk-off homer as the Mets prevailed 6-5.

Scott was back at it in Game Four on three days' rest, pitching a complete-game three-hitter with five K's as the 'Stros won 3-1.

Backman's difficulty with Scott was typical: he was 0-for-8 against him in the series, as opposed to 5-for-15, or .333, against the rest of the Astros staff. The Mets insisted to umpires and league officials, to no avail, that Scott's invincibility was the result of his scuffing the ball by some surreptitious means (sandpaper, nail, or thumbtack in his glove, for example).

This is as much as Scott would ever say about the issue, taken from MLB Network's "1986: A Postseason to Remember," which aired in 2011: "They can believe whatever they want to believe. Every ball that hits the ground has something on it. … I've thrown balls that were scuffed but I haven't scuffed every ball that I've thrown."

Game Five turned into a pitcher's duel between Ryan and Gooden. Strawberry tied the game 1-1 in the fifth with a laser-beam homer, and the score remained that way until the bottom of the 12th. Coming up clutch once again, Backman got on base with an infield single, went to second on a wild pick-off throw, and scored the winning run on a single to center by Gary Carter, who had been 1-for-21 in the series.

The Game

The epic, 16-inning sixth game against the Astros—which the Mets won to clinch the series and avoid a game-seven showdown with their nemesis, the talented Mr. Scott—had a weird sort of precedent.

The previous year, on July 4th, with many of the same players, the Mets battled the Atlanta Braves over 19 innings at Atlanta-Fulton County Stadium, with Keith Hernandez hitting for the cycle. The Mets scored a run to tie the game at eight in the ninth inning, and in extra innings they twice went ahead, only to be tied again by the Braves. In the 19th inning, the Mets scored five runs, but the Braves answered with two of their own before finally succumbing, 16-13, at around 4 a.m. A scheduled July 4th fireworks show followed the game.

Fast-forward 15 months and 11 days to October 15, 1986, Game Six of the NLCS, and the Mets played another road game with some eerie parallels. Perhaps the first experience prepared the team for the second?

This time, the Mets scored three runs to tie the game in the ninth, and went ahead in the 14th by one run, only to see Houston tie the game in the bottom of the inning. New York managed to bring home three runs in the top of the 16th, yet the home team battled back with two in the bottom of the frame. But it was not enough, as the Mets survived with a 7-6 win. ESPN has called it the greatest playoff series game of all time.

For Backman, it was the game of his life. "Because that's the game that got us into the World Series." And one other thing: "Everybody knew in game seven we were going to have to face Mike Scott, who was probably the best pitcher in the National League that year."

The Astros began the game as the '86 Mets had so often done, scoring three runs in the first off Bob Ojeda. The runs came home on a double by Phil Garner and singles by Glenn Davis and Jose Cruz. Ojeda yielded no additional scoring and was followed in the sixth by Rick Aguilera, who kept Houston off the board through the eighth.

Meanwhile the Mets were stymied through the first eight innings by lefty Bob Knepper, who gave up just two hits and a walk.

Facing defeat and a date with Scott, the Mets broke through against Knepper in the ninth. Leading off, pinch-hitter Dykstra tripled to center and scored on a single by platoon-mate Mookie Wilson. Mookie raced home on a double by Hernandez, who scored thanks to a Ray Knight sacrifice fly. That tied the game at three and sent it into extras.

Behind stalwart relief pitching by the Mets' Roger McDowell and the Astros' Larry Andersen, the game remained deadlocked until the 14th. Now facing Aurelio Lopez, Carter singled to right and Strawberry drew a walk. Knight's bunt forced Carter out at third, but Strawberry made it to second. Backman came up with a chance to put the Mets ahead. "I was thinking, *okay you got a chance*," he said. "Because nobody really hit that well in that series. I mean we faced quality pitching—Ryan, Knepper, Scott."

On an 0-1 count, Backman delivered a single to right field that scored Straw; Knight advanced to third and Backman to second on an errant throw to home by the right fielder, Kevin Bass. But, with only one out, the Mets plated no additional runs, which would prove costly.

Jesse Orosco came in to try and finish off the Astros in the bottom of the 14th. But after striking out Bill Doran, Orosco gave up a game-tying homer to Billy Hatcher down the left field line. In an echo of the 1985 Independence Day contest, an extra-inning game that looked won would continue.

Wally Backman

BuffaLutheran

Did Hatcher's homer deflate Backman? "You know what, I was on such a high because I was able to put us ahead," he said. "To get that big hit, I had a high for about 15 minutes. It was unbelievable. It was such a high."

As they did in '85, the Mets gave themselves a cushion in the top of the final frame, the 16th this time, scoring three times to go ahead 7-4, with Backman having a hand in the rally. Strawberry scored the first run on a Ray Knight single to right, which Backman followed with a walk. A wild pitch by Jeff Calhoun brought home Knight, and Backman scored on a single by Dykstra.

But, in a final parallel to the '85 classic, the home team did not go quietly in their last licks. The 14th inning Astros hero Hatcher struck again, this time with a run-scoring single to center, followed by another run-scoring single by Davis. The tying run was now on second, the winning run on first. "They were one hit away from tying it up again probably," noted Backman.

But Orosco, after a tense meeting at the mound with catcher Carter and first baseman Hernandez, struck out Bass swinging, and the game was over at last. There would be no third encounter with Mike Scott, and the Mets were World Series-bound.

"To win the game that put us into the World Series was by far the biggest game to that point that I played in," said Backman.

For Hernandez, it was the "worst, best, most nerve-racking game I was ever involved in," according to MLB.com.

Orosco might not have put Bass away were it not for the mound intervention by Hernandez, who ordered Carter not to use any more fastballs and to rely instead on the slider, famously warning, "If you call one more fastball, we're gonna fight."

"Keith was one of our big leaders and one of the big reasons we won," said Backman. "There were a lot of reasons — you have to have twenty-five guys playing hard together. But Keith was definitely a leader. He and Gary were the two biggest leaders and very, very huge factors in our success."

Still only 26 in 1986, Backman learned a great deal about the game from Hernandez and Carter. "Their whole mindset was winning," he said. "They taught a lot of us some of the different things it took to win. Baseball is a funny game because you're always learning something."

The Aftermath

The all-consuming intensity of Game Six left the Mets a bit depleted going into the World Series against the Red Sox. "I think it was because we got to such a high in Houston after winning Game Six and it took such a weight off our back—because we were picked to win—that there was a letdown," said Backman. This translated into a World Series performance that Backman described as "the worst seven games in a row that we played all season."

But Backman himself did well in the World Series, batting .333 in six games, with an on-base percentage of .429.

Losses to the Red Sox in the first two games of the series at Shea Stadium "put our backs against the wall," said Backman. While he agreed that adversity like this brought out the best in the team, "you never want to get there."

The Mets finally got their bearings in Game Three at Fenway Park, beating the Red Sox 7-1 after scoring four runs in the first. Backman contributed in the initial frame by singling and coming in to score on a double by Carter. The Mets evened the series with a 6-2 Game Four victory behind Ron Darling, with Backman scoring on one of Carter's two round-trippers. But the Red Sox came back with a 4-2 win in Game Five, in which Backman did not play.

Just as the Mets figured out how to survive extra-inning reversals in the 1985 July 4th game, they learned in Game Six of the NLCS how to come back in a do-or-die last-licks scenario requiring more than one run to tie. They would put that knowledge to good use in the historic Game Six of the World Series.

Backman got one hit in Game Six, beating out a single into the hole between short and third in the sixth inning. He advanced to third but was stranded there. In the bottom of the eighth, his sacrifice bunt moved Lee

Mazzilli to third, from which he would score on a sacrifice fly by Carter that tied the score at three.

The score remained tied at three after nine, but the Sox came back with two runs in the top of the 10th on a homer by Dave Henderson and a run-scoring single by Marty Barrett.

Backman led off the fateful bottom of the 10th with a flyout to left. Hernandez followed with a flyout to deep center, after which he retired to the clubhouse to have a beer, convinced that the Mets had lost the series. The scoreboard backed him up, congratulating the Red Sox.

But it wasn't over, as the Mets—in their most improbable comeback, in a comeback for the ages—scored three runs for the win, the last coming in on Mookie Wilson's immortal groundball through Bill Buckner's legs.

Backman, who was nursing a 103-degree fever that day, didn't retreat to the clubhouse after making the first out in the ninth. "I can remember seeing on the Diamond Vision, Congratulations Red Sox. I have a picture of that in my home," Backman said. "The game is never over until it's over. It was an amazing bunch of guys."

In the seventh game, Backman, pinch running for Teufel in the bottom of the sixth, scored the third run of the inning on a groundout by Carter. That tied the score at three, and the Mets tallied three more times in the seventh on their way to an 8-5 victory and their second World Championship. Backman wears his 1986 World Series ring every day.

He went on to play for the Mets through the 1988 season, hitting .273 in the NLCS that year against the Dodgers, to whom the Mets lost in seven games. Between 1989 and 1993, he played for the Twins, Pirates, Phillies, and Mariners, and then retired after 15 big league seasons.

Backman has spent his post-playing days largely managing minor league and independent league teams. The Arizona Diamondbacks hired him as manager in 2004, but a subsequent newspaper report about a bankruptcy filing, an arrest for DUI, and a domestic dispute caused the Diamondbacks to change their mind.

Backman has rebuilt his reputation since then with a series of successful managerial stints, including several with Mets farm teams. He interviewed to replace Jerry Manuel in 2011 as Mets manager, but the Mets hired Terry Collins instead. He remains a favorite among Mets fans, who love his unbridled devotion to the game; many would like to see him become the team's manager someday.

Backman's passion is on full display in some online videos made in 2007 when he was manager of the South Georgia Peanuts of the independent South Coast League; the videos were taken from a documentary television series called "Playing for Peanuts." In one example, he colorfully upbraids his players in the locker room for a lack of dedication to their craft, while in another he expresses his displeasure with an umpire by kicking dirt on home plate, and emptying the dugout of bats and balls.

In 2012 Backman was promoted to manager of the Mets' AAA Buffalo Bisons team. After the team relocated the next year to Las Vegas (as the 51s), he led it to two consecutive playoff berths in the Pacific Coast League, which named him manager of the year in 2014. He has groomed such core Mets as Matt Harvey, Juan Lagares, and Zach Wheeler, and in 2014, he helped steer some of the Mets' prized pitching prospects, such as Jacob DeGrom and Rafael Montero, to the big league squad. "Right now my job is to get those guys ready for Terry so they can go there and perform," said Backman.

Backman's managerial credo, molded when he was a Met, is to be ready for anything. "You could be losing by a couple of runs and get two runners on with two outs," he said. "Your worst hitter's coming to the plate and all of a sudden he hits a home run. You better be prepared to have your bullpen ready to come into the game because now it's a one-run game in your favor. You've got to be a few innings ahead as a manager."

Chapter 10

MOOKIE WILSON

Outfielder, 1980-1989
Throws/Bats: Right/Switch

The Game: October 25, 1986 vs. Boston Red Sox, at Shea
Stadium, Game Six, World Series

METS STATS	
GAMES:	1,116
AT-BATS:	4,027
HITS:	1,112
HOME RUNS:	60
AVERAGE:	.274
ON-BASE %:	.314
SLUGGING %:	.386
RUNS:	592
RBI:	342
STOLEN BASES:	281
FIELDING %:	.978
WAR:	20.7

The Run-up

All Mets fans of a certain age—you know who you are, and I am one of you—remember where they were sometime after midnight on October 26, 1986.

I myself was situated on the 23rd floor of a condominium tower in Cliffside Park, New Jersey, that overlooked the Hudson River, riveted to the television broadcast of Game Six of the World Series between the Mets and the Red Sox. Watching with me was the condo's owner, my late uncle Jules Herstone; my aunt Doris was sleeping.

At about 12:30 am, with two outs and a runner on second, Mookie Wilson, who had battled Red Sox reliever Bob Stanley through nine pitches, including a wild pitch that scored the tying run, chopped a ground ball down the first base line. The ball initially struck the ground near home plate and bounced up, landing in front of the first base bag. It bounced again, over the bag, and dropped a few feet in front of the first baseman, Bill Buckner, who had moved over toward the line from his original position a dozen feet into the second base hole. And then the ball abruptly stopped bouncing. It *rolled,* and kept rolling, toward Buckner, who might, for maybe an instant, have been primed for another bounce.

Buckner hunched over, his knees bent, his glove down, but the ball somehow skipped past the glove, through his legs, and kept rolling up the right field line. Wilson rounded first base and headed for second, though he didn't have to, because the runner on second, Ray Knight, was sprinting home with the winning run, third base coach Bud Harrelson by his side. After grabbing his helmet with both hands in seeming disbelief, Knight jumped on the plate and into the arms of his onrushing teammates.

The Mets had trailed 5–3 at the start of the inning. Their first two batters made outs. Both Wilson and Knight were down to their last strike. The scoreboard momentarily flashed, "Congratulations Red Sox." But the Amazins—the name truly fit—managed to string together three consecutive hits that produced a run before Wilson worked his magic to bring home two more.

It was a game that seemed all but lost, yet they had to win it to stay in the series and play a Game Seven. And they did win, 6-5.

At Shea Stadium, people were leaping, clapping, screaming, "in ecstasy," said a friend of mine who was there. Over in Cliffside Park, I had fallen to the floor in front of the TV, pounding my fist on the carpet.

The comeback was voted the No. 1 greatest moment in the history of Shea Stadium.

Stabbed in the heart as they were, the Red Sox seemed unlikely to recover in time to win a deciding Game Seven, though it was postponed a day due to weather. Yet they put up a resolute fight, scoring the first three runs of the game, and then, after falling behind by three, cutting the deficit to one in the eighth inning. But the Sox ultimately fell, 8-5, with Wilson singling and scoring New York's second run. The Mets became World Champions for the second time—a status they have yet, through 2014, to reclaim.

Of course, the Red Sox's agony was multiplied by its historical failure to win a World Series since 1918, 68 years earlier. It took a reversal of the digits—86 years—for them to finally break their "curse" in 2004.

The epic comeback of Game Six was as improbable as any in baseball annals. It became a cultural staple known as the "Buckner game" and, however unfairly, attached itself indelibly to the main protagonists of the affair, notably Wilson and, of course, Buckner.

Wilson and Buckner, who have become good friends in recent years, have come to accept their place in baseball history—easier for Wilson to do than Buckner. They have even been able to profit from their World Series experience through joint appearances and autograph signings. Still, neither likes being wholly defined by that one play.

"I felt I wasn't being given credit for the twelve years I put in; my twelve years were reduced to ten seconds," said Wilson during an interview in 2014 with documentarian Heather Quinlan for her documentary-in-process about the 1986 Mets, which will be released in 2016. "I think that's unfair. That may sound funny—why am I upset? Because like most athletes we want to be given credit for what we have accomplished on the field. That one moment—it wasn't how great I was; it was just one of those freak things that happen in baseball."

Wilson, who grew up on a farm in South Carolina, played for the University of South Carolina Gamecocks, coached by former Yankee second baseman Bobby Richardson. The Mets picked him in 1977 in the second round of the draft.

He performed well in the Mets' minor league system, batting .285 and stealing 164 bases over four years, and was named International League Rookie of the Year in 1979. The Mets brought him up the following year in September, and except for a minor-league rehab stint in 1986, he never looked back.

Wilson joined an early-80s team that was continuously mired at or near the bottom of the National League East. He added a welcome dose of speed and spunk, giving beleaguered Mets fans something to cheer about. His positive demeanor and aggressive style endeared him to fans, who serenaded him with "Moo" chants when he came to the plate.

In 1982, his first full season, he stole 58 bases—a Mets record at the time—scored 90 runs, drove in 55 runs, and batted .279. While patrolling center field, he led the National League in putouts, with 421, and double plays turned as a center fielder (four). In 1984 he pulled off six double plays to lead the league again, and became the team's all-time leader in stolen bases. (He was later surpassed by Jose Reyes in single-season and career stolen-base totals.)

As the Mets' fortunes started turning in 1983 and 1984 with the arrival of Darryl Strawberry, Keith Hernandez, and Dwight Gooden, Wilson continued to provide a spark at the top of the lineup. But a shoulder injury limited his playing time in 1985, and he began to platoon with newcomer Lenny Dykstra in center field, playing in left field as well in succeeding years.

From '86 through '88, while platooning with Dykstra, Wilson had his best hitting years with the Mets, batting .289, .299, and .296 while continuing to steal over 20 bases per season. In the '86 playoffs against the Astros, he didn't hit well (.115), but in the ninth inning of the crucial sixth and deciding game, he drove in the first run and scored the second as the Mets racked up three runs to tie the score and send it into extra innings, ultimately winning in the 16th.

The Game

That classic sixth game against the Astros proved that the Mets could be facing the abyss, trailing by multiple runs in their last turn at bat, and still manage to pull off a comeback. That capability came in handy on October 25, 1986, as the World Series, led by the Red Sox three games to two, returned to Shea Stadium for Game Six.

Game Six is mostly known for its ending, but much occurred during the first nine innings to make that ending possible.

Mets starter Bob Ojeda, whose strong performance in game three in Boston led the Mets to their first win of the series, gave up a leadoff single in the first to Wade Boggs, who scored Boston's first run when Dwight Evans doubled him home.

Ojeda yielded three more singles in the second inning, the last of which, by Marty Barrett, drove in pitcher Roger Clemens with the second Boston run.

Clemens, coming off his first dominant year as a starting pitcher, in which he led the league in wins (24) and ERA (2.48) and won his first Cy Young Award, held the Mets in check through the first four innings. The Mets didn't get their first hit until the fifth, but made it count as Knight singled home Strawberry, who had walked and stolen second. After Wilson singled, advancing Knight to third, Danny Heep's double-play grounder scored Knight to tie the score at two—the first Mets comeback of the game.

Boston regained the lead in the seventh off reliever Roger McDowell on a groundball out by Evans that scored Barrett for the third Red Sox run. A fourth run was prevented when Wilson threw out Jim Rice at home plate for the third out. But the Mets staged their second comeback in the bottom of the eighth as "The Kid," Gary Carter, lifted a sacrifice fly to left field off Red Sox reliever Calvin Schiraldi, scoring Lee Mazzilli and knotting the score at three.

slgckgc

Mookie Wilson

Should manager John McNamara have taken Clemens out of the game after seven innings of four-hit ball? It was one of several McNamara decisions later subjected to withering second-guessing by a crestfallen Red Sox nation. Clemens told the *New York Times* after the game that he was forced out of the game because of a blister on the middle finger of his right hand.

Mets reliever Rick Aguilera came in to pitch the top of the ninth. Because the pitcher's (ninth) spot in the order would be the fourth batter up in the bottom of the ninth, Mets manager Davey Johnson inserted Aguilera in the fourth spot occupied by Darryl Strawberry, who had made the last out in the eighth. Mazzilli, who had pinch hit in the eighth for reliever Jesse Orosco, remained in the ninth spot and took over in right field for Strawberry in the double-switch. Strawberry was exceedingly peeved about being removed from the game, and remained so even after the Mets won.

In any event, Aguilera retired Rice, Evans, and Rich Gedman in order in the ninth. In the Mets' half, Ray Knight led off with a walk and went to second on a bunt by Wilson, who made it to first on a bad throw by Gedman to second. Mets manager Davey Johnson opted to have Howard Johnson pinch hit for Kevin Elster, and asked him to bunt the runners over. But Hojo, not known for his bunting, failed to lay one down on the first pitch, then reverted to swinging and ended up striking out. Mazzilli then flied out to left, as did the next batter, Dykstra, ending the rally with the score still 3-3.

Dave Henderson, whose home run during the '86 American League Championship Series against the Angels had saved the Red Sox, led off the top of the 10th by drilling Aguilera's 0-1 pitch over Wilson's head and the left field wall. A double by Boggs followed by a Barrett single plated a second run, putting the Mets behind the eight ball, as they now trailed 5-3.

In the bottom of the 10th, Wally Backman led off by flying out to left off Schiraldi, and Keith Hernandez followed suit by flying out to deep center, after which he retreated to the manager's office. The situation looked grim for the Mets. The next out would be the last of the season, which had been, until now, a preeminently triumphant one, in which the Mets won a franchise-record 108 games that has yet to be surpassed. No one on the team wanted to make that out.

The next batter was Carter. "I don't want to be the last out," he said in an MLB.com video on the sixth game. "I don't want to be a trivia question." He laced a single to left.

But for the double switch, the batter now would have been Strawberry. But Aguilera had Straw's spot in the order. So manager Johnson asked Kevin Mitchell, a rookie who could play virtually any outfield or infield position, to pinch-hit, though Mitchell, a right-handed hitter, didn't normally bat against right-handers like Schiraldi. Mitchell had to be called in from the clubhouse, where he was making flight reservations for his trip home to San Diego. (Some believe that Mitchell had already removed his uniform and had to quickly put it back on; he insists the uniform never came off.)

Luckily for the Mets, Mitchell had an edge. He and Schiraldi, who started in the Mets organization, had been roommates in the minor leagues. Schiraldi enjoyed telling Mitchell in those days how he would pitch to him, Mitchell explained to documentarian Quinlan. Schiraldi would boast, "'Mitch, I know how to get you out," recalled Mitchell. "I'll start you with fastballs in, throw you sliders away.' He used to always say that."

As Mitchell prepared to face his erstwhile roommate, he wondered if Schiraldi would stick to the formula he had outlined years before. Sure enough, the first pitch was a fastball in, which he took for a strike. The next pitch was a slider away, which Mitchell reached out for and poked into center field for a base hit. "I said, this guy never forgot how he said he would pitch me, and I didn't forget."

Another factor going for Mitchell, known as a tough guy who grew up on the mean streets of San Diego, was that he was not fazed by the circumstances. "No fear," he told Quinlan. "Being scared is having a gun to your head. I wasn't scared at all."

And like Carter, Mitchell was determined not to make the last out of the World Series. "It's not gonna happen. I told myself, I'm gonna get a hit. I'm not gonna be no goat. Not in New York."

Knight came up next and stayed with the program, blooping a single to right-center, which sent Carter home and Mitchell to third, both running on contact with two outs. That was it for Schiraldi, who was replaced by Bob Stanley. Now it was Wilson's turn with the Mets still trailing, 5-4, but the tying run on third.

In his book, *Mookie: Life, Baseball and the '86 Mets*, he wrote that even while in the on-deck circle, waiting to see what Knight would do, he said to himself, "If I get a chance to bat, I can't make the last out. I CANNOT make the last out!" After Knight's hit, he kept repeating that admonition, like a mantra.

Wilson had a simple approach to hitting: look fastball, every pitch, and adjust to everything else. He brought that mindset to the plate, as well as something else: a singular focus on the at-bat. "Shea Stadium was rocking, but I didn't hear a thing," he wrote.

The ten-pitch at-bat that followed was the longest of his career. He fouled off the first pitch, took two high offerings, and then fouled off a ball into the dirt that he wished he had back. Like Knight, he was now down to his last strike.

He fouled off two more pitches and figured the next one would be on the outer edge. Instead it was inside—*way* inside. The catcher Gedman, who had called for and was expecting a sinker outside, reached for the ball, but it grazed the edge of his mitt and bounced diagonally away from the plate. Wilson leaned over the plate and, in dodging the ball, lost his footing and fell to the ground. Still on his knees, he began furiously waving home Mitchell, who burst down the line and stepped on home plate with the tying run as Stanley waited there for a throw from Gedman.

With the score tied at five, Wilson wouldn't be the last out, which ratcheted down the pressure considerably. Still, he was at the plate with a bat in his hands and Knight, the winning run, at second, and he could end the game right there against an undoubtedly shaky Stanley. The count was full, 3–2.

As Wilson fouled off another, Knight took a too-large lead at second. Stanley, not at his best, missed the pickoff sign and an opportunity to end the inning. Wilson fouled off his next pitch.

Mookie then hit the following pitch up the first base line, a slow bouncer. Stanley hesitated running off the mound to cover first, leaving Wilson, a very fast man, with a chance to beat Stanley and the first baseman Buckner in a race to the bag.

For Buckner, a proud and accomplished player with more than 2,700 career hits and a batting championship to his credit, Wilson's bouncer turned out to be a perfect storm. Buckner had a bad ankle, a long-term problem for him. The base runner was Wilson, whose speed demanded a rapid response to a ball that wasn't hit hard. Buckner was moving laterally to his left and couldn't plant his feet in time. The ball, which had bounced over first, perhaps hit a spot on the Shea turf—which had been ravaged by celebrating fans over the previous month—that turned it into a grounder. And it went through his legs.

In a 2011 ESPN documentary called "Catching Hell," Buckner said that, after studying the play in slow motion, he finally understood why he made the error: His glove, which he preferred to be "loose," closed up "automatically" as he moved to his left to field the ball. "So the ball went right by the right side of my glove," he said. "The ball didn't go underneath."

Added Buckner: "It didn't make anything better, but at least in my mind I knew why I missed the ball."

Wilson has long believed that even if Buckner had picked up the ball, he would have beat Buckner—as well as Stanley—to first. Knight, though, would have made it no farther than third and the score would have remained tied, with Howard Johnson coming up.

Many have raised the question: Why didn't McNamara replace Buckner with the younger, healthier Dave Stapleton? McNamara could have used Don Baylor to pinch-hit for Buckner in the eighth when the lefty Buckner faced left-handed reliever Jesse Orosco. Though McNamara had used Stapleton as a defensive replacement previously, he told the *New York Times* years later that he didn't trust him in that situation.

"Do I feel bad for Buckner," Wilson asked in the MLB.com retrospective on the sixth game. "Bill doesn't want anyone to feel sorry for him. Because what happened was baseball. It wasn't the first time something like

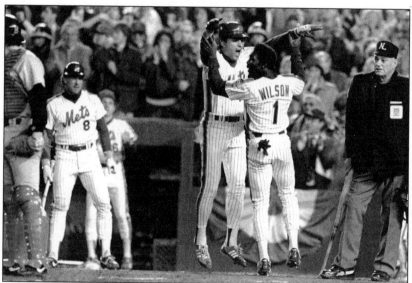

Fruits of Game Six: Mookie Wilson celebrates with Lee Mazzilli after they scored the Mets' first two runs in the six inning of Game Seven of the 1986 World Series, as Gary Carter (left) prepares to bat.

AP Photo/Rusty Kennedy

that happened to a ballplayer. And it's not going to be the last time if we stay in this game long enough."

If you believe in the "Curse of the Bambino," supposedly leveled on the Red Sox after they sold Babe Ruth to the Yankees in 1919, you would say it had something to do with Buckner's blunder. You might also conjecture that Buckner's fate was further darkened, if not sealed, by the presence of his "lucky" Chicago Cubs batting mitt (he won his batting title as a Cub) under his first baseman's glove. The Cubs' championship drought, still ongoing in 2014, began in 1908, a decade before Boston's. It was supposedly set in stone by the "Curse of the Billy Goat," imposed on the team by tavern owner Billy Sianis after he and his pet goat were asked to leave a 1945 World Series game at Wrigley Field. The goat's odor had apparently become an issue.

"So you've got all the bad Red Sox karma and all the Cubs karma slamming together," said Keith Olbermann during a conversation he had with Wilson on his ESPN2 show in May 2014. "They never had a chance."

But the ball that trickled by Buckner, which Wilson declined to keep after the game, had some positive karma, selling at auction in 2012 for $418,250.

The Aftermath

Wilson's right about the lasting impact that the sixth game of the '86 World Series and the Buckner play had on the rest of his career, and indeed, his life. It is forever his claim to fame, something he addresses in the very first chapter of his 2014 autobiography.

But he's also correct in observing that as a player he was far more than one game or play. His overall excellence as a hitter, fielder, and base runner produced a career WAR (wins above replacement) of 20.7—ninth all-time among Mets players. In 1996, the Mets recognized his accomplishments by inducting him into the team's Hall of Fame.

After 1986, Wilson played another two and a half years with the Mets, continuing to platoon in center field. When he struggled at the plate during the first third of the 1989 season, the Mets acquired Juan Samuel from the Phillies in exchange for Dykstra and Roger McDowell, relegating Wilson to backup duty. Not long thereafter, the Toronto Blue Jays acquired Wilson off waivers for reliever Jeff Musselman and minor league pitcher Mike Brady.

Wilson played his last two and a half seasons with the Blue Jays before retiring from baseball in 1991. He rejoined the Mets in 1996, serving as their first base coach for seven years, and returned to the role in 2011. He has also been the organization's base running coordinator, and managed its rookie league team in 2003 and 2004, as well as its single-A Brooklyn Cyclones squad in 2005. He was still a club ambassador in 2014.

One of the more eclectic ex-ballplayers, Wilson has driven trucks professionally and in 1996 earned a bachelor's degree from Mercy College. He is working on becoming an ordained minister, better able, perhaps, to explain miracles like Game Six.

Chapter 11

FRANK VIOLA

Pitcher, 1989-1991
Throws/Bats: Left

The Game: April 28, 1989 vs. LA Dodgers, at Dodger Stadium

METS STATS	
GAMES:	82
COMPLETE GAMES:	12
SHUTOUTS:	4
INNINGS PITCHED:	566.1
WINS:	38
LOSSES:	32
ERA:	3.31
WALKS:	141
STRIKEOUTS:	387
WHIP:	1.240
WAR:	9.7

The Run-up

Frank Viola and Ron Darling were Mets teammates for two and a half. But when their names are mentioned together, they are more often identified as having been mound opponents in what is widely regarded as the greatest college baseball game of all time.

The game took place on May 21, 1981 at venerable Yale Field, in West Haven, Connecticut, home of the Yale Bulldogs, who were squaring off against the St. John's Redmen (now Red Storm) in the first round of the 1981 NCAA Northeast Regional Tournament. There were about 2,500 fans in the horseshoe-shaped stands, including the incomparable baseball writer Roger Angell and his companion that day, legendary Red Sox pitcher "Smoky" Joe Wood, then ninety-one years old.

Viola, a twenty-one-year-old left-hander who was undefeated that season at 9-0, pitched for St. John's, while Darling, a twenty-year-old right-hander ranked as the best college pitcher in the Northeast, was on the mound for Yale.

Both pitchers more than lived up to their reputations, holding the other team scoreless through 11 innings. But Darling went much further, rendering the Redmen, a team of strong hitters, hitless as well.

Angell captured the contest in a classic piece in the *New Yorker* called "The Web of the Game." As the game entered its latter stages, he wrote, "The two pitchers held us—each as intent and calm and purposeful as the other. Ron Darling, never deviating from the purity of his stylish body-lean and leg crook and his riding, down-thrusting delivery, poured fastballs through the diminishing daylight.

"Viola was dominant in his own fashion, also setting down the Yale hitters one, two, three in the ninth and tenth with a handful of pitches."

The game finally turned in the 12th. St. John's Steve Scafa looped a ball over the Yale shortstop's head for his team's first hit, and proceeded to steal second and then third base. With a runner on first as the result of an error, Scafa scored on a double steal attempt. St. John's held on for the 1-0 victory as the Redmen relief pitcher in the bottom of the 12th, Eric Stampfl (who later played in the Mets' minor league system), shut down the Bulldogs. Despite his unparalleled brilliance, Darling was the losing pitcher, Viola the winner, but out of this experience the two forged a lifelong friendship.

"I was fortunate to get the win, and I pitched really well, but it wasn't about me," Viola told me at the Mets spring training camp in 2014. "Ronnie was just so dominant, it was about him."

As the web of Viola's career spun out over the 1980s, he would weave a record of great accomplishment with the Minnesota Twins, with whom he became known as "Sweet Music." And after he came to the Mets in 1989, Viola's most unforgettable game would be another 1-0, complete game triumph over another premier hurler, the Dodgers' Orel Hershiser, closing the loop on the '81 classic.

By his own admission, Viola was a late bloomer, pitching in formal competition for the first time in his junior year in high school as a fill-in for an injured player. With a fastball and a slow curve, his career took off, and he received a scholarship to pitch for St. John's, teaming up with future Mets reliever John Franco.

After being selected in the second round of the 1981 draft by the Twins, Viola made quick work of AAA and shot up to the bigs in June 1982. But he struggled in his first two seasons, compiling an 11-25 record and an ERA over 5.00. "I was so intimidated or in awe," Viola said in a 2014 interview on SNY's *Insider* show. "I was nitpicking and I was falling behind, ball one, ball two. Next thing you know I'm walking guys, giving up a two-run homer, a three-run homer."

Over time Viola came to the realization that if he trusted his stuff and threw pitches over the plate, the hitters would in many instances accommodate him by getting themselves out. That insight helped earn him 18 victories in 1984 and again in 1985.

But it would not be until he learned the circle change up in the mid-'80s from former Dodger ace Johnny Podres that Viola fully came into his own. It took him a year and a half to master the pitch, and he didn't start throwing it with confidence in a game until 1986. But then, in combination with his fastball, which he used to get ahead of hitters, it made all the difference. Already fooling hitters with, as Angell noted, "a constant variety of speeds," he would use the circle change to devastating effect, making it look like a fastball when in fact a much slower pitch was on the way. His strikeout totals pre-changeup, 149 and 135, grew over the next four seasons to 191, 197, 193, and 211.

"Until the changeup I didn't know what pitching was all about," he told SNY. "And once I got the changeup, I said, this is fun, this is what baseball is all about."

The changeup would lead Viola to lofty heights in 1987. He went 17-10 with a 2.90 ERA in the regular season, and led the Twins to their first world championship with a 3-1 postseason record, including a victory in Game Seven of the World Series. He was given the series MVP award—the same honor his mentor Podres received in 1955, when he led the Dodgers to their only world championship in Brooklyn.

Viola soared even higher in 1988, leading the American League in both wins (24) and winning percentage (.744), on the strength of a career-low 2.64 ERA. He was the overwhelming choice for the AL Cy Young Award.

But after a rocky first half of 1989, in which his record fell to 8-12, the Twins traded Viola to the Mets, minutes before the July 31st trade deadline, for five pitchers—Rick Aguilera, David West, Kevin Tapani, Tim Drummond, and Jack Savage (who came after the season).

"When I heard that I got traded to the Mets, I was going to miss Minnesota because I had some wonderful years there," said Viola on SNY. "But if there was any other team you want to go to, it's the team you [grew up rooting] for—it's the greatest thing in the world."

Viola came to the Mets toward the end of the Davey Johnson era as the team's heady mid-'80s run was beginning to wind down. After winning 100 games and finishing first in the NL East in 1988 (though losing to the Dodgers in a disappointing playoff series), the team came in second in 1989, six games behind the Cubs, and second again in 1990, four games behind the Pirates. In '89 the Mets parted ways with Lenny Dykstra and Roger McDowell, two vital cogs of their '86 machine, in exchange for Juan Samuel. Mid-'80s leaders Keith Hernandez and Gary Carter both left New York after the '89 season and Davey Johnson, voted the Mets' best manager of their first fifty years, lasted only 42 games into the 1990 season before he was replaced by former Mets shortstop Bud Harrelson.

Viola, part of a strong pitching staff, pitched to a 3.38 ERA during the second half of 1989 and then pulled off a stellar 1990 campaign with 20 wins and a third-place finish in the Cy Young voting. He made the All-Star Team in '90 and '91.

"We were so much better, we should've been in the playoffs every year, but for whatever reason it didn't pan out," Viola said. "When we got between the white lines, we just stopped playing as a team. We just never put it together. We were just too many individuals in a team-laden game."

But in his first go-around with the Mets in '89, Viola had a game to remember, one evocative of past glories.

The Game

Less than a month after the Mets acquired Viola, he was slated to start the first game of a series in LA against the Dodgers on August 28, a Monday night affair that drew a crowd of 38,820. The Dodgers, of course, were the group that knocked the Mets out of the postseason the prior year in the National League Championship Series, after the Mets had dominated them during the regular season. The Mets were only 3 ½ games behind the first-place Cubs as they arrived in LA, albeit in fourth place.

Viola's opponent: right-hander Orel Hershiser, the MVP of the '88 NLCS who closed out the Mets in game seven. But apart from that rather significant defeat, the Mets had done well against Hershiser, beating him twice already in 1989.

Most notably, the Viola-Hershiser matchup was the first ever between the NL and AL winners of the Cy Young award from the previous year—"a classic confrontation between a pair of ... aces at the top of their game," said the *New York Times*. Hershiser's resume also included setting the record for consecutive scoreless innings (59) in 1988.

The game took place in a ballpark—Dodger Stadium—redolent of pitching greatness, with the likes of Sandy Koufax, Don Drysdale, Don Sutton, Fernando Valenzuela, and now Hershiser.

As he did eight years earlier, Viola came out on top by a 1-0 score; except this time, he outpitched his rival, going the distance with five strikeouts (four in the first two innings) and no walks. He yielded a mere three hits, all singles—two to Jeff Hamilton and one to Mike Scioscia. Neither made it past second base. He threw only 85 pitches, including 61 strikes, and induced 13 ground balls.

No doubt frustrated by his team's anemic performance, Dodger manager Tommy Lasorda argued a first base call in the seventh inning with such fervor that he was ejected from the game.

For his part, Hershiser gave up just the one tally over eight innings, along with eight hits and a walk, while fanning four.

"I outdueled Orel, though we both threw the ball very well," Viola told me. "I was very comfortable pitching at Dodger Stadium. The history behind Dodger Stadium ... everything just fell into place. It was just one of those games where everything was smooth. That night everything was working."

The sole Met run scored in the top of the third on a single to center by Howard Johnson that chased home Gregg Jefferies, who had singled and taken second on a groundout. Jefferies was the new second baseman that year, having taken over with the departure of Wally Backman.

Viola even singled to center in the eighth, moving to second on an infield hit by Jefferies. It was his first big league hit, as a recent emigrant from the American League and its designated hitter rule. Not used to being on base, he got picked off at second on a throw from Dodger catcher (and future Angels manager) Scioscia to second baseman (and future Mets manager) Willie Randolph.

Frank Viola

Adam Rubin

I asked Viola to compare the Hershiser game to the one against Darling in college. "They were comparable. But I was probably better against Hershiser because when I pitched against Darling I didn't have my changeup yet," he said.

By beating Hershiser and the Dodgers, the Mets ended a five-game losing streak that began at Shea against the Giants and continued on the West Coast against the Padres. The Mets went on to beat the Dodgers in the next two games for the sweep, but then got swept themselves by the Giants in San Francisco. It was that kind of year.

Only one other Mets pitcher besides Viola pitched a 1-0 shutout in 1989—Bob Ojeda, on June 17 against the Phillies. The Mets suffered only one 1-0 defeat that season, to the Expos, on September 17. Mark Langston went the distance for the win. The loser? In an ironic echo of 1981, it was Ron Darling, who pitched seven innings this time.

The Aftermath

After his 20-win season in 1990, Viola made the All-Star game again in 1991 on the basis of an 11-5 record in the first half. But in the second half "all hell broke loose"—Viola's words—as he went 2-10 in his last 12 decisions and the Mets finished fifth with a 78-84 record. He left as a free agent after the season.

What made his final months in a Mets uniform especially uncomfortable was an imbroglio with radio shock jock Howard Stern, who called for a "suicide watch" on Viola. "Even growing up in New York and knowing the New York media and the New York market—and this is before all this networking and all this other stuff—I really got full force as to what kind of effect the press can have on you," he told SNY. "But it toughened me up long-term."

Viola signed with the Red Sox and won 13 games in 1992, followed by 11 in '93. But after 10 seasons in which he pitched more than 200 innings, his left arm broke down and he underwent Tommy John surgery, which sidelined him in 1994. Over the next two seasons, he tried unsuccessfully to catch on with the Reds and Blue Jays, and finally called it a career in May 1996—but not without some misgivings.

"[In Toronto] for the first time in my life they called me into the office and released me," he recalled on SNY. "And the words that bite at me to this day, was one of the guys said, 'Viola, you don't have it anymore.' And it hit me like a ton of bricks and I left that clubhouse totally deflated. And I went home and I told [my wife] Kathy, 'I'm done, I don't want to play anymore.'"

In retrospect, however, he believes that, as a finesse pitcher, he could have played another six or seven years. On the other hand, by retiring when he did, he got to spend more time with his family and burnish his relationship with this wife and three children, a son and two daughters, all of whom are athletes. (Daughter Brittany is an Olympic diver, daughter Kaley played Division I college volleyball, and son Frank III has pitched in the minor leagues.) "To this day they still want me around so I think something good has come out of it," he said.

After retiring as a player, Viola coached at an Orlando, Florida, prep school and in the Florida college summer league, and tried his hand at part-time broadcasting for the Red Sox. He came back to the Mets organization in 2011 as a pitching coach for the single-A Brooklyn Cyclones, and spent the next two years in that role with the single-A affiliate Savannah Sand Gnats.

In early 2014 Viola was all set to become pitching coach with the Mets' AAA Las Vegas 51s when he was hit with a series of serious personal setbacks. Within a month, both of his parents passed away, and then shortly after the start of spring training he was diagnosed with a serious heart ailment and underwent open-heart surgery in early April.

But he was able to recuperate and by June rejoined the 51s, where he has assumed a vital role preparing promising young pitchers like Noah Syndergaard and Rafael Montero for the major leagues. "The first thing I tell the boys is, I accomplished everything I wanted to," he explained to the *New York Daily News*. "I don't care about me, I care about you and I want all of you guys to make it as high up as you can get, and that's what I'm here for. The game of baseball has given me everything I've got and I want to give it back."

For inspiration, he harkens back to his changeup mentor and fellow World Series MVP, Johnny Podres, who died in 2008. "He told me the important stuff, which I take to this day and work with the kids," he said on SNY. "So I have Johnny Podres to thank more than anybody as far as what kind of coach I am today."

Chapter 12

ANTHONY YOUNG

Pitcher, 1991-1993
Throws/Bats: Right

The Game: August 5, 1991 vs. Chicago Cubs, at Shea Stadium

METS STATS	
GAMES:	101
COMPLETE GAMES:	2
SHUTOUTS:	0
SAVES:	18
INNINGS PITCHED:	270.2
WINS:	5
LOSSES:	35
ERA:	3.82
WALKS:	85
STRIKEOUTS:	146
WHIP:	1.367
WAR:	0.1

The Run-up

Baseball can be a cruel and capricious game, humiliating the most well-meaning and valiant among its ranks.

Consider Anthony Young, aka AY. Like anyone who cracks open the door to the big leagues, he was overjoyed at making it with the Mets in August 1991, and he delights in the memory of his debut appearance, which he considers the game of his life. Little did he know that day the vast ignominy that awaited him.

A tall, black, right-handed pitcher from Houston with dynamic stuff, he reminded people of his idol, Dwight Gooden. But unlike Gooden, whose first three years were among the best of any pitcher in history, Young stumbled into a 14-game losing streak in 1992. That was followed the next year by a 13-game losing streak, for a total of 27 consecutive defeats (14 as a starter, 13 as a reliever), which broke the major league record for pitching futility set eighty-two years earlier by Cliff Curtis. His 13 straight losses to open the 1993 season also set a National League record.

Perhaps worst of all for Young—and the many fans nationally who were supporting him—was the sheer longevity of his unfathomable streak, which lasted 465 days across 81 appearances and two seasons.

Curtis, a 6-foot-2 right-hander, managed to lose 23 consecutive games in 1910 and 1911 playing for the National League franchise in Boston, originally called the Beaneaters, but changed in 1910 to the Doves and in 1911 to the more aggressive-sounding Rustlers. (In 1912, the name changed again to the Braves, which was maintained, except from 1935-1940, when the team was known as the Bees. The Braves moved to Milwaukee in 1954, and to Atlanta in 1966.)

But Curtis's losing streak differed from Young's in an important way: Curtis started all of his losses, whereas Young started 14 and relieved in 13 others, when defeat would come swiftly in just one inning or less of work. One could argue that Curtis's uninterrupted failure was more improbable in that he and his team had more time to rally during his starts, while in many instances one misstep by Young in a relief outing was enough to spell doom.

"Some of those games I know I didn't deserve to lose," said Young, who, before press and fans, has always projected a quiet dignity and a balanced perspective about the streak. In some cases, he'd be in a position to win a game but "the bullpen would give it up," he recalled. In others, he was undone by his teammates' good intentions. "My teammates wanted to win so badly, they would screw up."

Ironically, for a pitcher to have a long losing streak, he actually has to pitch fairly well—well enough that his manager believes he can win and thus keeps putting him in games. His team also has to be seriously bad. In 1910, Curtis, who went 6-24, compiled a 3.55 ERA, which might have won him 20 games on a better team than the Doves, whose record was 53-100.

In 1992, the Mets were 72-90, but they were especially awful in September (when Young lost five games in relief), going 12-21. For the year, Young's ERA was 4.17, not great, but not bad enough to explain a 2-14 record.

The next year, the team hit a nadir they had not experienced since 1965 and have not repeated since, posting a record of 59-103. Meanwhile, Young's 1-16 mark was accompanied by a perfectly respectable 3.77 ERA.

It didn't help Young that the '92-'93 Mets were renowned for internal discord and bad behavior, which inspired Mets beat writers Bob Klapisch and John Harper to write a book titled *The Worst Team Money Could Buy: The Collapse of the New York Mets.*

Young was certainly good enough to win some games during his seemingly unending bout of losing. That he continued to fail suggested that, in addition to being on a bad team, he was the victim of some otherworldly bad luck, Murphy's Law run amok. To help him turn his fortunes around, fans by the droves sent him rabbit's feet, horseshoes, four-leaf clovers, and letters of support, including one from pitching great Bob Feller. "I still have everything," he said. He agreed the stash could someday fetch him a lot of money.

Of course, what Young really needed were base hits from his club. In 1992, in his first six losses, all starts, the Mets generated more than seven hits only once. Two defeats in June to the Montreal Expos (now the Washington Nationals) were especially telling. On June 6, at Olympic Stadium, Young allowed three earned runs in six innings, officially qualifying for a quality start. But Montreal's Ken Hill held the Mets to only one hit—an infield single in the fifth from none another than Young himself—and the Expos breezed to a 6-0 win.

A week later at Shea Stadium, Young pitched even better, allowing just two earned runs over seven innings. But the Mets could muster only three hits in losing 4-1.

Perhaps the oddest part of the '92 season for Young was that, in the midst of his 14-game losing streak, he converted 15 saves while filling in for injured closer John Franco. In fact, from July 7 through September 9, he earned saves in 12 straight appearances, while not suffering a single defeat in any other contest, a blessed reprieve. He helped his cause immensely during that period by pitching 23 2/3 consecutive innings in 20 outings without allowing a run.

Heading into September the Mets could reasonably believe that Young, despite his 2-9 record, was almost a lock coming out of the bullpen. But that belief only set up Young for further disaster as each of his last five losses of the year occurred after he blew a save in the late innings. (He did also save two games during that stretch.)

With 1992 finally behind him, Young could wipe the slate clean and hope for a better fate in the new season. But it was not to be, as he dropped his first 13 decisions in 1993.

In fact, defeat found a new way to haunt Young. In his first five losses, all in relief, three times he came into the game with the score tied and gave up a single run, which proved the difference maker.

On June 1, Young returned to the starting rotation in a game against the Cubs at Wrigley Field. He pitched six shutout innings and left with a slender 1-0 lead. But relievers Mike Draper and Mike Maddux obliterated his chances by giving up eight runs in the final two innings as the Mets fell, 8-3.

Over a 30-day period, Young started and lost seven more games. In four of those losses he turned in a quality start, including his 20th straight loss, a 5-1 setback to the Cubs on June 8 that broke the Mets' consecutive losses record for a pitcher, set by Craig Anderson from 1962 to 1964. Another quality start ended in a 6-3 defeat to the Expos that tied Curtis's 23-game streak; the Mets committed four errors in that game. Finally, on June 27, after a pedestrian 5-3 loss to the Cardinals, Young had the record for consecutive losing decisions to himself. (Around this time Young met Curtis's eighty-one-year-old daughter, who offered her sympathies.) In his next start, he lost a 3-1 game to the Giants that was called after five innings.

On July 7, the madness continued in heartbreaking fashion. Young yielded a leadoff single in the first and no other hits until the eighth, when Archi Cianfrocco bashed a two-run homer for San Diego's only runs. For their part, the Mets managed one hit, by Jeff Kent in the second, off the combination of Andy Benes and Gene Harris. That loss really sticks with Young. "I gave up a hit to lead the game off, first pitch of the game, back up the middle," he said. "I retired the next 23 straight."

Young's 27th and final loss in the streak came on July 24 against the Dodgers, when he pitched 2⅔ innings in relief before walking in the tie-breaking run in a 5-4 defeat.

He seemed primed for consecutive loss No. 28 on July 28. In a game at Shea Stadium against the Florida (now Miami) Marlins, in their inaugural season, Young entered in the top of the ninth for starter Bret Saberhagen in another tie game, 3-3, and gave up an unearned run on a two-out bunt single. But in their last licks, the Mets came back. Ryan Thompson popped a single over first to score Jeff McKnight from second and tie the game, taking Young off the hook. Eddie Murray then lashed a double to right to drive in Thompson, giving Young the win, no doubt the most highly coveted, deeply appreciated one of his career. Manager Dallas Green cracked open a bottle of champagne and the Mets celebrated as if the World Series had been won.

After ending a slump of any kind, players like to refer to "getting the monkey off my back." Asked how he felt once his losing streak was over, Young replied, "Not only is it a monkey off my back, it's a whole zoo."

Young also accepted an invitation to appear on *The Tonight Show* with Jay Leno, who had been making hay over Young's losing streak in his comedy monologues.

"He came in the green room and introduced himself and said, 'You know, I've been telling jokes about you,'" Young recalled. "He said, 'So you can talk about my [pronounced] chin.' I said, 'no, I don't have to do that.' But it was great. He was very nice."

The Game

While the victory over the Marlins that ended the losing streak will certainly remain dear to Young, his best memory as a Met was his first appearance, on August 5, 1991, at Shea Stadium against the Cubs. Many ballplayers, no matter what they accomplish in their career, hold a special place for their debut in the big leagues—the culmination of their childhood dreams.

Growing up in Houston, Young was compared in high school to Astros' flamethrower J.R. Richards, but in 1984 Mets rookie sensation Dwight Gooden became his touchstone and the Mets his team. During the Mets' tense battle with the Astros in the 1986 playoffs, Young, though attending the University of Houston, was pulling for the Mets "because Doc was my favorite player." To his great surprise and delight, the Mets drafted him the following year in the 38th round and he would eventually get to play with—and become good friends with—Gooden.

In his first few years in the Mets farm system, Young wondered how he would ever crack the team's solid pitching rotation of Gooden, Ron Darling, David Cone, and Sid Fernandez. But he worked his way up, reaching AAA Tidewater in 1991 after a spectacular AA season (15-3, 1.65 ERA) the year before. He pitched to a 3.73 ERA and a 7-9 record in AAA before getting called up to the bigs in August.

Anthony Young

Steve Aaronson

In that first game against the Cubs, left-hander Pete Schourek started for the Mets, giving up three runs in the initial frame. The Mets countered with one score in their half. Schourek settled down for a few innings but yielded a fourth run in the fifth and another in the sixth. Finally, in the seventh, after Schourek allowed one more unearned tally, manager Bud Harrelson called in Young to relieve him, with runners on first and second and two outs.

"When the [bullpen] phone rang, and they said, 'Get AY up,' it was like, you talk about butterflies! It was like, holy shit."

After the bullpen gate opened behind the outfield, Young began running toward the mound and taking in the moment, "I was amazed because we were still pulling fans in. It was crowded. It was a great feeling."

Young's first batter was shortstop Shawon Dunston, in his seventh year with the Cubs, and someone Young had watched play on TV. He threw him only fastballs (though he could also feature a slider or sinker). "I was just trying to throw strikes," he said.

Not familiar with Young, Dunston took his first pitch. "After I threw my first fastball, he stepped out of the box and looked towards the [Cubs] dugout and said phew." Young was pleased with Dunston's reaction. On an 0-2 count, he induced Dunston to hit a ground ball to shortstop Kevin Elster, who tossed to second baseman Gregg Jeffries for the force out, which retired the side.

In his next inning, the top of the eighth, Young struck out leadoff batter Rick Wilkins swinging, his first strikeout victim. He gave up his first hit to pitcher Frank Castillo, an infield single, but retired the next two batters.

In the top of the ninth, after walking Ryne Sandberg, Young struck out future Hall of Famer Andre Dawson, also swinging. "That was wonderful," Young said. But George Bell scorched a double down the left-field line, driving in Sandberg as Young yielded his first run. He then retired the next two batters, including Dunston for the second time, on a weak groundout to third.

The Mets scored once in the bottom of the ninth, which was not nearly enough as they succumbed 7-2. But Young had arrived as a pitcher in the major leagues.

The Aftermath

After three seasons with the Mets, the last two filled with trauma, Young was traded with Ottis Smith to the Cubs for Jose Vizcaino on the last day of spring training in 1994. He believes the Cubs were interested in him because "I always pitched decent against them for some reason." Mark Grace, the Cubs' All-Star first baseman, endorsed the trade, which "made me feel good," Young said. He pitched a scoreless inning in relief against the Mets in the third game of the year.

Young was put into the Cubs rotation and pitched fairly well for three months, with a 4-6 record and a 3.92 ERA. But then on July 26, in a game against the Pirates in Pittsburgh, he hurt his arm while striking out Midre Cummings in the bottom of the fourth. "I tried to go back out there and couldn't," he said. He opted to have Tommy John surgery around the time of the players' strike that ended the baseball season in August.

After rehabbing at the Cubs' training facility in Arizona, Young was able to pitch in the minors in May 1995 and rejoin the team in June, just 10 months after surgery. But rather than starting, he became the setup man for Cubs closer Randy Myers. Getting ready to pitch in the bullpen was harder for him post-surgery than it had been with the Mets; so to stay loose, he would play catch with the outfielders between innings. He finished the year at 3-4 with a 3.70 ERA.

In January 1996, Young signed as a free agent with the Astros, returning to his hometown of Houston. But he found it harder to focus there, and his ERA over 28 games in relief—and a 3-3 record—rose to 4.59, the worst of his career. In June, the Astros sent him to their AAA team in Tucson, where he reinjured his elbow and had more surgery, ending his season. After sitting out the 1997 season, he tried a comeback with the Cleveland Indians' AAA team in Buffalo, but ended up on the disabled list and was released. He called it quits and returned to Houston.

Following his playing days, Young, the father of three, pursued a dual career as a foreman at a chemical plant and a pitching instructor for boys ages 10-14. "I went to work at 5:00 in the morning [at the plant], got off at 1:30.

I had a chance to go home, take a nap, then I could start my baseball at 3:00 or 4:00 when the kids get out of school." He's also been a regular participant at the Mets' annual Fantasy Camp in Florida.

In June 2013, Young retired from the chemical industry. "I didn't like the smell of the stuff," he said. He has devoted himself to private pitching instruction under his own outfit, AY Enterprises, as well as to coaching youth teams.

His aim is to keep his students out of trouble and help them make their high school teams. "I've been very, very successful with that," Young said. He doesn't even mind when they tease him about his streak.

One of his prize students is his nephew, Barrett Barnes, an outfielder who was the 45th pick in the 2012 draft and entered the Pittsburgh Pirates organization.

Parents praise Young's ability to facilitate improvement in their children's baseball skills. "My thing is, as long as I see them getting better," he said, adding, with hard-earned insight, "It's not about winning all the time, it's about getting better."

Chapter 13

ERIC HILLMAN

Pitcher, 1992-1994
Throws/Bats: Left

The Game: July 25, 1993 vs. LA Dodgers, at Dodger Stadium

METS STATS	
GAMES:	49
COMPLETE GAMES:	3
SHUTOUTS:	1
INNINGS PITCHED:	232
WINS:	4
LOSSES:	14
ERA:	4.85
WALKS:	45
STRIKEOUTS:	96
WHIP:	1.422
WAR:	-0.5

The Run-up

In the history of baseball, five pitchers have stood upon the mound with the imposing stature of at least 6 feet, 10 inches: Chris Young (6-10); Randy Johnson (6-10); Andy Sisco (6-10); Eric Hillman (6-10); and Jon Rauch, height-wise (6-11) the king of the hill.

Johnson, AKA the "Big Unit," was the first mound giant to appear on the scene, in 1988. After a slow start, he became by far the most accomplished of the very-tall cohort and an almost certain future member of the Hall of Fame, for which he becomes eligible in 2015.

Johnson left the impression that great height results in great fastball velocity, but that wasn't so much the case with the other four pitchers (though Sisco could reach the mid-90s). Young, Rauch, and Hillman, all of whom played for the Mets during their careers, had more modest heaters, and had to develop complementary pitches.

Hillman, a left-hander who was drafted by the Mets in the 16th round of the 1987 draft, started off, like most major league pitchers of any height, dominating high school and most college hitters. But once he got into the Mets' minor league system, he found that hitters were no longer such pushovers for his mid-80s fastball. "I was used to getting a couple of strikeouts every inning," he said. "So I was getting frustrated." He would even look askance at ground ball outs.

Fortunately, Hillman's pitching coach, former Mets pitcher Al Jackson, helped him recalibrate his perspective. "I call him my dad," Hillman said. "I learned more from him than I learned from my own father, that's for sure. Not just about baseball but about everything."

One day Jackson came to the mound to calm down Hillman during a game. Speaking in his raspy voice, Jackson disabused the young Hillman of the notion that he had to go for strikeouts. "I'm just kind of pissed off and Al goes, 'Lefty, let me ask you, would you rather throw seven pitches and strike this guy out or would you rather throw three pitches and have him ground out to second base?'"

Hillman said he considered the question for a few seconds and replied that he would prefer the strikeout.

"And then Al said, 'God damn it, lefty, get your head out your ass! Don't you realize what you're doing?!'"

And thus Hillman began the process of changing from a self-styled power pitcher to someone who could employ know-how and artifice to get minor league hitters out—and justify being promoted to the big leagues. "Al really implored to me, just as you are thinking on the mound, they are thinking at the plate too," said Hillman.

Hillman's out pitch became a two-seam, high-80s sinking fastball, with which he was able to generate large quantities of ground balls. In one AAA game at Rochester in 1991, shortstop Tim Bogar, his Eastern Illinois University teammate and later his best friend on the Mets, scooped up 17 Hillman-induced grounders. "You just try to make guys hit the top half of the ball and beat it into the ground," Hillman said.

He used the sinker to great effect in his best games as a Met, including his sole shutout against the Dodgers, which he tabbed as the game of his life.

Hillman did consider his height to be of some advantage in that it gave him a very high release point, which was almost eight feet above home plate (including the height of the mound). "You have a baseball traveling almost 90 miles per hour and dropping six feet," he said. "So you really have some good downward trajectory."

Hillman worked his way up the ladder of the Mets minor league system, receiving his first call-up to the majors on May 18, 1992, just past his 26th birthday. Over the next three years, he would rotate between the big leagues, where he had mixed results, and AAA, where he always did well enough to justify a return to the Mets.

Like anyone who finds out he is going to the "show," Hillman, a native of the Chicago area, was ecstatic. "You have your dream as a kid, going to Comiskey Park, Wrigley Field. This is what I would love to do," he recalled. "You bust your butt, you put your time in the minor leagues. I get the call when I'm in Tidewater that I'm going up to meet the team in San Diego.

I'm crying as I call my mother to tell her that, 'Hey, I'm finally getting to the major leagues.'"

But Hillman's enthusiasm was tempered after he discovered that few of the '92 Mets shared his passion for the game, or at least the team. "You get up there and you're surrounded by a bunch of guys who just don't care," he said. "It's like, are you kidding me, this is what I've waited for my whole life?"

Indeed, the team he joined, despite (or perhaps because of) the presence of high-priced free agents, was riddled with dissension in the clubhouse, a paranoid attitude toward the press, and numerous tantrums and unprofessional, if not illegal, actions by players. That combination did not breed success, as the Mets finished the 1992 season with a dismal 72-90 record, in fifth place, 24 games behind the Pirates.

Still, Hillman had some success as a starter in the 1992 season, pitching eight shutout innings against the Pirates in mid-August, with six hits, four K's, and no walks, in a 2-0 win, his first in the majors; his sinker induced 18 ground balls, an outcome that Hillman would try to visualize in the dugout between innings, according to the *New York Times*.

By the end of August, Hillman had his second victory as the Mets prevailed 5-3 over the Giants. This time his sinker, mixed with a changeup and fastball, generated 16 groundball outs in 8 ⅓ innings. He finished the game with a 2.79 ERA, but two bad starts in September lifted it to 5.33 and a final record of 2–2.

As bad as the 1992 season was for the Mets, the '93 campaign was worse. The team finished with an abysmal record of 59-103—its worst in nearly thirty years—which put it dead last in the NL East, 38 games behind the first-place Phillies.

The season began with Bobby Bonilla's confrontation with Mets beat writer Bob Klapisch over how Bonilla was portrayed in *The Worst Team Money Could Buy: The Collapse of the New York Mets*, which Klapisch co-authored with John Harper. Shea fans grew to resent Bonilla and booed him mercilessly. Vince Coleman cemented his unsavory reputation by accidentally hitting Dwight Gooden on the shoulder blade with a golf club in the clubhouse while practicing his swing, and throwing a firecracker near a group of fans outside of Dodger Stadium. Bret Saberhagen contributed to the madness by setting off a firecracker under a table near reporters and, on another occasion, spraying bleach at reporters.

The chaos engulfing the Mets necessitated a managerial change 38 games into the season, with Dallas Green, known for his gruff, blunt manner, taking over from Jeff Torborg. Hillman took a dim view of Green's managerial skills. "The majority of managing is managing egos," he said. "Dallas never really did that. Dallas was a great GM—he knew how to procure talent, but he didn't know how to manage it on the field every day. He didn't know how to communicate with the players."

Nor was Green good at plotting in-game strategy several hitters in advance or anticipating the opposing manager's moves, Hillman added, though he acknowledged that Green's job was made difficult "with a bunch of slackeys like we had on that team who just didn't care."

As for his own performance, Hillman turned in a respectable 3.97 ERA in 1993. Moreover, his strikeout-to-walk ratio (60/24) was a solid 2 ½ to 1, and included 38 ⅔ consecutive innings without a walk. (The Mets record is 47.2 consecutive innings, set by Saberhagen in 1994). Over his three-year Mets career, he assembled a strikeout/walk ratio of 2.13, just under Jerry Koosman's 2.19 among Mets left-handers. Hillman's overall WHIP (walks and hits per innings pinched) was 1.42, just behind lefty Jon Niese's 1.36.

But in '93, on a team that finished 44 games under the .500 mark, Hillman could only muster a record of 2-9. He views those results philosophically, though with a touch of bitterness.

"I was proud of my career," he said. "Statistically, it wasn't the greatest. But you know what? The fact of the matter is, some days, it's not how you pitch but when you pitch. You can go out and lose 1-0 and the next start you can give up six earned runs and if your team scores eight you wind up the winning pitcher. That's the only thing that sticks in my craw a little bit."

But in the first of his two '93 wins, he gave the Mets the maximum opportunity to win—by pitching a shutout, in what he calls the game of his life.

The Game

The Mets began an 11-game West Coast swing on July 15, 1993, in San Francisco against the Giants, a game started by Hillman. He lasted only four innings, giving up four runs in an 8-1 loss.

But Hillman rebounded splendidly in San Diego on July 19 against the Padres at Jack Murphy Stadium. He pitched eight shutout innings, striking out three, walking none (he was in the midst of his walk-less innings streak), and inducing 14 groundball outs. He left the game with the Mets leading 1-0, on a Jeff Kent sacrifice fly in the second.

In the top of the ninth, the Mets failed to score. Though Hillman had thrown only 83 pitches, manager Green called upon relief pitcher John Franco in the bottom of the ninth to replace Hillman and secure the win. But Franco gave up a game-tying single to future Hall of Famer Tony Gwynn, blowing the save and sending the game to extra innings.

Fortunately, Charlie O'Brien, whom Hillman called the smartest catcher he ever worked with, smacked a solo homer to left in the top of the 10th. That gave the Mets a 2-1 lead, which Franco preserved in the bottom of the 10th, thereby earning the win instead of Hillman, who got a no-decision. "That was frustrating—it can be very frustrating as a starting pitcher," Hillman said.

The Mets' road trip concluded in Los Angeles with a four-game set against the Dodgers. Entering the final contest on Sunday, the Mets had split 10 games with the three California teams. Hillman got the start, still looking for his first win of the season. His mound opponent was Ramon Martinez.

This time Hillman secured the win, and more than that, the first and only complete-game shutout of his brief three-year big league career. Counting the previous game, he pitched 17 consecutive scoreless innings. "It's every kid's dream—no bigger thrill—than to come to the major leagues and pitch a shutout," he said.

He accomplished the job on just 104 pitches, scattering five hits, notching five K's, and, of course, allowing no walks. He outpitched Martinez, who gave up one run in eight innings. The Mets scored three in the ninth and won, 4-0.

With his sinker clicking, Hillman elicited 16 grounders. "The Dodgers knew sinkerballs were coming almost every time, and it didn't do them much good," wrote the *New York Times* in an account of the game.

"That's what Al Jackson taught me," said Hillman. "Throw it, and welcome contact. One pitch, one out. You can't get a better ratio than that."

So the Mets ended their West Coast road trip on the plus side of the ledger, with six wins and five losses.

For the first eight innings, the Dodgers game was quite similar to Hillman's previous performance against the Padres. In both contests, he kept the opposition off the boards while the Mets supplied just a single run, Kent's sac fly in the Padres game, and Joe Ursulak's sixth-inning homer against the Dodgers.

But in the Dodgers game, the Mets secured Hillman insurance runs off reliever Todd Worrell in the top of the ninth, on a run-scoring single by Kent and a single by Jeff McKnight that delivered two more runs. That relaxed Dallas Green enough to send Hillman back out in the bottom of the ninth. Hillman agreed that the four-run lead provided him with "a little room to go out and work the bottom of the ninth."

True to form, Hillman generated three groundball outs, the last two to his longtime buddy Bogar, whom he consulted on the mound before the last out, made by Dodgers slugger Eric Karros.

"I called him over to the mound, and I said, 'Bogie, can you believe this? This is everything I dreamed about as a kid.' He just said, 'Hey, let's get this last guy.' Sure enough, it was a ground ball to Bogie at short and he threw him out. So that was sweet."

Hillman was helped, he modestly noted, by the fact that he was relatively new, and "the Dodgers hadn't really seen me much."

Another plus was his battery mate, catcher Todd Hundley, whom Hillman called the best catcher he ever had, especially for a pitcher reliant on sinkers and sliders. "You could throw him anything, balls in the dirt," he said. "If you had a guy on second base or on third base, and you wanted to

Eric Hillman

Steve Aaronson

go low and in with a slider, you knew that he was going to block it, even if you bounced it in."

The catcher on the Dodgers that day was rookie Mike Piazza, who doubled in three trips. Piazza was Hillman's catcher the prior year in the inaugural season of the Arizona Fall League. Five years later he would come to the Mets and transform the franchise.

The game of Hillman's life should have been the main story in New York the following day. But the day before, Coleman threw his infamous firecracker near a group of fans, grabbing the headlines, and overshadowing Hillman. "That was just a snapshot, just the epitome of that team," Hillman said.

The Aftermath

Hillman picked up his second and final victory of 1993, a complete game, 2-1 win over the Cardinals, on September 30. He allowed one earned run and a walk, striking out three and producing 13 ground balls. It brought his final ERA under 4.00 (3.97) for the season.

The strike-shortened season of 1994 was Hillman's least effective, with no wins, 3 losses and an unsightly 7.79 ERA, despite also compiling a 10-1 record at AAA Norfolk. The following year he began playing in Japan with the Chiba Lotte Marines, managed by future Mets skipper Bobby Valentine.

Hillman said he liked playing for Valentine because he would always listen to his players rather than dictating orders. "Bobby likes to find out the psyche and the persona of the guys that he's managing," he said. "He likes the psychological aspect as much as anybody that I ever played for or against."

His two years with the Marines were the best of Hillman's professional life, starting with a 12-9 record in 1995. The next year, he won 14 games, posted a 2.40 ERA, had three times as many groundball outs as the next best groundball producer, and even held the great Ichiro Suzuki to a .206 average in 77 at-bats. For his 1996 accomplishments, he won the "best nine" award for the pitcher position as well as Japan's equivalent of the Cy Young award. He was also named MVP of the 1996 All-Star game.

Unlike American ballplayers, who may relish a chance to swing for the fences, regardless of circumstances, Japanese players always do what's perceived to be best for the team, Hillman observed.

"In Japan, there's no egos," he said. "Fundamentally, they are very sound. It's all station-to-station [base-to-base] over there. And because they bunt the leadoff man over, no matter what, there are really no big innings. If you look at the scores, it's always 3-2, 4-2. 3-1. There's no 10-5, 10-7 ballgames."

His exceptional 1996 season with the Marines landed him a two-year $7.5 million contract with another Japanese team, the Yomiuri Giants. But he spent most of 1997 on the disabled list with severe shoulder pain and missed all of 1998. Japanese doctors seemingly misdiagnosed him and he returned to the U.S. in July 1998 to have rotator cuff surgery.

After rehabbing his shoulder for a year, he tried a comeback with the Astros' AA Round Rock, Texas, team in 2000, but pitched in only one game before deciding to retire. He left the game "with a clean conscience" and no regrets, knowing that he had done everything possible to continue playing.

Aside from a stint as a TV analyst for the Colorado Rockies, Hillman's post-baseball career has centered around a Denver-based company he and his wife, Heather, started in 2006 called Pure Puppy, which manufactures and distributes pH-balanced, natural grooming products for dogs. The products are biodegradable and eco-friendly—something very important to Hillman. "I'm an environmentalist," he said. "On the back of my baseball card, it had 'if you weren't playing baseball you'd be' and I said 'a biologist, trying to lead the world in mandatory recycling.'"

Always fan-friendly, Hillman has been a regular at Mets' Fantasy Camp in Port St. Lucie, Florida, since his retirement from the game. He's even posted comments on the popular website "Ultimate Mets Database," addressing some fans who disparaged his pitching ability.

During his playing days, Hillman made a point of connecting with young fans. With their parents' permission, he would take kids from the stands on a 10-minute tour of the Mets dugout and clubhouse before games. It would make quite an impression.

"I would take little kids, eight- or ten-year-old boys. I'd pop him out and we'd walk down to the dugout. We'd grab some seeds, grab some gum, load up your pockets, and get ready for the game. I'm like, you thirsty? Come on, let's go in the locker room. We went through the tunnel at Shea, went into the big orange and blue locker room, with the huge Snapple machine. My locker's right here, there's Gooden's, there's Eddie Murray's. Kid would be standing there, amazed. Here is our weight room, the kitchen where we hang out. All right, grab a Snapple, any one you want, and we'll head back to the seats."

After Hillman led about ten children on his personalized tour, the Mets' public relations department informed him he would have to stop in deference to the legal liability the organization might incur if there were an accident. But Hillman may have planted a seed, because the Mets, in recent years, have offered a tour of Citi Field (adults pay $13; children under twelve, $9) that includes the clubhouse, dugout, field, press box, and scoreboard control room.

The implications of Hillman's kindness, at least in one case, transcended a mere guided tour. Years after his retirement from baseball, he was approached by a young man in his mid-twenties at Fantasy Camp.

"He goes, 'You probably don't remember me.' And I'm like, 'No I don't, how're you doing?'"

"He goes, 'My name's Justin and when I was nine years old you took me into the dugout and the clubhouse at Shea.'"

"And I said, 'Oh, right on!'"

"He said, 'I came here because I knew you were here.'"

"I'm like, 'Oh you live in the area?'"

"He said, 'No, I live in New York.'"

"And I'm like, 'So you came down here just to see me?'"

"He said, 'Yeah, I just wanted to personally thank you for the greatest memory that I've ever had in my life. I did not have an easy childhood, a lot of bad things happened in my life. But when I look back at my childhood, that's the greatest memory I have.'"

At this point, Hillman said, both he and Justin were in tears. "If I can make a difference in somebody's life. ... I wish I could've done it more," he told me.

It turns out that Hillman, large in stature, has an equally big heart—a legacy far greater than statistics and box scores.

Chapter 14

EDGARDO ALFONZO

1995-2002
Second Base, Third Base, Shortstop
Throws/Bats: Right

The Game: August 30, 1999 vs. Houston Astros, at the Astrodome

METS STATS	
GAMES:	1,086
AT-BATS:	3,897
HITS:	1,136
HOME RUNS:	120
AVERAGE:	.292
ON-BASE %:	.367
SLUGGING %:	.445
RUNS:	614
RBI:	538
STOLEN BASES:	45
FIELDING:	.980
WAR:	29.5

The Run-up

On Monday, August 30, 1999, in a night game at the Houston Astrodome, Mets second baseman Edgardo Alfonzo had the game of his life—and a game for the ages.

He came to the plate six times in the Mets' 17-1 blowout of the Astros and hit safely in each appearance, producing three home runs, a double, and two singles—a Mets record for hits in a game. (Since 1900, thirty-nine other players in the National League and forty in the American League have had six hits in a nine-inning game; only one—Rennie Stennett of the Pittsburgh Pirates, in 1975—has had seven.)

He scored a run in each at-bat for a total of six, a Mets record. (Just six other players in the major leagues have scored as many as six runs in a nine-inning game since 1900.)

His three home runs tied a Mets record shared with six others.

His 16 total bases set a Mets record and stands among the most ever recorded in a nine-inning game.

Yes, the Venezuela-born "Fonzie," as he is affectionately known, had a good day, arguably the best ever by a Mets position player.

"When you go four for four, it's amazing," he told me during a phone interview. "When you go five for five, it's unbelievable. I realized after I [went six for six], that was something. Wow, I said, wow." The video of the game remains "one of my favorites," he said.

Alfonzo's 16 total bases are particularly striking, putting him in the company of the some of the game's greatest hitters and hitting accomplishments.

For example, of the 18 players since 1900 who accumulated 16 or more total bases in a nine-inning game, fourteen of them did so by hitting four home runs, the major league record. The other four players—Alfonzo; Fred Lynn of the Boston Red Sox in 1975; Jimmie Foxx of the Philadelphia A's in 1932; and Ty Cobb of the Detroit Tigers in 1925—garnered their 16 total bases with three homers and a combination of other hits.

Of the 18 players with 16 or more total bases in a game, only four did it with six hits—Alfonzo, Foxx, Cobb, and Shawn Green, who in 2002 with the Dodgers outdid everyone with 19 total bases (the record), including four home runs, a double and a single.

Now consider some of the iconic sluggers who never amassed as many as 16 total bases in a game: Bath Ruth, Ted Williams, Henry Aaron, Joe DiMaggio, Stan Musial, and Mickey Mantle.

The other primary offensive statistic for a single game is runs batted in, which are dependent (as are runs scored) on what other players in the lineup do. In his 6-for-6 game, Alfonzo had five RBI, a considerable number, though less than the Mets record of nine set by Carlos Delgado in 2008, in a 15-6 Mets romp of the Yankees; in that game, Delgado went 3-for-5 with a grand slam, a three-run homer, and a double that drove in two. (The Major League single-game RBI record of 12 was set by two Cardinals—Mark "Hard-Hittin" Whiten in 1993 and Jim Bottomley in 1924; Whiten also hit a record-tying four home runs in his game.)

Alfonzo's 6-for-6 performance was not just a one-game oddity. He provided the Mets consistently excellent offensive production in both power and average, particularly in 1999 (when he won a Silver Slugger award) and 2000 as the team went to the postseason in back-to-back years for the only time in their history. He ranks fourth on the Mets career WAR (wins above replacement) list with 29.5. And in the postseason, his clutch hitting generated a team-record 17 RBI.

Complementing his offensive prowess, he was a premier defender, a vital part of the group—with shortstop Rey Ordoñez, third baseman Robin Ventura, and first baseman John Olerud—that in 1999 landed on the cover of *Sports Illustrated* with the headline, "The Best Infield Ever?" Alfonzo's defensive WAR (6.1) is the sixth best in Mets history.

For his overall contributions, he was named the second baseman on the Mets 50th anniversary All-Time Team.

The Game

As great as his 6-for-6 day was, it could have been even better if in his last at-bat he had homered instead of doubled; that would have put him in an elite group of players with four home runs in a game, including Hall-of-Famers Willie Mays, Lou Gehrig, and Mike Schmidt.

"[Manager] Bobby Valentine told me to try to go deep to make it four home runs," Alfonzo said. Leading 14-1 at that point, the Mets could afford to let Fonzie swing from his heels. "I was really concentrating to get my fourth home run. But I hit a line drive to the right side for a double."

Alfonzo's initial at-bat in the first inning resulted in a solo homer to deep left-center off starter Shane Reynolds. After singling off Reynolds and later scoring in the second, he launched a two-run bomb to deep left field in the fourth off Brian Williams, who had come in to relieve Reynolds. That made the score 9-0, a nice cushion for Mets starter Masato Yoshii, who pitched six scoreless innings.

By then, Fonzie realized he was in a rare zone. "[Williams] threw me two strikes right away. And then he threw me a fastball inside and I hit it to the upper deck in left field. I said wow. And then I knew I was right on it."

In the top of the sixth, facing the Astros' third pitcher of the day, Sean Bergman, Alfonzo drilled his third homer, a solo shot, on a 1-1 count. He singled off Bergman and scored in the eighth, and finished his evening in the ninth with the run-scoring double off Trever Miller, the 'Stros' fourth and final hurler.

I asked him to describe his state of mind during the game. "The thing is," he said, "you don't want the game to be over. You want to keep playing, you know?"

But when it was over, surrounded by reporters, he acknowledged his elation.

"I was so happy because I had a great game. I felt so good."

Not many visiting hitters were enamored of the Astrodome—considered to be a park that favored pitchers—but Alfonzo did well there and even enjoyed playing on AstroTurf. "You feel like you see everything perfect," he said. "That one and Dodger Stadium were my favorites."

Alfonzo batted second in the lineup that day, behind stolen-base king Rickey Henderson, who went 2-for-4. Fonzie would usually take a few pitches—but no more than one strike—to give Henderson a chance to steal second. (Henderson had no stolen bases that day.) Even with no one on base, he preferred not to swing at the first pitch in order to see what the pitcher had.

Where he batted in the lineup—he was sometimes in the third slot—didn't matter much to Alfonzo. "I've got to see the pitch the same way," he said. "I've got to wait for my pitch and try to play the game the way it's supposed to be played. If I bat second, the only thing that I have to do is let the guy in front of me try to get in scoring position. Other than that, just see the ball and hit it."

Hitting the ball was actually something Alfonzo had been struggling with leading up to his 6-for-6 game. In the previous 10 contests, he had accumulated the same number of hits—six—in 39 at bats, a .154 average.

He didn't do anything particularly different in the breakout game. But leading off with a home run gave him a jolt of confidence that carried over to the next at-bat, when he singled. "After my first home run, I felt so good there," he said. "I tried to keep that for my next couple of at-bats. That's what I did pretty much."

In dealing with slumps, he preaches hard work, patience, and staying positive. "You know what it is—162 games, every day. There's definitely going to be a bad week, so how are you going to take it? You have to be positive. You have to be confident when you play. Otherwise, forget it."

Most important, he said, is realizing that no player can control the game. Hard-hit balls get caught; broken-bat bloops drop in. That's just the way it is, so it's important to relax. "This is my thinking: If you let the game get to you, you're going to be in trouble."

To instill patience and selectivity at the plate, Alfonzo would mentally draw a strike zone from his knees to his chest. "You're going to select the pitch that you want," he said. "Sometimes it works and sometimes it doesn't."

Edgardo Alfonzo

Steve Aaronson

He would also think about the current circumstances—who's pitching, who's running, and who's hitting next.

In the end, he tried to strike a balance between remaining calm and being aggressive at the same time, like a cat waiting to pounce.

In the 6-for-6 game, he didn't wait long at the plate. Half of his hits came on just the second pitch, two on the third and just one—the fourth inning two-run dinger—on the fourth pitch, in a 1-2 count, his only two-strike count of the day.

He considered himself to be a good two-strike hitter—and many agreed. "I don't know what it was, but when I'm feeling good, I was letting the guy get me two strikes and then, boom, hit the ball." He hit seven or eight home runs that season in a two-strike hole.

At second base that evening, Alfonzo had two putouts, three assists, and no errors. In fact, Fonzie committed just five errors all season in 1999, for a .993 fielding average that led National League second basemen. On top of that, he did not mishandle a ground ball all year—the first second baseman in the history of the big leagues to accomplish that.

What's perhaps most remarkable about his defensive play is that this was Alfonzo's first season as a full-time second baseman. He had played third base the previous two seasons (as well as part-time during his first two years as a Met) and moved to second in deference to six-time Gold Glove third baseman Ventura when he joined the team in 1999. If Alfonzo missed receiving the Gold Glove for second basemen that year, it may well have been because he was still viewed as a converted third baseman. But he considered second base his "money" position.

Errors were sparse around the Mets' superlative 1999 infield, which combined for only 27 all year, the best in baseball history. Three-time-Gold Glover Olerud helped keep throwing errors by the other infielders to a minimum with his deft scoops of balls in the dirt around first base.

But the player whose defensive play most stood out in this "best infield ever" was Rey Ordoñez, whose streak of 101 consecutive errorless games in 1999 and 2000 set a major league record (later broken by Mike Bordick, with

110). Ordoñez left an indelible mark on Mets history with his preternatural quickness, ability to dive into the hole and throw powerfully from his knees, and fearlessness in attempting—and usually making—seemingly impossible plays. He was fortunate to have Alfonzo as his smart, nimble double-play partner.

"He was something else," said Alfonzo. "I had to be ready because he would do some crazy stuff, you know? With a man on first, I always had to be ready because you think he's never going to make that play and then he does, so I've got to be on [second] base."

Fonzie gained some experience reacting to Ordoñez while playing alongside him in the Mets minor league system. Foreshadowing his move from third to second with the Mets, Alfonzo had to shift from shortstop, his original position, to second in AA ball to accommodate Ordoñez. He later moved over to third to improve his chances of playing in the big leagues.

Alfonzo interacted well with Ordoñez (speaking to him in their native Spanish) and his other infield mates. In fact, he attributes the greatness of the infield to its capacity for communication. "With Olerud, I was telling him, 'hey, I'm going to be right behind you. I'll play here.' Same thing with Ventura and Ordoñez. That was the key."

The Aftermath

After beating the Astros 17-1 on Alfonzo's big day in late August, the Mets found themselves in second place, trailing the Atlanta Braves by 2 ½ games. They crept up to within a game of the Braves on September 19, but then were swept by Atlanta in a three-game series and lost three more to Philadelphia before falling to the Braves again, for a disastrous seven-game losing streak. Yet they were able to take three straight from the Pirates in the final weekend of the season to end in a tie for the Wild Card spot with the Cincinnati Reds.

Thus began Alfonzo's career as one of the most timely and productive postseason hitters in Mets history. When it was over, he would have the most postseason hits (26), doubles (eight), runs (15), and RBI (17).

In a "play-in" game against the Reds (officially game No. 163), Alfonzo socked a two-run homer in his initial at-bat of the game, and drove in the fifth run with a double in the sixth. The Mets prevailed 5-0 behind Al Leiter's masterful two-hitter.

The next night, the Mets opened the National League Division Series against the Diamondbacks in Arizona. Once again, Alfonzo delivered a solo homer in his first at-bat, this time against the powerful left-hander Randy Johnson, the 6-foot-10 "Big Unit."

How did Alfonzo approach Johnson, who finished his career with 4,875 strikeouts, first among left-handed pitchers? "Randy was a power pitcher. You don't have to think so much, you just have to react to this guy," he said. "He liked to challenge hitters. Throw the fastball and get right at you and then with two strikes come with a slider."

In that first at-bat, Johnson unleashed two fastballs and got ahead in the count with two strikes. But instead of throwing his hard, biting slider, Johnson came back with another fastball. "I hit it. My second home run in two days."

Alfonzo had hit a home run against Johnson once before so, unlike most, he wasn't intimidated by the Big Unit. "I think I was feeling good against Randy."

Alfonzo completed his heroics in the ninth inning of Game One, breaking a 4-4 tie with a grand slam off reliever Bobby Chouinard down the left field line. Chouinard fell behind in the count to Alfonzo, who put such a perfect swing on the home-run pitch that he didn't feel anything off the bat. "That's when you know you hit the ball good," he said. The grand slam proved to be the game-winner as the Mets triumphed 8-4.

As a Met, Alfonzo didn't start out hitting with power, but his home run totals gradually improved until in 1999 and 2000 they reached 27 and 25, respectively. He credits Mets hitting coach Tom Robson. "When he came to the Mets [in 1997] he told me he's going to make me use my power. And we worked on the way I set my legs to hit. And I think that was the key."

Another hitting advisor was his eldest brother, Edgar, who has managed several Mets minor league teams, including the Brooklyn Cyclones. "My brother is the one who teaches me everything," said Alfonzo. "Every time he watched a game, he tried to tell me about my swing."

In hitting the grand slam off Chouinard, Alfonzo, a right-handed batter, began his batting motion by lifting his left knee, his thigh parallel to the ground, and leaning back on his right foot. Then he uncoiled a powerful yet compact swing, eyes fixed on the ball, arms fully extended, as quick as a cobra snatching its prey.

There was no doubt the ball had enough distance, but, as it hugged the left field line, would it stay fair? This was reminiscent of Carlton Fisk's dramatic home run down the left field line in the 1975 World Series. But unlike Fisk, who frantically waved his arms to will the ball fair, Alfonzo just took a few steps and calmly watched. "I tried to move the fair pole—with my eyes," he said.

Once the ball was securely ensconced deep in the left field stands, he entered a serene home run trot around the bases; his only reaction came as he arrived at home plate, tap-tapping his chest and pointing to the sky before high-fiving his waiting teammates.

He became the first player in Major League history to hit a grand slam in his first postseason game. "That's a great feeling," he said. "After I went around the bags, oh my God!"

The Mets would go on to beat the Diamondbacks in the Division Series, three games to one, but lose to the Braves in the Championship Series four games to two.

The next year, further burnishing his clutch-hitting credentials, Alfonzo hit a two-run homer in the ninth inning of game two of the Divisional Series against the Giants, which the Mets won 5-4 in 10 innings. In game three, he doubled off the Giants' closer Robb Nenn to tie the game 2-2 in the bottom of the eighth. The Mets won again in extra innings on Benny Agbayani's walk-off homer in the 13th. Fonzie batted .444 against the Cardinals in the Championship Series, but a pulled groin in the final game limited him to hitting only .143 in the World Series vs. the Yankees.

"I almost didn't play in the World Series," he said. "I remember [manager] Bobby [Valentine] told me I shouldn't play because it's going to get worse.

I said, 'Bobby, you're crazy.' Everybody waits for this moment to play. So I wrap it up and then I play, even though I don't play 100%. It's everyone's dream to play in the playoffs and the World Series."

How was he able to come through so often in the clutch?

"I don't know," he said, laughing. "I don't think about it. I just concentrate. I know there's pressure, but I think if you concentrate on what you want to do, you make it easier."

Though he pulled the grand slam ball down the left field line, often when he came up with a runner in scoring position, he tried to hit the ball to right field (the other way for a right-handed hitter). He did this by waiting an extra tick—"staying back"—and using his hands to guide the ball to the right side, especially on an inside pitch. "You react to the ball. Your hands are going to react [automatically]," he said.

Born on November 8, 1973, in Santa Teresa, Venezuela, near Caracas, Alfonzo grew up playing baseball on weekends for local teams and later in high school. He didn't start playing every day until his first year in professional ball with the Mets organization, which signed him as an undrafted free agent when he was seventeen. "I remember after 15 days I wanted to go home," he said. "It was too hard for me."

He spent four years in the minors, winning the Eastern League batting title in his second season. Joining the Mets in 1995, he posted modest offensive numbers his first two years before maturing in 1997 with a .315 batting average and .391 on-base percentage. In 1998, his home run total reached 17, with 78 RBI—a sign of things to come. His next two years—in both of which the Mets made the postseason—he fully blossomed, achieving career highs in doubles (41 and 40), home runs (27 and 25) and RBI (108 and 94). In 2000, the season he was voted to play in the All-Star Game, he attained his peak batting average (.324), on-base percentage (.425), and slugging percentage (.542).

After hurting his back in 2000, Alfonzo saw his average plummet to .243 in 2001. "I had a little herniated disc. And it was hard for me to turn when I was swinging the bat." But he rebounded to .308 the next year, his last with the Mets, when he played third base again, this time in deference to new second baseman Roberto Alomar. He finished his eight years with the Mets with a .292 average, .367 on-base percentage, and .445 slugging percentage.

The San Francisco Giants courted him as a free agent and he joined them in 2003. "It was sad to leave New York," he said. "I had very great years with the Mets. And I'm always going to be a Mets fan."

As a tribute to Mets fans, he ran an ad on the top of taxis reading "Fonzie Loves N.Y." The gesture was "my way to appreciate the fans and the great support they gave me when I was here."

He played for three seasons with the Giants, through 2005. The next season, curtailed by knee problems, he split just 30 games between the Angels and the Blue Jays. It was his last year in the majors.

Only thirty-two at the time, Fonzie spent the next several years trying to make it back to the big leagues, including a brief tryout with the Mets' Norfolk Tides AAA affiliate in 2006. He played for several independent league teams and a few minor league teams, as well as in Japan, Mexico, and Venezuela. He finally retired for good in 2013.

Alfonzo, the father of two teenage boys, has stayed involved with the Mets, attending the last game at Shea Stadium in 2008 and becoming a club ambassador in 2013. He participates in many Citi Field events, such as a wiffle ball tournament held to benefit the Madison Square Boys & Girls Club.

He also managed top minor league prospects at Citi Field in the All-Stars Future Games, held prior to the All-Star Game in 2013. Still a highly popular presence in New York, where he resides, Fonzie hopes to be a coach in the Mets organization.

Alfonzo wants to be remembered as more than a superb ballplayer. "I would like people to recognize me or remember me as a great person," he said. "Because the game is going to be for a couple of years but after the game, who are you going to be? I can be a tremendous player, but if I'm a bad person I don't think it's going to matter."

Chapter 15

TURK WENDELL

Pitcher, 1997-2001
Throws/Bats: Right/Switch

**The Game: October 5, 1999 vs. Arizona
Diamondbacks, at Bank One Ballpark, Game One,
National League Division Series**

METS STATS	
GAMES:	285
SAVES:	10
INNINGS PITCHED:	312.2
WINS:	22
LOSSES:	14
ERA:	3.34
WALKS:	147
STRIKEOUTS:	259
WHIP:	1.299
WAR:	5.1

The Run-up

Throughout their history, the Mets have had iconoclasts of various kinds on their payroll—free spirits, oddballs, pranksters, eccentrics, cranks, double-talkers, and rebels.

Prominent among them: their first manager, Casey Stengel, whose offbeat wit and stream-of-consciousness "Stengelese" set the tone for his team of lovable losers; outfielder Jimmy Piersall, the troubled outfielder who in 1963 celebrated his 100th home run by running the bases facing backwards; Joe Pignatano, a coach in the late '60s and '70s who cultivated a vegetable garden in the Mets' bullpen at Shea Stadium; Tug McGraw, the ebullient reliever who inspired a pennant drive in 1973 by insisting "Ya Gotta Believe!"; Roger McDowell, another reliever who kept things lively for the mid-1980s Mets by lighting firecrackers in the dugout and planting gum laden with lit cigarettes on the cleats of unsuspecting teammates; and manager Bobby Valentine, who in 1999, after being ejected from a game, returned to the dugout wearing a fake moustache.

In 1997, the Mets acquired Steven John "Turk" Wendell, another free-spirited reliever, whose collection of superstitions—what he prefers to call "routines"—distinguished him from the crowd. In fact, *Men's Fitness* magazine named him the No. 1 Most Superstitious Athlete, ahead of Jason Giambi (who wears a bikini bottom during slumps) and Wade Boggs (who ate chicken before every game).

Wendell, the magazine said, "was a full-blown maniac when it came to superstition," citing such eccentricities as brushing his teeth between innings and wearing a necklace decorated with the sharp teeth of wild animals he had hunted and killed.

I asked him at the Mets 2014 Fantasy Camp if he still had the necklace. "No, it broke, but I have a couple of things," he said. "I have one elk tooth on me now."

Of course, Wendell was far more than his superstitions—he was an effective workhorse reliever who set a team record (since surpassed) of 80 appearances in 1999 and led the team with 77 outings in 2000; in 1998, he established a still-standing Mets record for pitching in eight consecutive games.

In a Mets career encompassing five seasons, he compiled an excellent 3.34 ERA along with a 22-14 record in 285 games, usually entering in the seventh or eighth inning to set up the closer. He had an outstanding pickoff move, once picking off two runners at first in one inning.

And in Game One of the 1999 playoffs against the Arizona Diamond-backs, he pitched to three batters in a scoreless eighth and picked up the win—his greatest memory as a Met.

Still, it was his eccentric habits—along with his approachable personality and outspoken comments—that made him a fan favorite.

Wendell brought several of his superstitions with him to the mound. One was his desire to have the umpire roll him the ball at the start of an inning so he could pick it up from the ground. For Wendell, this was necessary to start off each frame with "a clean slate," he said. "I always went to the pitching rubber first and scratched off where the opposing pitcher was. Then I would go pick up the ball once it stopped rolling."

Most umpires cooperated with his request, but if someone threw him the ball, he would knock it down with his glove, swipe the rubber, and pick up the horsehide.

Another mound habit was to draw three crosses on the dirt and say a prayer. Still another was to squat on the mound and wait for the catcher to arrive. Once the catcher assumed the squatting position, he stood up. He also liked to wave to his center fielder and wait for him to wave back before starting an inning.

As a Met he initiated a habit of picking up the rosin bag on the mound as he started an inning and slamming it to the ground, much to the delight of the fans.

Once all of these mound tasks were attended to, Wendell was "a normal pitcher like anybody else," he said in a video made early in his career with the Cubs.

After getting three outs, Wendell would leap over the baseline on his way to the dugout. He considers that more of a superstition than a routine, adding that "it got over-exaggerated"—a favorite term—"where I jumped higher and higher as the years went on."

Fans are accustomed to seeing baseballs and even a rare baseball bat fly into the stands. Wendell would occasionally throw his glove there. "If I pitched like crap, I figured all the luck was out of that glove and I'd need to get a new one," he said.

In the minor leagues and during his first two years as a Cub, Wendell was famous for eating wads of licorice during games and brushing his teeth in between innings. Like many superstitions, the teeth brushing started because of its association with success. "I had a bad taste in my mouth, brushed my teeth in between innings, and went out and struck out everybody," he said. But he decided to stop that routine after the '94 season.

Wendell firmly believed in the superstition forbidding anyone involved in or observing a no-hit bid, including broadcasters, from using the term "no-hitter." He chastised TV play-by-play announcer Gary Cohen on several occasions for breaking the rule. "If I ever used the words 'no-hitter,' I'd hear from Turk the next day," Cohen told radio announcer Howie Rose during a postgame on-air conversation after Johan Santana pitched the Mets' first no-hitter in 2012. "He'd say, 'What are you doing? You're jinxing us.' So I purposely kept saying it, just for him. And we never did get that no-hitter, until tonight."

In superstitious circles, the number 13 is devoutly to be avoided, but in a perverse turnabout Wendell embraced it as his uniform number. He wore number 99 on the Mets only because "Fonzie [Edgardo Alfonzo] had 13 and he wouldn't give it to me" and 99 "was a cool number." At his agent's prodding, he signed a deal in 2000 that had a total value, with incentives, of $9,999,999.99, in honor of his uniform number.

Superstitions may appear irrational, but Wendell had a perfectly rational explanation for his: They made him comfortable, allowing him to perform at his highest level. "Whatever it is in your walk of life, if you don't feel comfortable, you're not going to succeed as well as you could if you felt comfortable," he said.

Wendell, a native of Pittsfield, Massachusetts, became a standout pitcher at Quinnipiac University in Connecticut. The Atlanta Braves drafted him in 1988 as a fifth round selection, but in 1991 traded him with Yorkis Perez to the Chicago Cubs for Mike Bielecki and Damon Berryhill. He debuted for the Cubs in 1993.

After a shaky beginning, Wendell settled into the Cubs bullpen, appearing in 43 games in 1995 and 70 in 1996, when he earned 18 saves behind a strong 2.84 ERA. He garnered a loyal following among Cub fans, whom he regards as even more devoted to their team than Mets fans, considering the Cubs' inability to win the World Series in more than a century. "Mets fans are super-loyal too, but for Cubs fans to stick with them through all these years is remarkable," he said.

In 1997, after he pitched in 52 games, the Cubs traded Wendell, Brian McRae, and Mel Rojas to the Mets for Lance Johnson, Mark Clark, and Manny Alexander. He went on to help anchor the Mets bullpen as a setup man from 1998 through a good portion of 2001, and was a key cog on the only Mets teams to win back-to-back postseason berths, in 1999 and 2000.

Wendell would rather have been a starter (he started six games in his career) than a reliever; in the bullpen, he preferred being a closer to a setup man. But his least favorite role was long relief.

The '99 postseason was Wendell's first. He made the most of it with two wins in seven appearances, including a win in the first game of the playoffs—his most memorable day as a Met.

The Game

In 1999, the Mets stumbled in September, losing seven in a row, but they were able to take three straight from the Pirates in the final weekend of the season to finish in a tie for a Wild Card playoff spot with the Cincinnati Reds. The next day, they captured the Wild Card by handily beating the Reds 5-0 behind a complete-game two-hitter by Al Leiter.

"Al Leiter," said Wendell, never hesitant to poke fun. "Who's that?"

The following night, October 5, the Mets opened the National League Division Series in Arizona against the Diamondbacks. Their pitching opponent: Randy Johnson, the 6-foot-10 "Big Unit," fresh from a Cy Young season in which he was 17-9 and led the league in ERA (2.48) and strikeouts (364). On the mound for the Mets was the much shorter and less accomplished Masato Yoshii (6-foot-two, 12-8, 4.40 ERA, 105 strikeouts).

But the Mets were ready for Johnson, pounding him for two homers, a solo shot by Edgardo Alfonzo in the first and a two-run bomb by John Olerud in the third. They added a fourth run in the fourth on a bunt by Rey Ordoñez that brought home Robin Ventura.

Yoshii, however, gave up four runs of his own in a similar fashion, allowing Erubiel Durazo to connect for a solo homer in the fourth and Luis Gonzalez to follow with a two-run blast in the sixth. A sacrifice fly in the third accounted for the other run.

The Mets brought in Dennis Cook, another bullpen stalwart with 71 appearances in 1999, to replace Yoshii in the sixth. He permitted no runs for 1 ⅔ innings, which brought the Mets to the eighth with the score still tied 4-4. Now it was Wendell's time to set things up for closer Armando Benitez.

Wendell had an easy time of it in the bottom of the eighth. His first batter, Jay Bell, lifted a harmless fly ball to right. He walked Gonzalez but ended the inning by inducing Matt Williams to hit into a nifty 6-4-3 (shortstop to second baseman to first baseman) double play, executed by the premier infield of Ordoñez, Alfonzo, and Olerud. Those three, along with third baseman Ventura, formed what many thought was the best defensive infield of all time, on any team.

In the top of the ninth, Alfonzo, who was fast becoming one of the Mets' greatest postseason performers, socked a grand slam down the left-field line

Turk Wendell

Michael Garry

off reliever Bobby Chouinard to give the Mets a four-run cushion heading to Arizona's last licks. Johnson was responsible for three of the runs.

Closer Armando Benitez, famous for melting down in big situations, came through here, eliciting two fly balls and a popup to end the game. Wendell, for his one inning of work, was credited with the win, Johnson the loss.

Looking back on his career, Wendell wondered whether there was a particular game that stood out. "I don't know if I did anything spectacular," he said. "I'm kind of an average guy."

But after he reflected for a bit, the memory of game one against the D'backs remained gratifying.

"In the very first playoff game that I pitched in, I beat Randy Johnson," said Wendell. "I was the winning pitcher, he was the losing pitcher. That was pretty cool."

The Aftermath

The Mets went on to beat the Diamondbacks in the NLDS, three games to one, but lost the National League Championship Series to the Atlanta Braves, four games to two. Wendell pitched one more scoreless inning in the NLDS. In the NLCS he entered five games in relief, posting an ERA of 4.76, and picking up another win.

After a successful 2000 campaign in which he was 8-6 in 77 games with a 3.59 ERA, Wendell reprised his 1999 NLDS dominance in the 2000 NLDS against the Giants with two innings pitched and no runs allowed, followed by another scoreless 1 ⅓ innings in the NLCS against the Cardinals.

His sole postseason blemish came in Game One of the 2000 World Series against the Yankees when, after Benitez blew the save in the ninth, Wendell loaded the bases in the 12th and, with two outs, gave up a game-winning single to Jose Vizcaino. He made one other appearance as the Mets dropped the series four games to one. It was his last appearance in the postseason.

Overall, Wendell's postseason record for the Mets was 3-1, with a commendable 2.84 ERA.

In mid-2001, though Wendell had pitched effectively (ERA 3.51) in 49 games, the Mets traded him and Cook to the Phillies for Bruce Chen and Adam Walker. He struggled in 21 appearances for the Phils during the remainder of the year. In 2002, he missed the entire season due to an elbow injury but took part in 56 games for the Phils in 2003, featuring a solid 3.38 ERA.

He became a free agent after the 2003 season and signed a minor league contract with the Colorado Rockies, having made his home in Colorado. But after Wendell shuttled between the minors and the big leagues, where injuries limited him to 12 unproductive games, Colorado released him in July 2004. Unable to gain a spot the next year on the Houston Astros roster, he announced his retirement.

Wendell speaks positively of his thirteen-year career. "I loved it," he said. "I was very fortunate to get to play for the 10 minutes or whatever it was [in a relief appearance]. And I wanted to make the most of it."

Beyond his pitching and his superstitions, the multifaceted Wendell distinguished himself with his charity work aimed at children and his support for the military. Though he eschewed attention, the New York Press Photographers Association presented him with the "Good Guy Award" in 2000. Post-retirement, he made three trips to Iraq and Afghanistan to visit the troops.

Another area of distinction was his outspokenness on a wide spectrum of issues, though with his penchant for defining terms his way, he took issue with being called "outspoken." "I would just say that I tell it like it is."

One of the most famous examples of Wendell's candor was his commentary prior to the 2000 World Series: "Yankee Stadium? I don't give a hoot about it. We've played there before. It won't be a surprise. The Yankees have tortured us for years and years, and beating them would be sweet for me."

As Wendell explained it, these remarks stemmed simply from his having grown up a Red Sox fan in Western Massachusetts.

"But they used it as a rallying cry," I noted.

"Yeah," he replied.

"And when they won the World Series, they repeatedly toasted you."

"I heard all about it."

"How did that feel?"

"Not very good."

Another classic Turkism was his desire to structure his last Mets contract such that he would play his final season for free, as a "testament to the game." However, the players union got in his way.

"The union caught wind of 'free' and they said you're not doing that," he recalled. "Some of the guys said that if you played for free, some guys would think that if you lost the game you wouldn't care as much. But if you knew me, you'd know I wouldn't want to lose, regardless. I don't like losing at checkers."

Unlike most players who played in the 1990s and early 2000s, Wendell was not afraid to voice his opinion on steroids. He severely castigated players who were thought to be using them, notably sluggers Barry Bonds, Mark McGuire, and Sammy Sosa, and concurred with the revelations of steroid use in Jose Canseco's 2005 book, *Juiced*.

As a player, Wendell clearly outlined his goals in life: to play baseball, have a family, and own some land. All three have been realized: He has two children—his son Wyatt and daughter Dakota—and owns a ranch named after them, Wykota, a 200-acre camp for hunting and fishing (his passions) in Larkspur, Colorado. He also grows crops and raises farm animals there while various types of game fowl roam the land.

Perhaps all those superstitions paid off.

Chapter 16

TODD PRATT

Catcher, 1997-2001
Throws/Bats: Right

The Game: October, 9, 1999 vs. Arizona Diamondbacks,
at Shea Stadium, Game Four, National League Division Series

METS STATS	
GAMES:	276
AT-BATS:	555
HITS:	147
HOME RUNS:	17
AVERAGE:	.265
ON-BASE %:	.354
SLUGGING %:	.414
RUNS:	78
RBI:	87
STOLEN BASES:	3
FIELDING %:	.993
WAR:	2.7

The Run-up

"I wasn't the greatest hitter, said Todd Pratt. "I was just an average player. But I had power."

Pratt told me this on a bright, Florida-mild January day in the chain-link-bordered third base dugout at one of the practice fields that make up the Mets' Port St. Lucie, Florida, baseball complex. In a month, the major league team would commence spring training here, but this was the Mets Fantasy Camp, and a motley group of well-heeled fans, complete in personalized Mets uniforms, were squaring off. Pratt was a coach in this game, one of more than two-dozen former Mets participating in Fantasy Camp.

Pratt, whom I had met at lunch the previous day, promised he would talk to me and was true to his word, even though our 15-minute interview was punctuated by calls from fellow coaches urging him to get back in the game.

"Hey, Pratt, you gotta put a time limit on that," somebody yelled.

"No I don't," he said softly.

"Hey, Pratt, you've got to be involved here."

We kept talking, as memories of Pratt's heroics nearly fifteen years back floated through my head.

Well, that's hit well to center field. Finley goes back, back, back ... It's over! It's over! Todd Pratt, one of the most unlikely heroes ...

As indicated by Chris Berman's call, Pratt's journey through professional baseball—and to that particularly glorious afternoon on October 9, 1999, at Shea Stadium—was long, checkered, and, indeed, unlikely. It began when he was drafted by the Boston Red Sox in the sixth round of the 1985 amateur draft. He had just turned eighteen. He was a big kid, 6-foot-3, 195 pounds, a stature that would earn him the moniker "Tank."

He spent the next seven years toiling at various levels of the Red Sox's minor league system, with a brief detour in 1987 to the Cleveland Indians.

"I should have been a Red Sox [player], but I had some trials and tribulations in the minor leagues," Pratt said. "I played twenty+ years, and only fourteen of those were in the major leagues."

In the minors, Pratt developed a reputation as a good defensive catcher with hitting issues, which were exacerbated when the Red Sox decided he would skip rookie league in his first year. Some seasons he hit in the low .200s and struck out more than 100 times.

By 1990, the Red Sox gave up on Pratt and, unable to trade him, sent him to their AA New Britain, Connecticut, team to be a backup catcher and player-coach. After the 1991 season, he left the Red Sox organization for good as a free agent.

The Philadelphia Phillies rescued Pratt by selecting him in the Rule 5 draft. After hitting well at the AA and AAA levels, he finally reached the big leagues in September 1992 when the Phillies called him up to be their third-string catcher. Now twenty-five, he had spent almost eight years in the minor leagues.

In 1993, Pratt won the job as backup catcher to Darren Daulton and helped the Phillies make it to the World Series, which they lost to Toronto in six games. He reprised his backup role in 1994 but was hitting poorly when the players strike ended the season in August. In the offseason, the Phillies non-tendered Pratt, making him a free agent.

The Cubs invited him to spring training in 1995 and then assigned him to their American Association minor league team. He was called up to the big club in mid-season but hit poorly and became a free agent again after the season.

In 1996, after a spring training tryout with the Seattle Mariners didn't pan out, Pratt found himself out of baseball. He became an instructor at Bucky Dent's baseball school in Delray Beach, Florida, and even worked part-time for Domino's Pizzas. "The guy that fed Bucky Dent's [school] owned twenty Domino's Pizzas and he said, 'Todd, you're going to come work for me. You grind it out for a year and I'll make you a boss.'"

But then Pratt's fortunes began to turn in 1997. The Mets invited him to spring training, and he became the everyday catcher for the AAA Norfolk

Tides. He was called up later that season to serve as the backup to catcher Todd Hundley. In a foreshadowing of his most important moment as a Met, he hit a walkoff, extra-innings homer in his first at-bat with the club. He would remain with the organization through the 2001 season.

"The New York Mets organization pulled my career back together," said Pratt during a TV interview in the stands at Citi Field in June 2014 during a game against the San Diego Padres.

In his five years with the Mets, which included over 640 plate appearances, Pratt compiled very respectable numbers: 17 home runs, 87 RBI, a .265 batting average, and a .354 on-base percentage. His lifetime batting average over 662 games with the Phillies, Cubs, Mets, and Braves was .251.

During his first two years with the Mets, Pratt was the only catcher who had "options," which meant he could be sent to the minors. "It was tough for me in '97 and '98," he recalled. "At one point, Steve Phillips and Bobby Valentine called me in after a game and said, 'Todd, we have to send you down.' I just won a game against the Pittsburgh Pirates, and I'm hitting 320. I'm like, 'What do I have to do?' But I was never that player who said, 'Well, I'm going to take my three days [prior to reporting].' I said, 'Get me on a flight. I'm going to Norfolk. You better tell [Rick] Dempsey [AAA manager at Norfolk] that he better put me in the lineup tomorrow because I'm going to be there.'" Dempsey, he noted, helped him make it back to the major leagues.

After another stint in Norfolk in 1998, the Mets brought him up midseason, this time as an understudy to arguably the greatest offensive catcher in baseball history, Mike Piazza, whom the Mets had acquired from the Marlins for prospects.

In 1999, he won the backup job to Piazza in spring training and was with the major league club all season as the Mets returned to postseason play for the first time since 1988. He batted .293 in 71 games. The Mets won 96 games, finishing second behind the Braves, but tied with the Reds in the Wild Card race.

The Mets beat the Reds in a one-game "play-in" to the playoffs on the strength of a complete-game, two-hit shutout by Al Leiter. Now the Wild

Card winners in the National League, they immediately flew to Arizona to face Randy Johnson and the Diamondbacks in the National League Division Series, and split the first two games. Piazza injured his thumb so Pratt replaced him for the final two games—Game Three, which the Mets won behind Rick Reed, and Game Four, the clincher for the Mets, in which Pratt played the hero.

But he was almost the goat.

The Game

Game Four took place on a cloudy, 65-degree Saturday afternoon at Shea Stadium before a crowd of 56,177. The starting pitchers were Al Leiter, fresh from his triumph in Cincinnati, for the Mets and Brian Anderson for the D'Backs. The game was scoreless until the bottom of the fourth, when Edgardo Alfonzo cracked a first-pitch home run to lead off the inning.

Greg Colbrunn returned the favor in the top of the fifth, blasting a home run off Leiter to tie the score. It remained that way until the bottom of the seventh, when Benny Agbayani doubled to right field off Anderson, driving in Rickey Henderson from third with the go-ahead run.

In the top of the eighth, with the Mets ahead 2-1, Leiter retired the first two D'backs. But then he began to falter, giving up a walk to Turner Ward, who pinch-hit for Anderson, and a single to Tony Womack. With men on first and second, manager Bobby Valentine replaced Leiter with closer Armando Benitez, who was charged with earning a four-out save.

But Benitez, whose career as a closer for the Mets was sullied by numerous devastating meltdowns in big games, promptly gave up a double to Jay Bell, which scored Ward and Womack. After walking Luis Gonzalez intentionally, Benitez threw a 3-2 pitch that Matt Williams lined to left field for a single. Fortunately for Benitez and the Mets, Melvin Mora, who had replaced Rickey Henderson in left field at the beginning of the inning, threw out Bell at home plate for the third out, Pratt slapping the tag. But the D'backs now led 3-2.

In the bottom of the eighth, Alfonzo led off with a walk allowed by right-handed reliever Gregg Olson, who was replaced by left-hander Greg Swidell. Fonzie went to third after John Olerud hit a ball to right field that was misplayed by Womack, who had moved there from shortstop at the start of the inning. The next batter, Roger Cedeño, drove in Alfonzo with a sacrifice fly to center field, knotting the score at 3-3 and moving Olerud to third. So while the Mets' defensive move in the top of the eighth—inserting Mora in place of Henderson in left—saved them a run, the D'Backs' decision to put Womack in right cost them a run.

Swindell walked Robin Ventura intentionally and was replaced by Matt Mantei, the third pitcher of the inning for the D'Backs.

Up stepped Pratt, a right-handed hitter batting sixth in the lineup, who had been hitless in three tries to that point. A sacrifice fly would put the Mets ahead. But he just dribbled the ball to Mantei, who threw out Olerud trying to score at home.

"I could have easily been the goat," Pratt said. "I hit a 17- hopper right back to Mantei. All I had to do was get the ball into the outfield. And no one knows that. But if we had lost, they would've said 'Pratt had the chance in the bottom of the 8th to win the game.' But with my perseverance, I thought I was going to get another chance."

With Pratt now at first and Ventura at second, Mantei walked Darryl Hamilton to load the bases. But Rey Ordoñez struck out to end the inning.

Benitez had a 1-2-3 top of the ninth inning, and Mantei pitched out of trouble in the bottom of the ninth, so the game proceeded to extras. In the top of the 10th, John Franco, who replaced Benitez, retired all three batters he faced, setting the stage for the game's denouement in the bottom of the 10th.

Ventura started the inning by flying out to right field. The next batter was Pratt, trying to channel his inner Mickey Mantle (a better-known No. 7), though he had hit only three home runs all season in 160 plate appearances. He had some familiarity with Mantei. "I knew you couldn't fall behind on him," he said. "Very good pitcher—awesome pitcher. He was 99, 100 miles per hour. You know, ice, ice baby. Yeah, I knew who he was."

Mantei's first pitch to Pratt was a breaking ball in the dirt. He didn't swing. "It was like a 55-footer," he said.

Pratt knew the next pitch would be a fastball and he braced himself. "I was like, 'OK, just be on time, because it's going to be a heater now, he's not going to fall behind 2-0,' you know what I mean? So I said, 'Just be on time. Just don't be late, you got one chance.'"

Pratt guessed right. The pitch came in at 99 miles per hour, right down the middle, a little high. He raised his left leg slightly and swung, grimacing on contact, opening his mouth slightly in astonishment at the flight of the ball, his broad shoulders facing forward. "I was a lowball hitter, but I was on time."

The momentum of his backswing caused him to raise the bat over his head with the flourish of an orchestra conductor as he straddled home plate. He flung the bat to the ground and with a little hop over the plate, took off.

"Did you think it was gone?" I asked him.

"I knew it had a chance. I squared it up. I knew it had a chance."

As he ran towards first, Pratt watched center fielder Steve Finley, a five-time Gold Glove winner, go after the ball. "I'm thinking maybe it will go, but I'm seeing Steve line up the catch. I'm like, "Oh God, I hope I have enough.'"

Finley leaped, his glove extending slightly over the wall, and came down. For a brief, agonizing moment, the outcome was in doubt. Did Finley catch it? He peeked into his glove and saw ... nothing. His glove dropped dejectedly to his side. For a moment, he put his hands on his hips, then shrugged his shoulders, his pained expression like that of a teenager just rebuffed by his hoped-for prom date.

"Right when I'm about to reach first base is when he made the jump," Pratt said. "I've seen him do it a million times. Steve and I were kind of the same age. I thought he caught it. But all the fans, no one knew, 70,000 people didn't know."

Pratt realized the truth before the fans did. "He put his head down and looked [into his glove]. Right then, before he showed any more emotion, I knew he didn't catch it. Because he wouldn't have looked. He would've just

Todd Pratt celebrating his game-winning homer against the Diamondbacks in the 1999 NLDS, with Luis Lopez (right) and Rey Ordonez (left).

AP Photo/Bill Kostroun

run off. Before even the crowd knew, I knew, as soon as he went like that. I said, 'I GOT EM!' And then he shrugged his shoulders."

Pratt thinks Finely could have made the catch, but his fielding mechanics were off. "He bumped into the wall instead of going up over it," he said. "He went laterally instead of vertically and he kind of got short-armed."

Calling the play on the radio that day, Gary Cohen, the Mets TV play-by-play broadcaster since 2006, hesitated as he watched Finely make his leap. "Everybody held their breath," he recalled during a TV game broadcast in 2014. "Finley was a guy who was a great outfielder and a guy who robbed home runs with regularity. [He] caught this ball 99 times out of 100, but he stepped in that little hole right in front of the fence."

Pratt's blast was one of only six postseason series-clinching homers in baseball history—and the first by an understudy. But it was "no fluke," said Cohen. "He could hit. The only fluke was that Finley didn't catch it."

Whatever the interpretation, the Mets were victorious in 10, 4-3.

Rounding first, Pratt raised his right arm in triumph, then punched the sky with both arms in unison.

"Nobody had more enthusiasm for the game than Todd Pratt," said Cohen.

How did Pratt feel at that moment? There were two phases to his reaction. The initial, professional one recognized what he accomplished as a ballplayer for his team. "I was ecstatic, ecstatic. I rounded first; I got the home run. I was excited, but I still didn't really know what I did."

Then, as he rounded second and headed to third, he saw the fans. "I thought, 'Oh my God what did I just do?!'"

The stands at Shea were shaking; everyone was jumping up and down, even up in the rafters. "When I saw that, that's when I really started crying," he remembered. "My heart busted open at that point."

He cried, he said, not for himself but for the city he represented. "I saw the emotion of the fans, I saw fathers and sons ..."

"Hugging and high-fiving?"

"Yes, yes. I have a few pictures … " Pratt welled up with tears, right there at Fantasy Camp, more than fourteen years after the home run. "I'm getting all … I've looked at the pictures of me rounding third base. Me and my wife were so amazed to see fathers and sons …"

His teammates were a little excited too. They poured out of the dugout, running and leaping. John Franco raised his arms and took tiny, jig-like steps. With Luis Lopez and Rey Ordonez running behind him, Pratt arrived at home plate, a scrum of players forming around him; Benny Agbayani, on the periphery, jumped up and tried to reach Pratt. Fireworks dotted the sky. The champagne was waiting in the clubhouse.

The Aftermath

Beating the D'backs put the Mets into the National League Championship Series against the Atlanta Braves, their bitter rivals, who beat them for the top spot in the National League East. Pratt would play another memorable role in that series.

The Mets lost the first three games. Now, to win the best-of-seven series, they would have to prevail in the next four games, something no team in postseason history had ever accomplished.

But the Mets managed to win games four and five, the latter in 15 innings on the strength of Robin Ventura's "grand-slam single," in which Pratt played a key role. At the time, the game was the longest in elapsed time in postseason history, clocking in at five hours, 46 minutes. And the victory marked just the second time in baseball history that a team had come back from a 3-0 series deficit to force a Game Six. The other team: the Braves, who had done it during the prior year's NLCS.

It was all in vain, however, as the Mets succumbed to the Braves in the sixth game when Kenny Rogers walked in the go-ahead run in the 11th.

Still, the grand-slam single will go down as another indelibly wacky moment in Mets lore. Pratt, up in the bottom of the 15th with the bases loaded, walked on five pitches, forcing in Shawon Dunston from third and tying the score at 3-3. The Braves pitcher, big right-hander Kevin McGlinchy, then threw an injured and slumping Ventura a meaty fastball on a 2-1 count, which he launched through steady rain over the right-field fence. A grand slam, right?

Not so fast.

"I got so excited because I walked to tie the game. I was so fired up," Pratt said. "And Robin used to hit high fly balls [for home runs] but that one was a line drive. So I thought it was a long drive in the gap, a double. I'm like, 'OK, we won. All I got to do is tag second.' Robin's rounding first and he's going 'Dude!' and waving his arms, and I'm going, 'Dude, we won!' And I grabbed him. If you watch the video on that, we had twenty-five other guys right behind me [who mobbed Ventura]."

In the record books the grand slam was reduced to a single that scored the winning run from third (pinch runner Roger Cedeño). Pratt did have one concern following the game: the reaction of bookies, who had to pay bettors on both a 7-3 outcome as well as the actual 4-3 score. "I thought they might put a hit out on me," he said. He was not joking.

The following year the Mets won the Wild Card again and made it all the way to the World Series, with Pratt as Piazza's backup in 80 games in which he batted .275.

Pratt played in Game One of the 2000 World Series, against the Yankees, another unforgettable experience for him. He walked and scored, and was twice hit by a pitch as the Mets lost 4-3. In fact, he considered selecting game one as the game of his life, but decided on the D'backs game. "The home run is a better story," he said.

In midseason 2001, the Mets traded Pratt to his old team, the Phillies, for whom he played until 2005, when he left as a free agent. He played one more season as a backup catcher with the Atlanta Braves.

During his second run with the Phillies, he hit another extra-inning walk-off home run "with the packed crowd and all the drunks, and they went crazy, too." But what Pratt especially liked was the opponent. "That made it good. We beat the Red Sox."

In retirement, Pratt became known as a player of the online video game "Ultima Online," his picture appearing on the box of "Ultima Online: Renaissance." Since 2010, he has been the head baseball coach—for a program he started—at West Georgia Technical College, in Douglasville, Georgia. He and his wife, Tracy, have four children, Quade, Jake Ryan, Kolby, and Kamille.

Pratt is also the owner and former manager of the Douglasville (Georgia) Bulls of the Sunbelt League, a summer collegiate wooden-bat league partially sponsored by Major League Baseball. In 2014, he was named president of the Sunbelt League.

But he still aspires to be back with the Mets organization as a coach, he said in his June 2014 TV interview at Citi Field.

Pratt will be forever known for hitting the only walk-off, series-clinching home run in Mets postseason history. Even Ed Coleman, longtime WFAN Mets beat reporter, called that game the game of his broadcasting life.

When Pratt hit the home run against the Diamondbacks, he may have been helped by Steve Finely's awkward jump at the wall. Was that a little bit of luck?

"I think luck happens because you work hard for the opportunity," he said. "I don't believe in luck."

"It's preparation and opportunity," said my friend Steve, who was taking photos of Pratt during the interview.

"There you go," said Pratt. "I want you to put that in there. I totally believe in that. People ask me, 'Todd, how did you do it?' It was because I worked hard. I was ready for the opportunity."

Chapter 17

BENNY AGBAYANI

Outfield, 1998-2001
Throws/Bats: Right

The Game: October 7, 2000, vs. the San Francisco Giants, at
Shea Stadium, Game Three, National League Division Series

METS STATS	
GAMES:	322
AT-BATS:	937
HITS:	264
HOME RUNS:	35
AVERAGE:	.282
ON-BASE %:	.372
SLUGGING %:	.462
RUNS:	130
RBI:	129
STOLEN BASES:	15
FIELDING %:	.968
WAR:	1.5

The Run-up

Playing baseball in the major leagues may seem to the casual observer like a fun, carefree way to make a rather substantial living. It's play, after all, not work.

But for many players, especially at the outset of their careers, the reality is quite different. More than most people, ballplayers face a fraught, tenuous existence. Fewer than 10 percent of minor league players—who themselves have to be good enough to get drafted by big league clubs—make it to the majors. And once they get there, they have to demonstrate over and over that they deserve to stay, with plenty of others vying to take their place. Any significant drop in performance ensures a return to the paltry pay and ten-hour bus rides of the minors.

A case in point: Benny Agbayani, who in March 2000, despite having had some success with the Mets, seemed to be on the verge of being exiled to the farm.

The Mets' 30th round draft pick in 1993 and one of the few prospects to hail from Hawaii, where he starred for Hawaii Pacific University, Agbayani was a long shot to begin with. He spent four arduous years in the Mets' minor league system. In 1994, during the Major League Baseball players' strike, he was coerced into becoming a "replacement player" by a management dictate; if he refused, he would have been released. But in the end, he played a vital role on the 1999 and 2000 Mets.

What helped him to persevere in his early years was the advice of Len Sakata, a native Hawaiian and former major leaguer who coached and mentored Agbayani in the Hawaiian Winter League. "He knew what it took to make it to the major leagues," Agbayani told me during a phone interview. "He said if you want to make it, you cannot give up no matter how bad it gets. And he said it will get bad."

Another person who supported his rise was his wife, Niela, a former college softball player whom Agbayani married in the ballpark of the Mets' AAA affiliate, the Norfolk Tides, in a ceremony before the AAA All-Star game in 1998 (all expenses paid). She watched all of his games and offered constructive criticism. "She would tell me, 'hey, you better make some adjustments,'" he said. "I knew she was knowledgeable and just looking out for my best interests."

After having "a cup of coffee" with the Mets in 1998, he played in 101 games in 1999. Wearing number 50 for his home state, he acquitted himself admirably, despite laboring through an elbow injury in midseason. He finished the '99 season with 14 home runs (including 10 in his first 73 at-bats, a Mets record) and a .286 batting average. He had two games, a few days apart, in which he belted two home runs in each contest, and twice he hit homers in three consecutive games. And he contributed some key hits in the playoffs against Arizona and Atlanta.

The fast start was important to Agbayani. "Like they always say, the first impression is the best impression," he said. "I wanted to make an immediate impact."

Benny also wanted to justify manager Bobby Valentine's faith in him. Valentine, one of his managers in the minors, as well as on the Mets and later in Japan, was a mentor and unwavering supporter throughout Agbayani's career. In 1996, Valentine prevented him from being released from the minor leagues. "If somebody's fighting for you, you better go out there and do your job," Agbayani said.

Valentine and hitting coach Tom Robson helped Agbayani develop a front leg kick in his batting stance that enabled him to hit more home runs. (Robson helped Edgardo Alfonzo in the same way.) In *Big League Survivor*, an autobiography he published after the 2000 season, Agbayani wrote that the high leg kick "jump-started my career, making me a better hitter with lots more power at the plate."

His performance in 1999, coupled with his stocky everyman physique, round baby face, and underdog status, made Agbayani a fan favorite, dubbed the "Hawaiian Punch." After a home run, fans would chant "Ben-NEE, Ben-NEE," often imploring him to come out of the dugout for a curtain call. They would also serenade him to the tune of the Elton John song, "Benny and the Jets" as it played on the stadium sound system, substituting Mets for Jets. "Getting embraced by the fans of New York, you can't ask for anything else than that," he said.

It was a two-way relationship with Agbayani, who admired New York fans for their baseball savvy. "They know what's going on during the game; they know what you're supposed to do."

Throughout his career, Agbayani was extremely fan-friendly. He hopes current players treat fans well "because without the fans, there's no game."

Unlike some players who play in New York—the media capital and the biggest market in the country—Agbayani never felt overwhelmed. On the contrary, "I loved it," he said. "And like everyone says, if you can play in New York, you can play anywhere."

But in 2000, he found himself on the bubble as the Mets tried to figure out whom among a crowd of eight outfielders to keep on the big league roster. "I didn't want to play in the minors," he said. "You get a little frustrated."

Despite this uncertainty, he tried to maintain his poise on the field. "The mental part of the game is the toughest part," he said. "Being in a professional sport, you're going up, down. It wasn't a secure thing for me. All I could do, all I could control, was how I performed on the field. Hopefully someone liked it and I still had a job."

And perform he did. In fact, 2000 turned out to be the year in which Agbayani, ever the "Big League Survivor," rose to some remarkable heights, both during the regular season and especially the postseason, which included the game of his life.

The season began on March 30 in Tokyo of all places, in a two-game set against the Cubs, Major League Baseball's first-ever regular season series outside of North America. In front of a sold-out crowd of 55,000 at the Tokyo Dome, Agbayani belted a pinch-hit grand slam to straightaway center field in the 11th inning off Cubs reliever Danny Young to win the second game of the series.

For hitting the grand slam, he came away with the series MVP award, a Shogun trophy, and a $10,000 check for the charity of his choice. More important, that timely blast, combined with a foot injury to outfielder Darryl Hamilton, kept him on the roster as the team headed back to the states. After the Mets released Rickey Henderson—Agbayani's idol as a kid as well as a friend and mentor on the Mets—his position on the team became more secure.

How did he manage to come off the bench after sitting for 13 innings and hit the ball out of sight? He certainly wasn't trying for a grand slam. "In that situation as a player, you want to be the hero, but on the other hand you want the ball club to win the ball game," he said. "You kind of relax. I just told myself to do the best I can. That's all you can do because you're facing great pitching. All you can do is go up there and wish for the best."

While in Japan, he visited the Shinto shrine with Niela; they were also taken out to dinner by Konishiki, a noted Japanese sumo wrestler.

As the 2000 campaign rolled on, Agbayani continued to perform well for the Mets. By season's end, he had racked up career highs in games (119), at-bats (350), hits (101), home runs (15), RBI (60), batting average (.289), and on-base percentage (.391).

There was, however, one incident in the outfield, during a Saturday evening game in August against the Giants at Shea, that Agbayani would rather forget.

In the top of the fourth inning, with the Mets leading 1-0 and left-hander Mike Hampton on the mound, the Giants loaded the bases. Catcher Bobby Estalella lofted a high fly ball to Agbayani in left. He caught it easily and, thinking it was the third out, handed the ball to a young boy wearing a Mets T-shirt in the stands.

The only problem: there were two outs, not three. Realizing his mistake, Agbayani went back to the stunned kid, grabbed the ball from his hand, and fired it into the infield. However, once the fan touched the ball, the play was officially dead, and all three runners were awarded two bases. Jeff Kent and Ellis Burks scored while J.T. Snow went to third.

The Giants now led 2-1, but a Todd Zeile two-run double gave the Mets the lead again and this time they held on to win. So Agbayani didn't cost them the game. Still, he was mortified.

"Benny had a mind block," said Mets radio announcer Gary Cohen. Right after the play, Agbayani covered his face with his glove. In the clubhouse after the game, speaking to reporters, he said, "It's already done. You can't take that back. Got to go out there and play the game."

It was the first and last time he ever did something like that, he told me.

Such was the level of his popularity that when he came up to bat in the bottom of the fourth, the crowd, instead of lambasting him for his error, applauded and chanted "Ben-NEE, Ben-NEE." He was human and the fans quickly forgave him, though forgiveness is not something New York fans commonly offer players who fall short.

He also made amends with the young fan in the stands, bringing him an autographed baseball when he returned to left field in the top of the fifth.

The Game

Agbayani more than made up for his defensive flub with his exemplary play in the 2000 National League Division Series, in which the Wild Card Mets played the Western-Division-winning Giants, the team with the best record in baseball (97-65). He batted a solid .333, getting hits in all four games, including one that was particularly consequential.

The Mets and Giants split the first two games of the series in San Francisco, and Game Three was held Saturday evening, October 7, at Shea Stadium.

The Giants went ahead 2-0 in the top of the fourth inning on RBI singles by Bobby Estalella (who had hit the ill-fated fly ball to Agbayani in August) and Marvin Benard, off Mets pitcher Rick Reed. The Mets came back with a run in the sixth courtesy of Timo Perez's RBI single, and another in the eighth, thanks to Edgardo Alfonzo's RBI double. The score remained locked at 2-2 heading into the 13th inning.

In the top of the 13th, Barry Bonds, who would end his controversial career with more home runs (762) than any other player, popped up to second baseman Edgardo Alfonzo with two runners on base for the third out.

The first Mets batter in the bottom of the frame, Robin Ventura, grounded out, bringing up Agbayani.

Batting sixth in the lineup that night, Agbayani had five fruitless at-bats leading up to this one. Three times he lifted fly balls to the outfield—once in the bottom of the 11th with runners on first and second and no outs—to no avail. But he was unbowed. "You can't dwell on what your [previous] at-bat was," he said. "You've got to wait for your next at-bat and try and do better."

Now in the bottom of the 13th, Agbayani was facing hard-throwing rookie left-hander Aaron Fultz, the Giants' sixth pitcher of the day, who had entered in the 12th. Valentine told him as he left the dugout, "C'mon, do the best you can and win it for us."

Agbayani had never faced Fultz before and took the first pitch to see what he had. On the next pitch, with the wind blowing out in left field, he nailed a fastball down the middle from Fultz over Barry Bonds's head and the left-center-field wall and into the picnic-area bleachers for a walk-off homer that gave the Mets a 3-2 victory. The homer sent 56,000 fans—nary a soul had left—into a paroxysm of individual and communal joy as chants of "Ben-NEE, Ben-NEE" reverberated around a shaking Shea Stadium. He was greeted at home plate by a massive scrum of Mets, who jumped up and down in unison and, like a large sea creature, enveloped and carried him off the field to the strains of "Rock and Roll Part 2." A framed photo of that scene still hangs in Agbayani's home.

This homer was a bookend to the one in Japan that started the season, also an extra-inning job that won the game. As before, Agbayani wasn't thinking about hitting a home run, just about trying to get on.

"I was looking for something over the plate that I could hit, and it was just in my wheelhouse," said Agbayani, who always prepares for a fastball and adjusts when it's something else. "I didn't even feel it when I hit it. I kind of felt that I hit it pretty good."

So good that he felt certain it was going out. "But you never know at Shea," he said. "I saw Barry playing back like he was going to catch it. Then

Benny Agbayani

slgckgc

he kept on going back and the ball kept going. And once it went over, you know ..."

Seemingly light years from the start of the season when he was hanging onto the roster for dear life, he felt now like he was on top of the world, the heady recipient of universal acclaim. "Being with the fans and your teammates, you could not ask for anything better than that."

The Mets now led the best-of-five series two games to one, with a chance to wrap it up at home the next day—or travel across the country to play a deciding game in San Francisco. "Coming off a high like that, it kind of revved everybody up," said Agbayani. "It gave us that boost of confidence that we're going to just win it and take it home."

And win it they did, 4-0, behind one of the most masterful pitching performances in Mets history, Bobby Jones's one-hitter. Agbayani contributed two hits, continuing his postseason hitting streak.

He kept on hitting in the next series against the St. Louis Cardinals, batting a robust .353 with three RBI and getting knocks in all five games as the Mets took the series four games to one. Meanwhile, their crosstown counterparts, the New York Yankees, were winning their playoff series in the American League, setting up the first "Subway Series" between New York teams since the Yankees beat the Brooklyn Dodgers in 1956.

"It was a wish come true for any New York fan, to have the Yankees and the Mets in the World Series," Agbayani said. "Speaking for myself, I was really excited. To see the Mets and Yankees fans come together and cheering at one end and cheering at the other end. I can just imagine households where they have Mets and Yankees fans. It was a moment where you had to be there. This was a thing you could not miss."

Still a young player not cognizant of the ways athletes can be exploited by the media, he let slip a prediction that the Mets would win the series in five. Instead, they lost it in five, though the games were all close and the Mets were positioned to win Game One at Yankee Stadium until closer Armando Benitez blew the save. "We should have won the first game," he said, laughing. "Should have, could have. Eh, you know." Agbayani maintains that the season was still a success for the Mets, what with their Wild Card victory and the National League pennant.

In the Mets' lone World Series victory, in Game Three at Shea, Agbayani sliced an RBI double to left-center field off Yankee starter Orlando "El Duque" Hernandez (who lost for the first time in the postseason) in the bottom of the eighth to give the Mets the lead, 3-2. The Mets scored another in the inning and held on for a 4-2 win.

Given the setting, he considers this the biggest hit of his career apart from the 13th-innng game-winner. Agbayani had now hit in all 12 of the Mets' postseason contests in 2000 (and the last one in 1999), though the streak would end in the next game.

The Aftermath

Hampered by hamstring injuries in 2001, Agbayani played in only 91 games. His offensive numbers declined as he hit just six homers and drove in 27 runs, though his average was a respectable .277.

Over the course of his time with the Mets, Agbayani compiled an OPS (on-base plus slugging percentage) of .833, the eighth-highest in team history for batters with at least 1,000 plate appearances. But it wasn't enough for the Mets, who traded him to the Colorado Rockies after the '91 season.

"I was kind of disappointed because I came up through the Mets' system," he said. "I wanted to be [in New York] and finish up my career there. But in this business you never know what's going to happen,"

Agbayani played in Colorado and Boston in 2002, helping the Red Sox in their stretch drive. The next year he spent with the Kansas City Royals' AAA team in Omaha. Then he made the big jump in 2004 to Japan, playing for the Chiba Lotte Marines under Bobby Valentine. "I thought I needed a change," he said.

It was Valentine, his enduring advocate, who recruited him. "He said if I was interested he wanted me to come and work out over there," said

Agbayani. "I hadn't been in the majors [for a year] so they wanted to see what kind of player I was. I took the opportunity and got a contract."

His first year with the Marines was his best as a pro. He whacked 35 home runs and knocked in 100 runs with a .315 batting average and a .426 on-base percentage. The following year he cooled off, but the Marines won the Japanese championship. He and Valentine both continued on the team through 2009.

Like the fans in New York, Japanese fans embraced Agbayani, perhaps even more so. At games, a horde would lavish him with an extended chant— "Oh Benny, Oh Benny"—while standing and clapping.

"The [Japanese] fans are really into it," he said. "Like I always tell everybody, if you really want to see fans, you need to come. I can't explain how they are. These fans are into it from day one to the last day of the season."

In 2009, at age thirty-seven, Agbayani retired from the game and returned to Hawaii, where he grew up playing soccer, baseball, and football. The following year, he began working as an educational assistant at Mililani High School, in Oahu. (He recently left that position.) The job encompassed everything from tutor to guidance counselor to security officer.

His students were aware of his status as a former big league ballplayer, but he didn't make too much of it. He did try to convey the message that sustained him through his career—to try your best and never give up. "There's a future for these youngsters out here in Hawaii."

Agbayani is also heavily involved with his own children, coaching his two daughters, ages thirteen and ten, on a softball team with his wife. His six-year-old son is starting to play baseball. "I thought I was retired, but I'm on the field seven days a week!"

Chapter 18

BOBBY JONES

Pitcher, 1993-2000
Throws/Bats: Right

The Game: October 8, 2000 vs. the San Francisco Giants, at
Pacific Bell Park, Game Four, National League Division Series

METS STATS	
GAMES:	193
COMPLETE GAMES:	10
SHUTOUTS:	4
INNINGS PITCHED:	1,215.2
WINS:	74
LOSSES:	56
ERA:	4.13
WALKS:	353
STRIKEOUTS:	714
WHIP:	1.323
WAR:	9.8

The Run-up

"Here's the pitch on the way to Bonds ... Fly ball to center ... Can he run it down? ... On the run, Payton ... Makes the catch ... It's all over ... The Mets win it!!! Jay Payton makes the catch ... A one-hit shutout by Bobby Jones ... And they're all racing to the mound and mobbing Bobby Jones ... What a magnificent game ... The Mets have never had a better game pitched in their thirty-nine-year history than this game pitched by Bobby Jones." –Mets' Hall of Fame radio announcer Bob Murphy

Bobby J. Jones, a right-handed pitcher for the Mets in the 1990s and 2000, shares some pre- and post-career biographical trivia with none other than Tom Seaver. They both went to Fresno (California) High School and they have both turned a lifelong love of wine into a winery business in Northern California.

Of course, their baseball careers differed significantly. Seaver was the iconic "franchise" player with a blazing fastball who turned "lovable losers into world champions," to quote his Hall of Fame plaque, while Jones was a solid starter with a tantalizingly slow curve who posted 74 wins for the Mets, good for ninth on the team's all-time win list, which is headed by Seaver's 198 wins.

But Jones did have one thing on Seaver. While Tom Terrific pitched many memorable playoff and World Series games in 1969 and 1973, he never threw a one-hitter in the postseason and he never pitched a postseason series-clinching victory. Bobby Jones did both, in one game, on Sunday, October 8, 2000, at Shea Stadium, the only one-hitter in Mets postseason history. (The team has had 37 one-hitters during the regular season.)

Making his first playoff start, Jones pitched to just three batters over the minimum in that series-deciding Game Four, advancing the Mets past the San Francisco Giants in the National League Division Series and on to the National League Championship Series vs. the St. Louis Cardinals. (The Mets would defeat the Cardinals but lose to the Yankees in the "subway" World Series. Jones started Game Four in each series, with a no-decision against the Cards and a loss to the Yanks.)

Jones's one-hit gem on that cloudy and chilly evening was easily one of the greatest pitching performances—and just the sixth one-hitter—in baseball's postseason history, up there with Don Larsen's perfect game for the Yankees in the 1956 World Series; Roy Halladay's no-hitter for the Phillies in the 2010 National League Division Series; and Jim Lonborg's one-hitter for the Red Sox in the 1967 World Series.

A strapping 6-foot-4, 210-pounder who turned thirty that year, Jones almost didn't pitch in Game Four. There was speculation that Mike Hampton, the Mets' ERA leader, would pitch on three days' rest, or that left-hander Glendon Rusch would step in, but manager Bobby Valentine ultimately decided to go with Jones. "He had faith in me and stuck with me," Jones told me during a phone conversation.

Jones's wife, Kristi, also had faith in him. The night before Game Four, she ran into Valentine in the tunnel leading to the Mets' dugout and told him, "Don't worry, my husband is going to have the game of his life." Valentine later referred to her prophecy in post-game interviews.

Jones and his wife have three children—two girls, Shaylee and Avery, and a boy, Breyton, a high school senior in 2014 with whom Jones was working on pitching. Besides his budding wine business, Jones is a barbecue aficionado who has created his own sauce recipe and is thinking about writing a cookbook. He coached in 2006 for his alma mater, Fresno State (for which he was an All-American), and these days offers private pitching instruction to kids ten years old and up.

Jones is linked to another Mets icon—Darryl Strawberry. Selected by the Mets with the 36th pick in the first round of the 1991 amateur draft, Jones was the compensatory pick the Mets earned when Strawberry left the team that year as a free agent to join the Dodgers.

After a highly successful run in the minors, Jones was called up to the Mets in August of 1993 at age twenty-three. He won his debut game against the Phillies on August 14, spinning his signature 70-mph curve ball as he allowed just one run over six innings. Jones learned how to throw a curve from his father, Bob Sr., when he was just nine—well before it's advisable for a youngster to start throwing a breaking ball, due to the curve's strain on the arm. It became his favorite pitch.

For the most part, Jones's fastball crossed the plate at a modest 85 miles per hour, though "when I was a little younger, it was little harder than that." He threw a slider and changeup as well and helped his cause with excellent fielding, leading the National League in fielding percentage in 1994 and 2001. "It's your ERA out there," he said. "Nobody wants to jump out of the way of a ball and let it go up the middle." He was also proficient with the bunt, leading the league in sacrifice hits with 18 in 1995.

In his one-hitter, Jones stuck to his usual arsenal of pitches. "It wasn't like I was overpowering or had a couple of extra miles per hour on my fastball," he said. "It was just that I had that focus—the ability to just put the ball where I felt I wanted to." And he credited his fielders for rescuing him when he made a pitching mistake. "You've got to have a lot of luck on your side, and some speedsters in the outfield to run those balls down for you." Jones had popular late-season call-up Timo Perez in right field, Jay Payton in center, and game-three hero Benny Agbayani in left.

I asked him how he and catcher Mike Piazza prepared for Game Four.

"We sat down and had a very good game plan just like any other game," said Jones. "We knew exactly what we wanted to do with each hitter, in certain situations."

But he emphasized that the art of pitching is keeping your best cards hidden until you really need them. "You're not going to go to your best stuff in a 0-0 ballgame in the third inning," he said. "But when it's the sixth or seventh inning and you've got a couple of runners on, then you go to that game plan and remember, this is where we're going to get them out. If you show them that early, they're going to be aware of it and make adjustments."

For any pitcher, but particularly one like Jones who can't physically overpower a hitter, pitching is very much a mind game.

Jones became a mainstay in the Mets' rotation from 1994 through 1997, winning at least 10 games each year. His peak came in 1997 with 15 wins and his only All-Star Game appearance, in which he retired all three batters he faced in the eighth inning, including back-to-back strikeouts of heavy-hitting Ken Griffey, Jr. and Mark McGuire.

He remembered returning to the dugout after the strikeouts and being congratulated by fellow All-Star pitcher Curt Schilling, who told him, "You know what? Your son is probably one of the only kids that can say my dad struck out Griffey and McGuire back-to-back." That quote endures as an All-Star Game memory "that still stands out for me today."

In 1998, Jones missed double figures in wins by just one game. He slumped the next year when a back injury limited him to three wins in 12 starts, and he was left off the Mets' roster for the postseason, the team's first in 11 years. To be left off the roster was a bitter disappointment for Jones, who toiled all those years for the Mets when they weren't making the playoffs.

In 2000, Jones continued to struggle, posting a 1-3 record with a 10.19 ERA after eight starts. At mid-season he accepted a demotion to the Mets AAA affiliate in Norfolk, the Tides.

"I remember getting just beat up at Yankee Stadium and the coaching staff asking me if I would accept assignment down to AAA to work out the problems I was going through," said Jones. "As a veteran of eight years, it was kind of hard to swallow. But I knew it was something that I needed to do—go down to a place where I was a little more relaxed and I could work on things to get back and help the team."

His visit to Norfolk lasted two weeks, long enough to make some key adjustments. His family remained in New York, and he commuted back and forth while making all of his starts for the Tides.

"Sometimes you've got to swallow your pride and do what's best for the team," said Jones. "If it's going to make me better, it's going to help me help the team. Fortunately it did for me."

What Jones needed to improve in Norfolk was "command," the ability to put the ball where he wanted it, give or take a few centimeters. It's what distinguishes major league pitchers, whether speed merchants or junk ballers, from the rest of the universe.

"I wasn't an overpowering guy," said Jones. "I had to have command to be able to hit spots and have all my pitches working. And when I didn't, I had to find other ways to be successful. But for somebody who is not an overpowering pitcher, sometimes that can be tough."

Pitching command requires much more than physical talent, which most major league players have in abundance; it also calls for self-confidence. This is what Jones was really working on in Norfolk—the mental side of the game, often neglected if not entirely downplayed in the macho culture of professional sports.

"You have to trust yourself and your ability to go out there and perform," he said. "And if you don't—if you have any doubt whatsoever—that's where you're going to run into problems."

Part of the mental challenge of pitching is shrugging off the vicissitudes inherent in the path of a batted ball.

"A good pitch that's hit between short and third—it could have been a routine ground ball to the shortstop or the third baseman," Jones said. "It's true what they say—baseball is a game of inches. As a pitcher, you've got to be able to realize, hey, there's a lot to just getting the right bounce. You have to be able to shove that off and not worry about it."

Jones doesn't think he necessarily pitched any better in the one-hitter than at any other time, except that he didn't pay for his mistakes. "Pitchers make four or five mistakes a game and if two of them get fouled off and one of them gets caught in the outfield, well maybe you have a great game. Sometimes you get away with them and sometimes you don't."

After returning to the Mets from Norfolk in late June, Jones began winning on a regular basis, going 10-3 the rest of the season and ending with 11 wins—testimony to the wisdom of accepting his assignment to the farm. "I was blessed the coaches came up with that idea, because as a player I probably would not have recommended it."

If 2000 was the year of his greatest triumph, it was also his final year with the Mets. He signed as a free agent with the San Diego Padres and played two more seasons before retiring in 2002.

Bobby Jones during the ninth inning of his one-hit shutout of the San Francisco Giants in the 2000 National League Division Series.

AP Photo/Mark Lennihan

The Game

Unlike 1999, Jones made the postseason roster in 2000 as the fourth starter. The Mets, Wild Card winners with 94 wins and 68 losses, faced the San Francisco Giants, the Western Division champions and holder of the best record in baseball (97-65), in one of the two National League Division Series. The first two games of the best-of-five series took place at the Giants' palatial Pacific Bell (now AT&T) Park, then in its inaugural season by the San Francisco Bay.

The Giants cruised to a 5-1 Game One victory. The Mets bounced back with a 5-4, 10-inning win in Game Two, which ended when reliever John Franco struck out Barry Bonds looking, on a 3-2 changeup, Franco's signature pitch.

Convening at Shea Stadium for Game Three, the Mets won another extra-inning affair, this one in 13 innings, on Benny Agbayani's walk-off home run.

The Mets wanted to close out the series at Shea rather than have to cross the country and play a deciding fifth game, and they handed the ball to Jones. His pitching opponent: fellow Fresno State alum Mark Gardner, a close friend and neighbor in California. Jones and Gardner later started the "Step to the Plate" Foundation to support cancer patients at the Stanford University Medical Center. "I knew him really well; he's one of my good buddies," said Jones.

The Mets asked Mike Hampton, the possible starter in Game Four until Jones was chosen, to fly to San Francisco the day of Game Four in the event that the teams would play a fifth and deciding contest. But Hampton said he preferred to remain in New York "and be part of the celebration," said Jones. "I had everyone on my side."

Jones woke up on October 8, 2000 keenly excited about what lay ahead. "The playoff atmosphere, my first year being active in the playoffs, getting that opportunity to start—it was just the place to be," he remembered. "The playoffs in New York are pretty intense; it's a pretty special environment."

The Mets got off to a grand start in Game Four as Robin Ventura's two-out home run produced a two-run first-inning lead. Those early runs helped Jones's mindset.

"[An early lead] makes a huge difference, at least to me," he said. "Some pitchers may say differently, but whenever there is a little bit of a cushion, you don't change your game plan but there's a little more room for error; you don't have to be as fine, maybe. That just helps me when I'm on the mound to relax a little bit. It's just, I do what I've got to do, and I don't worry about it. Just trust your stuff, have faith in your stuff, and go do it."

And Jones did, in spades. In every inning but one, he was perfect, retiring the side in order. The only exception was the fifth inning, when he gave up his lone hit—a leadoff double to former Met second baseman Jeff Kent that went off the glove of a leaping Robin Ventura, the third baseman, into left field.

Jones mused about what might have happened if Ventura "was two inches taller" and caught Kent's drive. "It would've been totally different if it wasn't a hit. Who knows?" As for the player who got the hit, Jones likes to point out, tongue-in-cheek, that after playing behind Jones for many years at second for the Mets, Kent "knew every pitch that I threw."

But Kent wasn't the final base runner for the Giants that inning. After retiring right-fielder Ellis Burks on a fly ball to right field that advanced Kent to third, Jones walked first baseman J.T. Snow. The next batter, shortstop Rich Aurilia, was in a position to score Kent with an out. But Jones got him to fly out to shallow left field, not deep enough to allow Kent to tag up from third.

Now with two outs, Jones intentionally walked catcher Doug Mirabelli to load the bases, and faced his good friend Gardner. "It was still early in the game and he was a pretty decent hitter so they stuck with him." Gardner popped up to second base. The inning—and the Giants' only offensive output of the game—was over with no runs scored.

Gardner only pitched to four more batters in the bottom of the fifth before being taken out of the game, making Giants manager Dusty Baker's decision to let him hit in the top of the fifth with the bases loaded a rather dubious one, in retrospect.

But the bigger out was Aurelia. "If you look at his numbers, he probably did pretty well off me," said Jones. "He was a tough out for me." Jones got him by "doing things differently."

Jones was part of the rally in the bottom of the fifth that added two more runs to the Mets tally. He struck out, swinging, at a pitch in the dirt that went to the backstop, and he was able to make it safely to first base. "I struck out a lot but I never seemed to get on base that way." Then he scored, with Timo Perez, on Edgardo Alfonzo's double to center field.

Score after five: Mets 4, Giants 0, the two new runs more salve for the pitching psyche. "When you are able to increase that lead, that puts momentum on our side and weakens it for them," Jones said.

Jones said he prepared for that at-bat in his usual manner, assuming he would hit. "I get my helmet on and get in the on-deck circle until somebody tells me differently. That's kind of the starting pitcher's mentality. I'm not coming out of there until somebody yanks me out of there."

By the ninth inning, the 56,245 fans (I was one) knew they were on the verge of witnessing something special in Mets history—a one-hit shutout in a playoff-series-clinching win. It was Jones's moment and they were on their feet calling out his name throughout the ninth.

"Even now," he said, "it brings chills just to remember hearing the sold-out crowd chanting, 'Bobby! Bobby! Bobby!'"

Was it hard to focus with that going on?

"No. You hear it, but you don't. It's almost like you have earplugs in. But once that final out is made, somebody rips your earplugs off and now it's amplified super, super loud. Then you can actually take it all in and go, wow, that was pretty cool." But first he had to retire Barry Bonds one last time.

Pitching to Bonds was undoubtedly Jones's biggest challenge that day. Though Bonds had yet to garner the statistics that would make him the poster child for the steroids era—73 home runs in 2001, a .370 batting average in 2002, to cite a few—he was still in 2000 a fearsome offensive force, with a career-best-to-that-point 49 home runs and a .306 batting average. But he also had a rep for coming up small in the playoffs (which he later erased, though he was never part of a World Series winner).

In the first inning, Jones struck out Bonds swinging on a 2-2 pitch. In the fourth, he struck him out looking on a 2-2 pitch. Bonds finally put the ball in play in the sixth, but just flied out to left field. And in the ninth, Bonds, with two outs and the last hope for the Giants, hit a screaming line drive that Jay Payton ran down in center, ending the game and prompting Bob Murphy's joyful radio call.

"The way I always tried to get Barry out was to throw hard, up in the zone, inside, trying to get him to chase," Jones said. But first he threw the big, slow curve, changing Bonds's eye level as the ball started up in the strike zone and then broke down. With two strikes, Jones elevated the fastball, which, in the optical illusion conjured by crafty pitchers, looked like a blazer compared with the slow curve. On that day, Bonds was his.

"The crowd really cheered when you got Bonds out," I said.

"Yeah, yeah. I always loved that."

How did he feel when Bonds took his final swing?

"When he hit it, I thought he hit it a lot harder than he did. So when I turned around and saw the ball come down and the final out, it was a little like I didn't know what to do. I was kind of in shock."

At that moment, two hours and 48 minutes after he threw the game's first pitch, Jones found himself at the center of the baseball universe, mobbed by his teammates, the crowd screaming, the fireworks popping, The Baha Men's "Who Let the Dogs Out?" blaring. "People were going crazy and it was kind of cool, you know?"

He ended the game with 116 pitches, 73 for strikes, including five strikeouts. He came up in the bottom of the eighth with runners on first and second and two outs—a prime opportunity for manager Valentine to insert a pinch hitter and take Jones out of the game. But he was allowed to hit, and struck out swinging.

The Aftermath

In a postgame interview on the field, a reporter with CNNSI wanted Jones to recap the pivotal fifth inning, when he gave up his only hit and his two walks. How did he get out of that?

Still shell-shocked, and not hearing the question too well because the crowd was still so loud, Jones could only reply that he didn't remember the fifth; he only remembered the last out of the game.

In the raucous player celebration after the game, Mets pitcher Al Leiter told the press how proud he was of Jones for having that performance. "I think they all understood what I went through," Jones said. "To come back and have that game, one of my last games in New York as a Met, was pretty special. Emotionally it was just huge. I think to this day that's what New York remembers me [for]."

And, of course, that it was the series clincher made Jones's accomplishment even bigger. "Yeah, that was it," he said. "We were going on to St. Louis."

Chapter 19

MIKE PIAZZA

Catcher, 1998-2005
Throws/Bats: Right

The Game: September 21, 2001 vs. Atlanta Braves, at Shea Stadium

METS STATS	
GAMES:	972
AT-BATS:	3,478
HITS:	1,028
HOME RUNS:	220
AVERAGE:	.296
ON-BASE %:	.373
SLUGGING %:	.542
RUNS:	532
RBI:	655
STOLEN BASES:	7
FIELDING %:	.990
WAR:	24.5

The Run-up

That's frankly one of the most unforgettable swings of a baseball bat I've ever seen in my life. –Mets Broadcaster Howie Rose, on Mike Piazza's home run in the first game played in New York after 9/11/01

The fans and players who gathered at Shea Stadium on September 21, 2001, were not quite sure how to feel. They wanted to move on with their lives, to enjoy an early fall, Friday night ballgame, yet they were living in the aftermath of one of the most traumatic events to ever be visited upon a great American city.

The baseball circumstances of the game—the Mets were playing their archrivals, the Atlanta Braves, whom they were trailing in the standings by five games—were almost an afterthought. What really mattered was that this was the first professional sporting event to take place in New York City since the September 11th terrorist attacks. Would people show up? Would they feel safe? Could they enjoy themselves? Ambivalence abounded.

"When September 11th hit, if they had cancelled the season, I would have been fine with it. I just couldn't even conceive of going back to play baseball," said Howie Rose, the Mets radio broadcaster, bard, and chief historian, during SNY's June 2012 broadcast announcing the Mets All-Time Team, which included Piazza as the catcher.

The Mets were not in New York City on September 11th; they were in Pittsburgh, waiting to play the Pirates that evening, just 80 miles from Shanksville, Pennsylvania, where the last terrorist-captured plane, United Airlines Flight 93, went down. After the attacks, Major League Baseball cancelled all of its games for the foreseeable future, and the Mets took a bus back to New York City the next day.

As it approached Manhattan on the New Jersey side near midnight, the bus drove within view of Ground Zero, past the floodlights and the black smoke and acrid odor—and the suddenly missing buildings. In the ensuing days, Piazza and his teammates tried to help New Yorkers get back on their feet, visiting the afflicted and packing up supplies at Shea Stadium's parking lot, which had become a staging area.

"You just wanted to help out any way you can," said Piazza at a ceremony in 2008 commemorating Shea Stadium's greatest moments. (Piazza's performance in the September 21, 2001 game was voted No. 2, after the 1986 World Series game-six comeback.) "Every day we were going to visit people in the hospital. We saw fire people in the hospital who were in the [9/11] event."

Ten days later, Piazza wasn't sure about this first game back at Shea. "To get back on the field again, we really were very confused," he said. "We didn't think baseball had a place in that event. But we also knew there was a time eventually when we'd have to try to get on with the season and get on with our lives."

As he stood on the field during the pregame ceremonies and listened to the bagpipes play, he started praying. "I said, 'Please, God, give me the strength to get through this.' It was so hard to hold it together emotionally."

By September 2001, Piazza was already a legend in New York, the rare catcher who could hit for power and average, on his way to securing his place as the greatest hitting catcher in baseball history.

After seven remarkable years as a Dodger—in his last full season, in 1997, he slugged 40 home runs, drove in 124, and hit .362, the highest average ever by a National League catcher—he came to the Mets in 1998 by way of a trade with the Florida Marlins, who had acquired him from LA. For Piazza, the Mets sent the Marlins prospects Preston Wilson, Ed Yarnall, and Geoff Goetz, arguably the most lopsided trade on the positive side in their history.

"I remember when we first traded for you and I was like a little twelve-year-old," said former Mets pitcher Al Leiter, in a video speech at Piazza's Mets Hall of Fame ceremony at Shea Stadium in September 2013. "I was a Mets fan growing up. We got Piazza!"

By the time he came to the Mets, Piazza had long since blown away any notion that, after being just a 62nd round pick (1,390th overall) in the 1988 draft, he was in the big leagues only because Dodgers manager Tom Lasorda was childhood buddies with Piazza's father, Vince.

In 1998, the Mets signed Piazza to a $93 million, seven-year contract. Unlike many other free agents who have played for the Mets, he lived up to his contract, hitting 40, 38, 36, and 33 home runs in his first four full seasons, and, in 1999, setting the single-season team record for RBI (124), which was later tied by David Wright. His .542 slugging percentage is tops in Mets history.

On May 5, 2004, Piazza hit his 352nd home run as a catcher, surpassing Carlton Fisk for the most homers as a catcher in major league history. Piazza ended his career fourth in RBI among catchers.

Like Gary Carter before him, Piazza "came over to what was a good team and made it a potential championship team," said Gary Cohen during the broadcast of the Mets All-Time Team.

Piazza's Achilles' heel was throwing out base stealers; his career caught-stealing percentage was 23%, well below the 35.5% caught by his catcher teammates.

In other respects, his catching prowess, though often criticized, stands up to scrutiny. In 2000, his .997 fielding percentage (which he repeated in 2005) led National League catchers. Most significantly, he got the most out of his pitching staff. Over the course of his career, his pitchers' ERA was 3.80, compared to 4.34 by catcher teammates handling the same pitchers.

After his contract expired, Piazza left the Mets as a free agent and signed a one-year contract with the Padres in 2006. In his return to Shea on August 8, 2006, he received an immense outpouring of affection from Mets fans, including frequent standing ovations. He singled in the Mets 3-2 victory, and the next day homered twice and came close to a third time as the Mets won again, 4-3. (He was vigorously applauded after the first homer, noticeably less so after the second.)

At his induction to the Mets Hall of Fame, Piazza chose his return to Shea as a Padre—and especially the embracing response from Mets fans—as his greatest Mets-related memory.

"Yeah, we hit some great home runs, and had some great games and some great teams," he said. "But the relationship we've had, the love that we've shared, and the love you've given me and the support, words cannot describe how special it is to me. ... When I came back here in 2006, with San Diego, you guys cheered for me. And you pulled for me. That just shows what we have and what we have shared."

But he was a Padre when that happened. As a Met, the memory of what he did on September 21, 2001, looms large for Piazza as well as for baseball fans, New Yorkers, and anyone touched by the events of September 11. He has called it "one of the most emotional nights of my life."

The Game

This was clearly no ordinary regular season ballgame. The pregame ceremony featured a 21-gun salute salute and bagpipes playing "Amazing Grace." Diana Ross, joined by a local gospel choir, delivered a stirring "God Bless America," followed by Marc Anthony's spirited national anthem, accompanied by the fans. (During the seventh-inning stretch, Liza Minnelli sang "New York, New York," arm in arm with police and firefighters.) Red, white, and blue ribbons were painted on the grass. Lines at security checkpoints delayed the start of the game.

The Mets, who wore caps with insignias of the fire and police departments in place of the usual intertwined NY, donated their salary for the game to the New York Police and Fire Widows and Children's Benefit Fund Foundation. Piazza's contribution was $68,306.01.

There were even pregame hugs between Mets and Braves players, normally the most bitter of rivals.

"It was different," said Atlanta manager Bobby Cox in an MLB.com video clip. "They weren't such an enemy after all ... for maybe ten minutes. Once the game started, it was a game."

Despite his feverish emotions, Piazza tried to put his game face on. But this game clearly meant more to him than a typical ballgame, even one that had playoff implications, even one against the Braves. "We *had* to win that ballgame," he wrote in his book, *Long Shot* (emphasis in the original).

The game remained scoreless through the first three innings (though Piazza doubled to left in the first), a pitchers duel between the Mets' Bruce Chen and the Braves' Jason Marquis, a New York native. In the fourth, Chipper Jones singled and came home on a double to right field by Ken Caminiti, Piazza dropping the throw to the plate while putting a tag on Jones.

Piazza, a devout Roman Catholic, immediately atoned for his mistake by doubling in the bottom of the fourth, moving to third on a single by Robin Ventura, and scoring on a sacrifice fly by Tsuyoshi Shinjo.

The score remained tied 1-1 until the eighth. After securing the first two outs, John Franco, in for Chen, allowed a walk and a single. Manager Bobby Valentine brought in closer Armando Benitez to face the next batter, Brian Jordan, who doubled home a run on Benitez's first pitch, making it 2-1 Braves. Benitez then walked a batter before finally retiring the side on an Andruw Jones fly ball to center. It was very reminiscent of the Mets' historic struggles against Atlanta.

But Piazza was due up in the bottom of the eighth. After Matt Lawton grounded out to short, Edgardo Alfonzo worked out a walk on a 3-2 count off reliever Mark Karsay, who, like Marquis, was from New York (Queens, in particular). At Piazza's Mets Hall of Fame ceremony, he showered considerable praise on Alfonzo's ability to deliver in the clutch. "If I wasn't the guy up there with the game on the line, I wanted it to be Fonzie," he said. "Because I knew he came through, sometimes a lot more than I did."

But this time it would be Piazza with the game on the line, as he sauntered to the plate, tugging his jersey. "Here's the man the Mets want up in this spot, down a run, late in the game," said Rose during the TV broadcast. "Karsay has seen Piazza four times previously; Mike is 1 for 4 against him."

He didn't offer at Karsay's first 96-mile-per-hour fastball, a pitch he could have hit. But the next pitch, another heater, was a different story. Piazza squared it up and connected with his patented swing, honed over innumerable childhood practice sessions in the backyard with his father, strengthened by his assiduous workouts, the incessant squeezing of a hand grip that others couldn't budge.

"And it's hit deep to left-center," said Rose, his voice rising. "Andruw Jones on the run. *This one has a chance.* Home Run! Mike Piazza! And the Mets lead, 3 to 2!

The crowd exploded.

Piazza rounded the bases almost casually, seemingly oblivious to the uproar he had just ignited. As he crossed the plate, he and Ventura executed an over-the-head, double high-five. He returned to the dugout, but the vociferous crowd, waving American flags, demanded a curtain call, and he obliged, lifting his helmet with one hand, kissing his fingers and pointing skyward with the other.

"People found a way to find some sort of joy or happiness or inspiration," he said at the Shea Stadium's greatest moments gathering. "But for me I try to keep it in perspective."

For the record, Benitez gave up a lead-off single in the top of the ninth, but got a double play grounder to end the game. The Mets won, 3-2, as they *had* to. They moved to 4 ½ games behind the first-place Braves in the NL East. They would end the season six games behind, in third place.

The Aftermath

Just as this was no ordinary game, Piazza's blast was no ordinary home run. Home runs, especially of the go-ahead variety, always make the home fans happy, but these fans needed that jolt of happiness more than they knew. Piazza's lightning strike in the night penetrated the darkness of the post-9/11 gloom and, for a brief moment and more, gave the 41,235 on hand and the millions observing electronically a feeling of genuine exultation few expected to experience that night. Amid the tears, the laughter, the yelling and cheering, the clapping and hugging and jumping and flag waving and USA chanting, there was palpable relief—we're going to be all right. Normally our refuge, baseball became our catharsis.

Carol Gies, who lost her husband, Ronnie, a firefighter, at the World Trade Center on 9/11, attended the game with her three sons. When Piazza hit the homer, she saw her boys "jumping up and down and screaming and smiling again for the first time," she told the *New York Daily News*. After the game, they met in the dugout with Piazza, who told the boys their father was "a true hero."

Broadcaster Rose put it this way during SNY's All-Time Team program: "When he was circling the bases, I remember seeing a shot of a couple of

Mike Piazza gestures to fans after the Mets' 3-2 win over the Atlanta Braves in the first game played in New York after the 9/11 attacks. His two-run homer in the eighth inning put the Mets ahead to stay.

AP Photo/Jeff Zelevansky

uniformed firemen who had undoubtedly in that 10-day period lost comrades, friends, God-forbid relatives or children. But they were smiling! And it made such a profound impact on me that after the most devastating event that most of us had ever lived through in this town, that if those firefighters who had suffered such deep personal loss can get some happiness from Mike Piazza hitting a home run in a game against the Atlanta Braves, then not only did baseball make the right decision to come back, it made the only decision. Mike Piazza galvanized the city on that night. I didn't think it was possible before he hit that home run, but afterward it became crystal clear, not even what Mike's impact was on the Mets, but what that home run meant to this entire city. And that's frankly one of the most unforgettable swings of a base-ball bat I've ever seen in my life."

Though he has come to understand the magnitude of what he did that night, Piazza is generally subdued in his appraisal. "I was fortunate that I found the strength to at least hit a home run in that situation," he said in his presentation at the Greatest Moments at Shea gathering. "The true heroes were New Yorkers in general and this organization, how everyone reacted. I was just very blessed to run into one."

In *Long Shot*, he expresses professional and personal satisfaction in his accomplishment that night, and some amazement at the timeless reverbera-tions it set off. He never imagined that a regular season home run "could resonate so far beyond the boundaries of baseball," he wrote.

Piazza ended his career as a twelve-time All-Star and a ten-time Silver Slugger and one of the greatest hitters the Mets ever had. He and the team's greatest pitcher, Tom Seaver, were chosen to officially "close" Shea Stadium in 2008 and "open" Citi Field the next year.

Piazza is hoping to join Seaver at another venue—the Hall of Fame. In 2014, his second year of eligibility, he garnered 62.2% of the votes cast by sportswriters. That's below the 75% threshold for entry, but close enough that his induction seems inevitable, though unproven rumors of steroid use may get in the way. If he does enter the Hall, he will go as a Met, the only position player in team history to be inducted.

Chapter 20

DAVID WRIGHT

Third Base, 2004-present
Throws/Bats: Right

The Game: October 19, 2006 vs. St. Louis Cardinals, at Shea
Stadium, Game Seven, National League Championship Series

METS STATS (THROUGH 2014)	
GAMES:	1,508
AT-BATS:	5,707
HITS:	1,702
HOME RUNS:	230
AVERAGE:	.298
ON-BASE %:	.377
SLUGGING %:	.494
RUNS:	907
RBI:	939
STOLEN BASES:	191
FIELDING %:	.955
WAR:	49.7

The Run-up

Over the team's first 53 seasons, 153 players—from Kurt Abbott to Don Zimmer—have taken the field at third base for the New York Mets. Longtime Mets radio broadcaster Howie Rose has described the position as "something of a black hole" for the team.

It's therefore a little ironic that the player who has become the face of the franchise over the past decade is a third baseman named David Wright.

Since joining the Mets in July 2004, Wright has rewritten the team's record books. Entering the 2015 season, he had compiled the most at-bats (5,707), RBI (939), total bases (2,819), extra-base hits (631), runs (907), hits (1,702), doubles (375), hit-by-pitches (45), sacrifice flies (65), and walks (713) in team history. He also leads all Mets in career and single-season WAR (wins above replacement) with 49.7 and 8.3, respectively.

With 1,508 games played, Wright is still second to Ed Kranepool, who participated in 1,853, and with 230 home runs he is runner up to Darryl Strawberry, who hit 252, but he could pass both during the next three seasons. If he stays healthy, he should be able to burnish his existing records and break a few more over the course of his 2012 contract, which keeps him in a Mets uniform through 2020. At almost $140 million, the contract is the richest in Mets history.

Add to that Wright's seven All-Star Game appearances, two Gold Glove awards, two Silver Slugger awards, and membership in the 30-30 club comprising players who have hit at least 30 homers and stolen at least 30 bases in the same season. (Wright did both in 2007.)

Wright was named the Mets' captain, the fourth in team history, in 2013, when he also became known as "Captain America" for his exploits on behalf of Team USA in the World Baseball Classic. And in 2014, he even won the "Face of MLB" contest.

He has also been recognized for his philanthropy, winning the Sports Humanitarian of the Year award in 2008, among other honors. His David Wright Foundation aids children in need in the New York City and Norfolk, Virginia, areas.

Yet, for all of his accomplishments, Wright lacks the one thing that would gratify him the most as a player—a World Championship.

When he appeared on SNY's June 2012 broadcast announcing the Mets All-Time Team—he was selected at third base, to no one's surprise—Wright expressed his gratitude for being included with franchise icons like Tom Seaver, Jerry Koosman, Darryl Strawberry, and Keith Hernandez. But he made a point of separating himself from those players because of their championship pedigree.

"You have guys that have World Series rings, who have been to the World Series and have won here. I haven't experienced that. That's where I want to be."

A championship, he added, is "what I yearn for. That's ultimately why you take the field to play this game."

Wright has so far had only one opportunity to win a championship—in 2006, when the Mets won the National League East and beat the Dodgers in the National League Division Series, but lost to the Cardinals in the National League Championship Series, thus missing the World Series. Just getting a taste of postseason baseball for the first time was enough for Wright to say on the All-Time Team broadcast that the 2006 playoffs represented his most memorable experience as a Met.

"Just running out on that field for the first time and looking at Shea Stadium and particularly the upper deck," he said. "Literally, it shakes. When [the fans] get up and down, I mean it shakes." The audience at the 92nd Street Y in Manhattan, where the All-Time Team broadcast was held, burst into applause.

Wright added, "I never experienced anything like that in baseball and I want to experience that again."

Growing up in Chesapeake, Virginia, Wright rooted for the Mets, whose AAA team played in nearby Norfolk. His favorite player, however, was the Orioles' Cal Ripken, Jr., whom he would get to watch at Baltimore's Camden Yards. "I loved the way he played the game," Wright said on the David Letterman Show in July 2006.

But the Mets came first. "I have a tremendous pride when I put that uniform on every day because I grew up in Norfolk where our AAA team is," he said on the All-Time Team broadcast. (The AAA team has since relocated to Las Vegas.) "I grew up a Mets fan. I worshipped those players before me."

The Mets selected Wright, who was a superb high school ballplayer, in the 2001 amateur draft during the supplemental round as compensation for the team's loss of Mike Hampton to the Colorado Rockies as a free agent. He pushed up the ranks of the Mets' minor league system until a breakout season in 2004, when he hit .341 at the AA and AAA levels, and earned a call-up to the "show" in July.

Though a highly touted rookie, Wright didn't have any special privileges. He carried Cliff Floyd's luggage and fetched coffee for veterans. On the All-Time Team broadcast, he cracked, "I probably shouldn't say this on air but John Franco used to make me wash his back. It was good because it molded me and made me appreciate not having to wash people's backs now."

Wright quickly established himself as a player capable of hitting for both average and power, batting .306 with 27 homers and 102 RBI in his first full season in the majors in 2005. Though he made 24 errors that year, he also showed off some flashy defensive moves, particularly in an August game in San Diego.

With one out in the seventh inning, Padre Brian Giles lifted a pop fly over Wright's head into shallow left field. Running at full speed with his back to home plate—like Willie Mays making his classic over-the-shoulder catch in the 1954 World Series—he reached out with his right, bare hand and caught the ball in full stride, his momentum bringing him to the ground. After coming to a stop, his chest flat on the grass, his legs curled up, he thrust his right hand into the air clutching the baseball.

"David Wright just guaranteed that he will be seen on scoreboards around baseball for the next 20 years," said Mets TV announcer Ted Robinson in reacting to the play. Wright's grab won MLB.com's Most Outstanding Play of the Year Award, based on fan votes, in 2005.

Wright has three younger brothers, Stephen, Matthew, and Daniel, who "keep me pretty level-headed," Wright said on the David Letterman Show in 2006. He added that after his great catch, they left him a phone message. It said that, given his 24 errors the previous year, "it was a good thing I didn't try to use my glove or I probably would have dropped it."

In 2006, Wright became an All-Star for the first time, and finished second to Ryan Howard in the home run derby. He had a series of game-winning hits in May, including a single off Yankees reliever Mariano Rivera; in the Mets Hall of Fame Museum at Citi Field, the third base bag used in the game is on display, autographed by Wright.

Wright finished 2006 with outstanding numbers: 26 homers, 116 RBI, a .311 average and an OPS (on-base plus slugging percentages) of .912. The team did well, too, dominating the NL East and matching the Yankees for the most regular season wins in the major leagues—97.

Wright and the Mets continued to thrive in the NLDS against the Dodgers, despite losing two starting pitchers to injury—Pedro Martinez and Orlando (El Duque) Hernandez. Wright had his best game of the postseason in Game One, with two doubles and three RBI, as the Mets edged LA 6-5.

The next day, Wright contributed a single in the Mets two-run sixth (though he was forced out at the plate), his only hit in the team's 4-1 win. He had a run-scoring single as part of a three-run first-inning rally in the third and final game in Los Angeles, as the Mets won 9-5, completing the sweep and qualifying for the NLCS against the Cardinals, whose 83-78 regular season record was the worst of any playoff team.

Wright went hitless in nine at-bats in the first three games against St. Louis, which took a 2-1 series lead. But prior to Game Four, Mets manager Willie Randolph predicted, "Tonight is the night I feel he's going to bust out."

Sure enough, in Game Four at Busch Stadium, Wright stroked a solo homer to left-center field in the third to give the Mets a 2-1 advantage. He also walked and scored in the Mets' six-run fifth inning, on the way to a 12-5 victory.

Wright doubled in Game Five, which the Mets lost 4-2, and singled in Game Six, which they won 4-2, beating Cardinals ace Scott Carpenter. Thus was established the decisive Game Seven, on October 19, 2006, a misty Thursday night, with a trip to the World Series at stake. There were 56,357 raucous fans at Shea Stadium—just the way Wright liked it.

The Game

"I've never experienced an atmosphere, a craziness that is playoff baseball in New York until [2006]," Wright said at the All-Time Team broadcast.

In an SNY commercial on his most memorable moment as a Met that aired periodically during game broadcasts in 2014—part of a series of such commercials featuring Mets players—Wright again reflected on the 2006 playoffs. "The passionate Mets fans. To go out there and give them October games is a feeling I'll never forget. I want that feeling again. You talk about the feeling on opening day; times that by a million, and you'll get playoff baseball in New York."

The atmosphere at Shea was intense throughout the playoffs, but it reached a perfervid peak in game seven. Wright said in a *New York Post* retrospective on that contest, "The playoffs in '06, especially game seven, from pregame on, we would go take the field for warm-ups and the place would literally be, like, swaying back and forth, kind of. It was incredible."

"Fifty thousand people are booing our batboys, for Christ sakes," Cardinals manager Tony La Russa told the *Post*.

Wright put the Mets on the scoreboard in the first inning of Game Seven with a bloop single to right field off Cards starter Jeff Suppan, driving in Carlos Beltran, who had doubled. "I had been pressing a little bit and to get one to flare in there gave me a lot of confidence," he told the *Post*. "And obviously to take a lead early on in game seven, that was big for us."

But St. Louis immediately responded in the top half of the second against Mets southpaw Oliver Perez, as Ronnie Belliard's squeeze bunt scored Jim Edmonds from third, tying the game at one.

David Wright

Michael Garry

The Mets' two hits in the first turned out to be all they would collect off Suppan across seven innings, though he did walk four. In the eighth, Cardinals reliever Randy Flores pitched a 1-2-3 inning with two strikeouts.

As for Wright, after his first-inning hit, he would only ground out in the fourth, reach on an error in the sixth, and strike out in the eighth.

Meanwhile, Perez surrendered just the second-inning run through six, though he was saved by a monumental catch by left fielder Endy Chavez in the top of the sixth.

With Edmonds on first, Scott Rolen slammed a fly ball to left that had all the earmarks of a home run. But Chavez, leaping from the warning track as if from a trampoline, reached high over the left field wall to snare the ball at the tip of his glove, the force of the ball pulling the webbing back. Upon landing back on terra firma—in front of a sign saying "The Strength To Be There"—he unleashed a throw to shortstop Jose Reyes, who fired to Carlos Delgado at first to double up Edmonds, who had already rounded second, never dreaming that Chavez would make such a catch. The inning was over.

Its rafters shaking, Shea Stadium bathed Chavez in a standing ovation. Every Met on the field waited near first base to congratulate him.

"When he first hit it, I remember that Endy had a great read on it," said Wright to the *Post*. And right after the catch, "I just thought double play."

Chavez's catch is etched into Mets fans' consciousness, but it also has a visual representation at Citi Field, above the entrance to the left field stands, in the form of a navy-blue metal silhouette of a fielder making an over-the-fence, tip-of-the-webbing catch. Ron Swoboda's headlong diving grab in the 1969 World Series is similarly depicted at the right field entrance.

Chavez had a chance to cement his immortal status in Mets lore in the bottom of the sixth when he came up with the bases loaded, but he hit Suppan's first pitch directly into the glove of center fielder Edmonds.

The Cards were held in check as well, as Perez's replacement in the seventh, Chad Bradford, set down the Redbirds in order, and reliever Aaron Heilman followed with a scoreless eighth.

But there was still the ninth.

With the score still tied at one, manager Willie Randolph elected to stay with Heilman rather than use his closer, Billy Wagner. Heilman struck out his first batter, Edmonds. But Rolen singled and then notorious Mets killer Yadier Molina drilled a backbreaking two-run homer to left. The Cards led 3-1 going into the bottom of the ninth. "It just seemed like an eternity for [Molina] to round the bases," Wright told the *Post*.

Adam Wainwright, a twenty-four-year-old, 6-foot-7 right-handed rookie reliever (he would later become a dominant starter), came in to pitch the ninth for the Cards, wielding a devastating curveball. He had made 61 appearances in 2006, with a 3.12 ERA.

The Mets' first two batters Jose, Valentin and Chavez, both singled, putting the Mets in a promising position. Randolph sent up slugging outfielder Cliff Floyd, who had been nursing an injured Achilles tendon, to pinch-hit for Heilman, but Wainwright struck him out looking. After Reyes lined out to center field Paul, Lo Duca worked out a walk, loading the bases. Up came switch-hitter Beltran, who had homered three times in the series and had a reputation for postseason heroics based on his gargantuan performance for the Astros in 2004.

Like mighty Casey in Ernest Thayer's classic poem, Beltran quickly fell behind, no balls, two strikes—the first on an out-of-the-blue changeup that flummoxed him. Wainwright then uncorked his most knee-bending curveball, the force of his follow-through thrusting his body toward first base. Crossing the plate, the pitch dropped abruptly to the outside corner, at Beltran's knees. He froze. Strike three. The Cardinals won the pennant.

There was no joy in Sheaville, as the formerly boisterous crowd fell into morbid silence. The Cards celebrated and went on to beat the Tigers in the World Series.

Looking back at the 2006 NLCS, Wright rued the lost opportunity. "Multiply whatever we accomplished that year by a million more and that's the kind of regard we would have been held to in our city's National League history," Wright told the *St. Louis Post-Dispatch* in 2011. "That's what it would have meant to us."

But he recognized the futility of dwelling on the past, and made sure to deflect blame from Beltran. "You can't look at one at-bat and say that's the one that signifies everything that happened," he said. "There is so much more that could have happened that we could have done better."

In the *New York Post*, he disputed the notion that Beltran should have swung at Wainwright's last pitch. "It might look like you can do that," he said. "You can't. If you know the guy's throwing 94-95 with a curveball that just buckles you, you have to look one or the other. You can't go up there and hit both."

Though it took Wright a while to get over the sting of losing, he could still appreciate what had transpired. "I just remember thinking that's the coolest thing I've ever experienced—the playoff baseball in New York and a game seven in the NLCS."

The Aftermath

Wright's brilliant career continued in 2007. He fashioned a 26-game hitting streak (started the prior season), and finished the season with an OPS of .963, the highest of his career. He also became the third Met to join the 30-30 Club, along with Darryl Strawberry and Wright's mentor, Howard Johnson.

"Hojo was incredibly helpful in my whole development," Wright said on the Mets All-Time Team broadcast. "He coached me through the minor leagues. I had him for a few years in the big leagues. He was one of those original 30-30 guys, and coming up, that's what I wanted to be. I wanted to play good defense, I wanted to hit for power, hit for average, steal bases, and he kind of instilled at a young age that I could be that type of player. Not to mention just the winning aspect of it. He knew what it was like to win. He taught me how to win at a young age. I'll forever be grateful for that."

But the Mets didn't win enough in 2007. They were in first place, up by seven games, on September 12, and proceeded to have two five-game losing streaks over the next two weeks. Still with a chance to make the playoffs on the last day of the season, they lost 8-1 to the Florida Marlins, at Shea Stadium, completing one of the worst collapses in baseball history.

Wright had another tremendous season in 2008, reaching career highs in home runs (33) and RBI (124, which tied Mike Piazza for the most ever by a Met). But the Mets once again flubbed an opportunity to make the postseason, playing shabbily down the stretch (not quite as badly as they did in '07) and once again being eliminated on the last day of the season by the Marlins in an almost inconceivable case of déjà vu. Wright led off the ninth inning of the final game—the last ever at Shea—with a popup to second as the Mets fell 4-2.

For all the anguish and disappointment of 2006 through 2008, Mets fans would look back upon that period as the "good old days," when the Mets were at least in contention. Beginning with the inaugural 2009 season at Citi Field—adjacent to where Shea Stadium was located—the team has labored through six straight losing (under a .500 winning percentage) seasons, winning between 70 and 79 games.

Wright did not foresee in 2006 that the team would decline as it did. "There is no question that I thought [2006] was going to be the first of many playoff experiences and exciting Game 7s," he told the *St. Louis Post-Dispatch*. "That just hasn't been the case for a number of reasons."

One might be that Wright had a hard time adjusting to the cavernous dimensions at Citi Field, socking only 10 homers in 144 games in 2009. The new ballpark was also the scene of Wright's worst moment as a player, when he was struck on the head by a 93-mile-per-hour fastball thrown by the Giants' Matt Cain on August 15, 2009, and suffered a concussion.

But Wright, if not the team, rebounded in 2010 with another vintage year, slugging 29 homers and 103 RBI, though his average slipped a bit to .283. After a stress fracture in his lower back limited him to 102 games and a .254 average in 2011, he returned to form in 2012 and 2013, hitting over .300 both years.

In 2014, however, Wright's production slipped alarmingly as he hit only eight homers and knocked in 63 runs in 134 games while batting just .269;

his on-base percentage (.324) and slugging percentage (.374) were both career lows. A bruised rotator cuff in his left shoulder—caused by a headfirst slide into second on June 12 at Citi Field—may explain the falloff. It didn't help that he was drilled by a pitch near his sore left shoulder on August 16 and had to sit out a game. The Mets finally shut Wright down for the season on September 9 after an MRI revealed inflammation in the shoulder. There remained the possibility of surgery in the off-season.

Mets fans in 2014 were left hoping, perhaps praying, that Wright—whose contract runs through 2020—would regain the hitting prowess that had him on a sure path to the Hall of Fame, especially on a team that has often struggled offensively. While the Mets have been able to stockpile a number of talented young pitchers—notably Matt Harvey, Zack Wheeler, Jacob deGrom, and Noah Syndergaard—they need Wright's hitting as well as his veteran leadership to contend in 2015 and beyond.

Wright understands the position he is in. "I'll be the first one to tell you that when we're winning and we're playing well, I love the perks, I enjoy everything New York has to offer," he said on the All-Time Team show. "And vice versa, you have to understand—and I learned this as a young player—that when things aren't going so well, when you're struggling or the team's struggling, you have to be held accountable."

Looking over his team, which also includes emerging young players like Lucas Duda, Juan Lagares, and Travis d'Arnaud, a dependable hitter in Daniel Murphy, a veteran home-run threat in Curtis Granderson, and a solidifying bullpen, Wright told the *Newark Star-Ledger* near the end of the 2014 season that "we're getting close to that [point] where we are a piece or two away." The Mets acquired one of those pieces in November 2014 when they signed outfielder Michael Cuddyer—a former National League batting champion and a close friend of Wright's from Virginia—to a two-year contract.

Perhaps before it finally ends for Wright, he will be able to see if postseason success makes Citi Field shake as hard as Shea.

Chapter 21

DANIEL MURPHY

Second Base, First Base, Outfield, 2008-present
Throws/Bats: Right/Left

The Game: September 27, 2008 vs. Florida Marlins,
at Shea Stadium

METS STATS (THROUGH 2014)	
GAMES:	773
AT-BATS:	2,855
HITS:	827
HOME RUNS:	48
AVERAGE:	.290
ON-BASE %:	.333
SLUGGING %:	.419
RUNS:	366
RBI:	329
STOLEN BASES:	55
FIELDING %:	.980
WAR:	10.9

The Run-up

I met Daniel Murphy at the Mets Spring Training facility in Port St. Lucie, Florida, on a sunny day in late Mets' spring training just after everyday players had reported. He was informally clad in a grey T-Shirt with "Mets Baseball" on the front, blue shorts with an orange stripe, and a baseball cap emblazoned with "Mr. Met" on the front.

Murphy, selected by the Mets in the 13th round of the 2006 draft, was patiently signing autographs for a group of fans lined up behind a chain link fence, near the practice fields. He was also posing for pictures with fans, each time putting his arm around someone's shoulder.

"Have a good one, brother," he told one group. "Thanks, you guys, for staying out here. I know I kept you guys out here forever."

He was unfailingly solicitous of the children in the group, always looking for a "high-five." In six weeks, he would become a father for the first time, and miss the first two games of the regular season in order to be with his wife and newborn son, Noah—which raised some eyebrows in New York sports talk radio circles.

Murphy was one of the longer-tenured Mets on the 2014 squad, having made his big league debut in 2008. Pitchers Jon Niese and Bobby Parnell came up that year as well. All, of course, are outranked by team captain David Wright, a Met since 2004.

Murphy cut his teeth as a third baseman, but needed to play somewhere else given Wright's lock on that position. The Mets started him in left field in 2008, moved him to first base the following year, and finally decided in 2010 that he would play second base. He took slowly and at times painfully to that position, but has become a fixture there since 2012.

Far more than for his defense, it is as a hitter who sprays hits across the vast dimensions of Citi Field where Murphy has found his identity. His hitting excellence earned him his first All-Star Game selection in 2014.

After he finished with this group of fans, I asked Murphy if he could talk to me about the game of his life up to this point as a Met. I had some ideas about which game it might be.

"Was it your first game as a Mets where you singled in your first at-bat against Oswalt in '08? Was it your walk-off single against the Nats in 2012? Your two-homer game against the Cubs in '12 after that long homer drought?"

"No," he said. "It was when Johan [Santana] threw like a one-hitter [actually a three-hitter] against the Marlins with two games left in the year in '08."

At first I thought he must have meant Santana's no-hitter in June 2012, the first in Mets history after more than a half-century and 8,019 games. But then it hit me. Of course! That Marlins game was as close as Murphy has come to the postseason with the Mets. By winning that game, they kept their playoff hopes alive for at least one more day.

I asked him if he did anything special in that game, not knowing that he was hitless in three trips. He gave me a deeply aggrieved, incredulous look. "Not much, but it's not about how I did," he shot back. "It's about the team."

But then he paused to consider. "If I had to say another one a little more personal, it would be ..." But he stopped there.

Certainly Murphy has had far more productive games as a Met. But, like Wright, what he wants most of all is to play in the postseason with a chance to win it all. Since he joined the Mets on August 2, 2008, no game in which the team was victorious had more playoff relevance than Santana's gem. The victory also meant that this group of Mets, largely a carryover from '07 when the team blew a sizable first-place lead in September, might redeem themselves, burying the shame and heartbreak of the previous year.

Sadly, the next day—it was both the final game of the season and the last ever played at Shea Stadium—all of that promise was extinguished as the Mets fell to the Marlins, 4-2. After the game, despite the gloom visited upon the remaining fans, the Mets held a ceremony featuring many of their former greats, including Tom Seaver and Mike Piazza, who officially "closed" the stadium. Murphy was the only current Met who came out for the ceremony. He "walked behind home plate, scooped up some dirt and returned to the dugout to scattered applause," reported the *New York Times*.

The Mets' fall in '07, when they were seven games up, in first place, with 17 left to play, was more precipitous than that of '08, when they squandered half as many games with 17 to go. (Indeed, '07's collapse ranks with the worst in baseball history.) But '08's final two games were an eerie reprise of '07's, confounding Mets fans who, in their most jaded moments, would never have foreseen the same sequence happening in two consecutive seasons.

With two games left on the schedule in 2007, the Mets faced the Marlins at Shea, still with a chance to take the National League East from the Phillies. They needed a brilliant effort and they got one from rookie pitcher John Maine, who had a no-hitter going until two outs in the eighth, when he yielded an infield hit to pinch-hitter Paul Hoover. The Mets provided him an ample cushion, scoring 13 runs on 19 hits. If only they could have saved some of those runs for the next day.

The Mets needed another victory on Sunday, September 30, the last day of the season, to keep pace with the Phillies. They didn't get one. In perhaps the worst performance of his Hall of Fame career, Tom Glavine gave up seven runs in the first inning while recording only one out. The Mets responded with one run in the bottom of the first, but nothing more, as Florida won 8-1. After the game, Glavine said he was disappointed but not devastated, a distinction that was lost on most Mets fans.

One year later, like Maine before him, Santana threw a masterpiece on the penultimate day of the season, giving the Mets hope that they could catch the Milwaukee Brewers in the Wild Card race (the division had already been lost again to the Phillies.) But again, on the last day, while the Mets were far more competitive than the previous year, the result was the same—a loss, 4-2, to the same team, the Marlins. The Brewers won their game, eliminating the Mets.

But until Santana's no-hitter in 2012, his three-hit shutout on that second-to-last day was his greatest Mets performance, one that lives on for many Mets fans as well as for Murphy.

The Game

Facing season-ending elimination—perhaps a little like facing execution—concentrates the mind. And so it was on September 27, 2008, for Santana, who posted a note next to the Mets' lineup card that read, "It's time to be a MAN."

It was time for the Mets to put aside their regrets and frustrations and focus on the task at hand. It was also time for them to overlook minor injuries or lingering fatigue, especially in Santana's case, since, as Murphy pointed out to me, "he threw on three days' rest" for just the second time in his career. In his previous game, he had thrown a career-high 125 pitches, but he still insisted on making this start. It turned out that Santana's grit was even greater than just starting on short rest. After the game, doctors found that he had a torn meniscus in his knee, and he had surgery on it a few days later.

In any event, on this next-to-last-day of the season, the two-time Cy Young winner was indomitable, striking out nine (eight on the changeup) and scattering three hits while walking three on 117 pitches. The result was a 2-0 shutout, the sixth of his career.

Murphy, called up just the previous month, played left field that day and made one putout, in the seventh. He was relieved in the ninth by Endy Chavez, famous for his homer-robbing catch in the 2006 playoffs.

Santana faced only two threats. In the fifth, after a single by Cody Ross, he walked Jeremy Hermida and intentionally walked heavy-hitting shortstop Hanley Ramirez, but then got John Baker to line out to right field. And in the ninth, after yielding a one-out double to Josh Willingham, he fanned Dan Uggla and induced Ross into lining a ball to deep left field that Chavez caught on the warning track to end the game.

Murphy, while going 0-3, contributed to the Mets' second run in the fifth by getting hit by a 1-2 pitch thrown by Marlins starter Ricky Nolasco. He scampered home after the next batter, Ramon Martinez, drilled a double to deep right-center field. The Mets' other run came on a sacrifice fly by Carlos Delgado that scored Jose Reyes.

Daniel Murphy

Michael Garry

"Wow, wow, wow, wow," Mets manager Jerry Manuel told the *New York Times* after the game. "I think if I had to describe that one, I'd say that was gangsta. That's gangsta. That's serious gangsta right there."

The Aftermath

Since 2008, the Mets have never come as close to the postseason as they did that year. Their first six years at Citi Field have all resulted in losing seasons.

However, the Mets have been developing a core of talented young players who, along with veterans like Murphy and Wright, offer the hope of better days ahead. Unlike Wright, though, Murphy's long-term future remains in doubt; he became eligible for arbitration after the 2014 season and will become a free agent after the 2015 season, making him a frequent subject of trade speculation. The Mets have an up-and-coming second baseman, Dilson Herrera, waiting in the wings.

Murphy's bat would be hard to replace. Over the past few years, he has settled in as one of the better-hitting second basemen in the National League. Usually batting second in front of Wright, he has become what baseball observers like to call "a professional hitter."

From 2011 through 2014, he hit .320, .291, .286, and .289. He finished second in the National League in hits with 188 in 2013 while supplying some power as well with 13 home runs and 73 RBI. Moreover, he has hit over .300 with runners in scoring position.

His walk totals have been on the low side, but he boosted his on-base percentage to .332 in 2014, and it's an area he is trying to improve.

Defensively, Murphy is still a work in progress at second base, though the progress has been substantial since he began playing the position in 2010. That year, during a June game with the Mets' AAA affiliate in Buffalo, New York, he suffered a season-ending MCL (medial collateral ligament) tear while trying to turn a double play. In August 2011, his season was again ended prematurely by an MCL injury after the Braves' Jose Constanza slid into him feet-first while stealing second base.

But Murphy has played mostly full-time at second base since 2012, albeit while committing 15 errors in 2012 and 16 in 2013, the second-most in the league both years. In 2014 he led the league with 15 errors at second base. On the other hand, in 2013 he was third in second-base assists (391) and in double plays turned at second (86), as well as second in putouts at second (263). In 2014, he finished second in and double plays turned.

"I'm getting more comfortable at second base," Murphy told me at spring training. "Each game you play, there are certain intricacies that you haven't seen before." He credits infield coach Tim Teufel and former Mets utility infielder Justin Turner with helping him learn the position. "During the year last year, Turner helped me a lot," he said. "He was good to talk to about second base."

Though he has been criticized for sometimes being careless on the base paths, Murphy has proved to be an adept base stealer, swiping 23 bases while being caught just three times in 2013, for a league-leading 88.5% success rate. He finished the season with 22 consecutive steals, the second longest such streak in team history. In 2014, he added 13 steals in 18 attempts. "I'm sneaky, elusive," he said.

Murphy drew attention to himself in an unexpected way in 2014 when he decided to take a three-day paternity leave—his right according to the MLB collective bargaining agreement—at the end of spring training to be with his wife for the birth of their son. By missing the first two games of the regular season, he elicited some critical comments from a few radio talk-show hosts, notably WFAN's Mike Francesca, though Murphy had the full support of Mets management.

"You see the birth and you get back," said Francesa. "What do you do in the first couple days? Maybe you take care of the other kids. Well, you gotta have someone to do that if you're a Major League Baseball player."

But many people, including Mets manager Terry Collins, rallied to Murphy's side. As for Murphy himself, he held firm to the importance of being with his newborn son and wife, who had experienced a C-section, during and after the birth. "My wife and I discussed it and we felt the best thing for our family was for me to try to stay for an extra day," he said in a locker room interview on SNY, the Mets' cable network. "She was completely finished, she was done. Having me there helped a lot."

On June 9 (an off day for the Mets), Murphy spoke about being a new father at the White House as part of a Working Families Summit. "Long after they tell me that I'm not good enough to play professional baseball anymore, I'll be a father," Murphy said. "And I'll be a husband. So that was a reason, on the front end, that I wanted to be there for my wife and for my son."

Chapter 22

JON NIESE

Pitcher, 2008-present
Throws/Bats: Left

The Game: June 10, 2010 vs. San Diego Padres, at Citi Field

METS STATS (THROUGH 2014)	
GAMES:	149
COMPLETE GAMES:	3
SHUTOUTS:	2
INNINGS PITCHED:	891.2
WINS:	52
LOSSES:	51
ERA:	3.87
WALKS:	265
STRIKEOUTS:	713
WHIP:	1.354
WAR:	6.2

The Run-up

Although the Mets have had only one no-hitter in their history, one-hitters have been fairly plentiful.

Through the 2014 season, Mets pitchers, either individually or collectively, have thrown 38 one-hitters. Of those, 29 were by a single pitcher.

But a closer look at those 29 one-hitters reveals that two of them were particularly special. In those cases, the solitary hit allowed was the only thing separating the pitcher from a perfect game. The pitcher in those games faced 28 batters, just one over the minimum number who would come to the plate in a nine-inning game. By comparison, in the Mets' solitary no-hitter, Johan Santana faced 32 batters because he allowed a base on balls to five of them.

The first pitcher to hurl a near-perfect one-hitter was the Mets' only Hall of Famer, Tom Seaver, in the "Jimmy Qualls game," on July 9, 1969, at Shea Stadium. Demonstrating the competitive seriousness of the heretofore laughable Mets, Seaver ran a perfect game against the Cubs until one out in the top of the ninth when Qualls, an otherwise undistinguished outfielder and pinch-hitting specialist, struck a clean single to left-center field. Seaver retired the next two Cubs, thereby facing a total of 28 batters in the Mets 4-0 win.

The next—and, as of the start of the 2015 season, only—time a Mets pitcher missed perfection by one hit was on June 10, 2010, when southpaw Jon Niese did it against the San Diego Padres.

I tracked down Niese at spring training in 2014 after he finished participating in a bunting drill conducted by former Met Wally Backman, manager of the Las Vegas 51s, the Mets' AAA team. Niese, Zack Wheeler, Jacob deGrom, Rafael Montero, and other Mets pitchers were taking turns laying down bunts on balls thrown by a pitching machine controlled by Backman.

After explaining that I was talking to Mets players about the game of their life, I suggested that his might be that one-hitter against the Padres.

He agreed.

Niese's association with the Mets began on the day of his birth, October 27, 1986, the same day the franchise clinched the second of its two

World Championships. Fittingly, the Mets selected him in the seventh round of the 2005 draft.

He made his major league debut on September 2, 2008, against the Brewers in Milwaukee, becoming the first pitcher in Mets history to give up a homer to the first batter he faced (Rickie Weeks). But in his next start, his first at Shea Stadium, he earned his first win, pitching eight shutout innings in a 5-0 whitewashing of the Braves that kept the Mets in the playoff hunt. "That was the one-year anniversary of my buddy passing away," he said. "A bunch of fans were chanting my name. It was pretty surreal."

Both in the minors and with the Mets, Niese has been a solid left-handed starter, albeit somewhat prone to injury. His minor league record, mostly encompassing 2005 to 2009, was 40-32 with a 3.72 ERA. Through the 2014 season, his major league stats since arriving in 2008 are not too different: 52-52, with a 3.87 ERA.

But his ERA, after starting in the 4.00s, dropped to the 3.00s between 2012 and 2014, including a career-best 3.40 in 2012 (to go with a career-best 13 wins that he matched in 2014). In 2012, he set a franchise record by making 17 straight starts where he pitched six or more innings and walked two or fewer batters.

In 2013, he finished with the fourth highest WHIP (walks and hits per inning pitched) in the National League. That year he also threw his second complete-game shutout, a three-hitter against the Phillies on August 27. He became the second Mets pitcher to pitch a shutout and drive in three runs, a feat previously accomplished by Pete Falcone in 1981, also against the Phillies.

Niese is more likely to help with his bat than most pitchers. In 2012, he led all Mets hurlers with 12 hits and a .218 batting average. He's also skilled at preventing runners from stealing bases; he finished 2013 having allowed the eighth-fewest stolen bases (18) in the majors since 2008.

But Niese has been continually hampered by injuries of varying types and degrees. He was placed on the 60-day disabled list in 2009 with a torn right hamstring tendon, which required season-ending surgery. Since then, he's been on the 15-day DL in 2010 (hamstring strain), 2011 (intercostal

Jon Niese

AP Photo/Tony Dejak

strain of the right side), 2013 (partial tear of the left rotator cuff), and 2014 (left shoulder strain).

The Game

Despite a hamstring strain in May that put him on the 15-day DL, Niese made 30 starts in 2010, winning nine, in what was effectively his rookie year. He led all National League rookies in strikeouts, with 148.

His finest moment came on June 10 in the second game of a day-night doubleheader at Citi Field against the Padres. In the opener, San Diego topped the Mets 4-2 as Johan Santana allowed four runs over 6 ⅔ innings.

But Niese quieted the Padres in the nightcap, yielding nothing except one hit, a third-inning leadoff double down the right field line by center fielder Chris Denorfia on a 3-2 count. That early in the game, catcher Rod Barajas didn't want to walk the leadoff batter, and called for a fastball over the plate. If it had been later in the game and Niese had been working on a no-hitter, he might have called for a cut fastball, he told the *New York Times*.

"He had no-hit stuff, and if he had gotten ahead of Denorfia early on—something special did happen, but something a little more special could have happened," said Barajas.

After Denorfia's hit, Niese struck out the next two hitters and got Jerry Hairston to fly out to deep right field, ending the threat. He proceeded to retire the next 18 hitters in order, for a total of 21 straight to close out the game—a franchise record. He struck out six, walked none, and induced 14 groundball outs on a total of 108 pitches as he guided the Mets to a 3-0 victory. It was the first shutout and the first complete game of his career.

"I hit my spots," Niese told me. "It was one of those things where you're in the zone so much. You're focusing on the task at hand."

After the game, "I was just happy I had a shutout," he said. He knew he had given up only one hit but didn't realize he had finished just one over the minimum until after the game when "a media guy told me."

The Mets scored early for Niese that day against Padres starter Jon Garland. In the second, left fielder Chris Carter led off with a double to deep right-center. A single by Barajas advanced Carter to third, from which he dashed home on a single by Jeff Francoeur.

With Francoeur on first and Barajas on second—two slow runners—second baseman Ruben Tejada came up, and on an 0-2 count hit into the tenth triple play in the Mets' 48-year history. It was a grounder to third baseman Chase Headley, who stepped on third to force out Barajas and threw to second baseman Lance Zawadski to force out Francoeur; Zawadski's throw to first beat Tejada for the third out. As of the start of the 2015 season, the Mets, who have executed 11 triple plays of their own, had not hit into another.

In the bottom of the third, the Mets padded their lead. Niese himself led off with a walk. He advanced all the way to third after Padres catcher Yorvit Torrealba picked up a ball bunted by Jose Reyes and threw wildly to first; Reyes wound up on second. Niese came home on a groundout by David Wright and Reyes followed when Ike Davis singled to right. That made the score 3-0, where it remained until the end.

The best the Mets could do after the third was leave the bases loaded in the sixth. But they didn't have to do anything else, given Niese's dominance. After he got the final out, a pop-up in foul territory that Barajas caught, the crowd of 28,072 applauded resoundingly. "I couldn't keep a smile from my face," Niese told the *Times* after the game. "It's great to have the fans behind you like that. It's just a great feeling."

One advantage Niese had that day was that he used a cut fastball for the first time. "They didn't know I had it," he told me.

The Aftermath

Since then the cut fastball, traveling between 87 and 89 miles per hour, has become one of the most effective pitches in Niese's repertoire, which includes a four-seam and two-seam fastball, a curveball, and a changeup. "The cutter has come a long way," Niese said in 2014 on SNY. "The cutter is one of those pitches where, if I feel I'm off, it can get me back on track. I've just been real confident with the cutter."

Niese signed a $25.5 million, five-year contract extension in April 2012; it includes two club options that could keep him on the Mets through 2018. But his success over that span will hinge on his health.

Niese's most recent injuries have centered on his left shoulder. When he went on the DL with a partly torn rotator cuff in June 2013, there was speculation over whether he would need surgery. But after resting his arm, he returned and pitched effectively.

In our 2014 spring training chat, he told me he felt good, adding, "I just want to stay healthy and get innings this year. I'm working out all the kinks and soreness." But a few days later he flew to New York to have an MRI test on his shoulder, which was negative.

He got off to a strong start in 2014, but in July was struck in the back by a line drive and placed on the disabled list with the left shoulder strain. He struggled upon his return, his velocity diminishing, but then put together a string of good outings in August. He finished 2014 with a 9-11 record and a 3.40 ERA.

Mets observers were left wondering whether Niese should have rotator cuff surgery to improve his future prospects with the team. Some speculated that he would be on the trading block after the 2014 season.

Niese seems to appreciate what he's accomplished and the opportunities ahead. "I never take it for granted," he said in 2012 on an SNY program called "Riding Shotgun with Jon Niese," filmed in his Dodge truck as he drove to Citi Field. "When I get on this highway, I look at [Citi Field] all the time. It's crazy. I look at it and it's just like 'wow, I play in a big league stadium.' It's crazy to think about. It does hit me every day."

Chapter 23

DILLON GEE

Pitcher, 2010-present
Throws/Bats: Right

The Game: September 7, 2010 vs. Washington Nationals,
at Nationals Park

METS STATS (THROUGH 2014)	
GAMES:	106
COMPLETE GAMES:	3
SHUTOUTS:	0
INNINGS PITCHED:	639.2
WINS:	40
LOSSES:	32
ERA:	3.91
WALKS:	205
STRIKEOUTS:	464
WHIP:	1.288
WAR:	5.4

The Run-up

When Tom Seaver, the greatest pitcher in Mets history, made his debut on April 13, 1967, against the Pirates at Shea Stadium, he pitched fairly well: 5 ⅓ innings, six hits, two earned runs, four walks, and eight strikeouts. He received a no-decision as the Mets won, 3-2.

Another giant of Mets pitching, Dwight Gooden, had a similar line in his inaugural appearance in the major leagues against the Astros in Houston on April 8, 1984: 6 ⅓ innings, five hits, one earned run, one walk, and six strikeouts. Gooden got the win in the Mets' 3-2 victory.

Dillon Gee outdid them both when he made his first start for the Mets on September 7, 2010, against the Nationals in Washington, D.C. The right-hander took a no-hitter into the sixth and all told allowed two hits over seven innings while striking out four. He earned his first win as the Mets prevailed, 4-1.

Gee did not hesitate in selecting his extraordinary debut as the game of his life with New York when I met him at the team's spring training headquarters in 2014. He had just finished signing autographs for hordes of fans and was on his way to the locker room.

The first game, he told me, fulfilled "my dream as a kid" to play baseball—which he had been doing "all of my life"—at the highest professional level. Like Gooden and Seaver before him, he was jittery at the beginning, with a dozen or so family and friends in the ballpark. But once he threw his first pitch to the Nationals' Nyjer Morgan, he "settled down and got down to business."

Gee pitched for the University of Texas Mavericks in 2005 and 2006, helping the team reach the 2006 NCAA tournament. The Mets selected him the following year in the 21st round of the amateur draft. After a strong start in the minors, he suffered a torn labrum in his right shoulder in May 2009 while playing for the Mets' AAA Buffalo Bisons. The Bisons shut down Gee for the remainder of the season—a harbinger of the kind of injury issues he would have with the Mets.

Dillon Gee

Michael Garry

Gee bounced back in 2010, posting a 13-8 record for Buffalo while leading AAA with 165 strikeouts in 161 ⅓ innings, though his ERA was on the high side—4.96. He was still an unheralded prospect when the Mets decided to call him up in September to pitch in place of an injured Johan Santana.

The Game

In his debut game against the Nats, Gee faced Yunesky Maya, who was also starting his first game in the majors, the first such rookie faceoff in Mets history. But only 13,835 showed up to see the fourth-place Mets and fifth-place Nats.

The Mets' first baseman Ike Davis immediately took some pressure off Gee by belting a three-run homer off Maya in the top of the first inning. In the next inning, Gee, in his first at-bat, hit a run-scoring single, becoming the first Mets pitcher to record an RBI in his major league debut. He had been 0-22 at the plate in the minors that year. "Everybody made fun of me, so it was really nice to get one here," he told the Associated Press.

Those four runs were all Gee would get—or need. He breezed through the Nats' lineup, mixing his slider (his curve wasn't working) and a well-placed fastball, and didn't allow his first base runner until a walk in the third. In the fourth, he employed 12 pitches to strike out the side—Ian Desmond, Ryan Zimmerman, and Adam Dunn, the heart of the Washington lineup, all swinging at strike three for his first big league Ks. He maintained his no-hitter in the fifth, allowing just a walk to Danny Espinosa.

Washington finally broke through in the sixth as the leadoff hitter Willie Harris—a longtime Mets nemesis—drilled a homer over the wall in right-center. Unfazed, Gee was determined to "put it behind me," he said, and got through the rest of the inning with only a walk to Desmond, Gee's third and last free pass.

Gee yielded his second and final hit, a single to pinch-hitter Kevin Mench, in the seventh. Though Gee had thrown only 86 pitches, manager

Jerry Manuel wanted him to leave the game on a high note. Mets relievers Pedro Feliciano and Bobby Parnell handled the Nats in the eighth and Hisanori Takahasi, after putting two runners on base in the ninth, finished off Washington, giving Gee his first W and the Mets a 4-1 victory.

"That went better than I expected," he told media after the game. "I kind of blacked out, I think. I don't even know what happened out there."

Gee described it to me as "being in the zone, doing my best."

Gee collected a plastic grocery bag full of baseballs to give away to his family and friends who attended the game. He also had a few keepsake balls, "my first pitch, my first hit, and my first strikeout," he said.

The Aftermath

After Gee's impressive debut, Manuel gave him four more starts in 2010, which he finished with a 2-2 record and a slender 2.18 ERA. That earned him a starting job in 2011, and he took advantage of the opportunity as few other pitchers in Mets history have.

Beginning on April 17, Gee reeled off seven consecutive victories, becoming the first Mets rookie to win his first seven decisions as a starter. He finished the 2011 season at 13-6 (with a 4.43 ERA), tying Gary Gentry for the fifth-most wins by a Mets rookie. Among first-year pitchers with at least 15 decisions, his .684 winning percentage is the best in team history for a single season.

The following season, after a 6-7 record and a 4.10 ERA in the first half, Gee complained of numbness in his fingers, and a test revealed a blood clot in his pitching shoulder. He had surgery to remove the clot, and didn't pitch again in 2012.

But Gee came back healthy in 2013 and lasted the entire year. After a wobbly start, he had his best overall season, with a 12-11 record, a 3.62 ERA, and 142 strikeouts. Working efficiently, he averaged just 3.55 pitches per batter, the second best in the majors.

His high-water mark came on May 30, when he struck out a career-best 12 in a 3-1 Mets win at Yankee Stadium. This was in the last of four Subway Series games against the Yankees (two at Citi Field, two at the Stadium), and by winning the Mets swept the series for the first time.

"I needed that on so many levels, it's crazy," said Gee to the media after the game. "Obviously, it's fun to go out there and pitch like that."

Gee's 12 strikeouts were the most ever recorded by a Met against the Yankees. Moreover, Gee became only the second opposing pitcher in Yankees history—the other was Boston's Pedro Martinez—to strike out 12, walk none, and allow four hits or fewer. That performance set him on a strong course as he finished the season pitching at least six innings in 17 straight starts.

Gee started out 2014 splendidly, going 3-1 with a 2.73 ERA, when in mid-May the Mets announced he was going on the disabled list with a strained right lat muscle (in his back) and considerable soreness. He spent two months on the disabled list and in his return pitched erratically, finishing the season with a 7-8 record and a 4.00 ERA.

Gee, who made $3.6 million in 2014, is eligible for two more rounds of arbitration in 2015 and 2016. Will he spend those years with the Mets? The Mets have put together a rotation laden with talented young pitchers, such as Matt Harvey (expected to return in 2015 after having Tommy John surgery), Zack Wheeler, and 2014 Rookie of the Year Jacob deGrom, as well as the still-unproven Rafael Montero and Noah Syndergaard. Where Gee and another injury-prone veteran starter, Jon Niese, fit into this group remains one of the intriguing questions for the franchise going into 2015.

Chapter 24

JOHAN SANTANA

Pitcher, 2008-2010, 2012
Throws/Bats: Left

The Game: June 1, 2012 vs. St. Louis Cardinals, at Citi Field

METS STATS	
GAMES:	109
COMPLETE GAMES:	9
SHUTOUTS:	6
INNINGS PITCHED:	717
WINS:	46
LOSSES:	34
ERA:	3.18
WALKS:	203
STRIKEOUTS:	607
WHIP:	1.201
WAR:	15.2

The Run-up

Success has never come easily to the Mets, so when it does arrive, the effect is spectacular.

The team was historically woeful during its first four years, and marginally better the next three. Then, in 1969, the Mets did something that seemed as extraordinary as the moon walk that took place that year—they won a World Championship.

They went through another long, fallow period in the late 1970s and early 1980s before winning a second World Championship—in the most intensely dramatic way imaginable.

So the Mets and their fans have enjoyed these two, relatively rare, moments of euphoria. What they had not experienced, from 1962 until 2012, over 8,019 regular-season games, was one of their pitchers throwing a no-hitter. But when that finally happened, it sure felt good.

Through the 2014 season, there had been 244 no-hitters (including 21 perfect games) pitched in the major leagues since the start of the modern era in 1901. Because it is so unusual, difficult, and historic, a no-hitter is like a World Championship encapsulated within a single game. Every fan dreams of attending a no-hitter in person.

For Mets fans, though, a no-hitter was an achievement more than fifty years in the making. It had become a kind of obsession—when would we get a no-hitter? Would we ever get one? In every game, until the opposition struck its first hit, Mets fans would wonder, could this be *the game*? A website, NoNoHitters.com, tracked the phenomenon.

After all, every other team in the major leagues, save the San Diego Padres, had at least one no-hitter. Even teams that didn't come into existence until the 1990s—the Diamondbacks, the Marlins, the Rays, and the Rockies—all had at least one.

Needless to say, the Mets themselves have been no-hit six times, though not since September 8, 1993, when Darryl Kyle of the Astros did it.

What made not having a no-hitter particularly grating—and a little absurd—was that the Mets' pitching staff has been blessed over the years with outstanding hurlers such as Tom Seaver, Jerry Koosman, Nolan Ryan, Jon Matlack, Dwight Gooden, Ron Darling, Frank Viola, David Cone, Sid Fernandez, Al Leiter, and Pedro Martinez, among others. It was a contradiction wrapped in a conundrum.

Rubbing salt in the wound, seven pitchers—including Seaver, Cone, and Gooden—would execute a no-hitter for another team after leaving the Mets. And in the cruelest twist of fate, the pitcher with the most no-hitters in history, Nolan Ryan, threw all seven of them after the Mets unwisely traded him away.

There were also ten pitchers—Warren Spahn, John Candelaria, Bret Saberhagen, and Al Leiter, among them—who had no-hitters before coming to the Mets. Hideo Nomo managed to hurl a no-no both before and after his stint with the team.

It's not as if the Mets had not come close. Through the 2014 season, the team's pitchers, either individually or collectively, had thrown 38 one-hitters. Tom Seaver took a no-hitter into the ninth inning three times but couldn't seal the deal. Four times, Mets pitchers entered the eighth inning with a no-hitter, but settled for a one-hitter, most recently John Maine in 2007.

The only no-hitter-less streak worse than the Mets' fifty-plus years of futility was set by the Philadelphia Phillies. They went without a no-hitter for more than 58 years and 8,945 games, from May 3, 1906, until June 21, 1964, when Jim Bunning threw a perfect game against, of course, the Mets. But at least Phillies fans had that 1906 no-hitter (and some before it) to sustain them, not to mention the seven that have taken place since Bunning's masterpiece.

A no-hitter just didn't seem in the cards for the Mets. And yet we kept hoping. Well, most of us. "I've always said this, that I don't think it will ever happen," said Mets TV play-by-play announcer Gary Cohen, in an on-air discussion on WFAN with his radio counterpart and fellow Mets-fan-for-life, Howie Rose, in June 2012. "Part of that is a defense mechanism—because you don't want to be disappointed—but part of that I really believed."

And then along came Johan Santana, the Venezuelan southpaw whom the Mets acquired from the Minnesota Twins in a blockbuster trade in 2007 and signed to a six-year, $137.5 million contract.

He had never thrown a no-hitter before coming to the Mets—not at any level of competition, not even "in video games," he said. Yet he was a pitcher of surpassing talent, the owner of a devastating circle changeup, and the winner of two Cy Young Awards with the Twins. In 2006, he topped the majors in wins, ERA, and strikeouts, the pitching equivalent of the Triple Crown. In his first season with the Mets in 2008, he led the league with a 2.53 ERA, finished third in the Cy Young voting, and set a Mets record for strikeouts by a left-hander with 206.

On the other hand, he was not a frequent finisher of games (few pitchers are these days), with just 13 complete games in 272 starts, including eight shutouts, prior to 2012.

But he was certainly capable of throwing a no-hitter.

Most problematic for Santana was his health. After joining the Mets, he suffered a series of injuries of increasing severity. In 2008, after pitching a masterful three-hit shutout on three days' rest against the Marlins that temporarily saved the Mets' season, he was found to have a torn meniscus in his left knee. He underwent surgery a few days later. In August of the next year, he underwent season-ending surgery to remove bone chips in his left elbow. But his worst setback occurred in September 2010, when he had Tommy John surgery to repair a torn anterior capsule in his left shoulder, and missed the entire 2011 season. Unlike surgery to repair a torn ligament, Santana's surgery was uncommon and did not promise a high likelihood of recovery.

But he got off to a good start in 2012. On May 26, he pitched a complete-game shutout against the Padres, striking out seven and improving his record to 2-2 with a 2.75 ERA over ten starts.

Still, no one, least of all Santana, expected a man not far removed from major elbow surgery to pitch the first no-hitter in Mets history on June 1 at Citi Field, against the Cardinals. Yet it happened. With Mets fans praying, their anxiety at a fever pitch, Santana struck out David Freese swinging with a nasty 3-2 changeup for the final out in the ninth. The Mets won, 8-0, and Santana did not give up a solitary hit. Johan became "No-Han" in headlines everywhere.

It was only the eighth no-hitter in baseball history against a defending World Championship team. It is, to date, the singular high point for the Mets at Citi Field.

"Coming into this game, I had no clue, I had no sense that I would throw a no-hitter," said Santana after the game at a press conference. "Tonight was a night I wasn't even thinking about it. It just happened. I knew that we had a good chance to win this ballgame; that's the approach that I had. I never had in my mind that I would throw a no-hitter. Never."

If he was surprised, the shock among fans and observers was palpable, the euphoria uncharted.

In their radio conversation after the game, Rose asked Cohen if, the first split second after Freese swung, he was in a state of utter disbelief (as Rose was).

"Yes," replied Cohen. "At the point when that last pitch came to Freese, I was still expecting to see a hit."

Even Mets catcher Josh Thole, in his first game back from the disabled list, "turned around to check with the umpire before he went out to hug Santana," Cohen observed. "Because even he was making sure it was real. And it was. And it was almost impossible to believe."

What made the no-hitter especially remarkable, apart from the fact that it happened, was that Santana, in his return from Tommy John surgery, was under a strict pitch-count limit of up to 115 pitches. But by the time he approached that number in the seventh inning, the no-hitter was in sight; neither Santana nor manager Terry Collins wanted to interfere with the possibility of making history that night, though Collins agonized over whether Santana would suffer any ill effects from the effort he was making. By the end of the contest, his pitch count totaled 134, nine more than he had ever thrown in a game.

The Game

The threat of a downpour hung over Citi Field, along with occasional rain drops and gusts of wind, throughout Friday evening, June 1, 2012. But the skies would not open up—under an injunction from the baseball gods—until after the completion of the game.

Over the first three innings, neither Santana nor his mound counterpart, Adam Wainwright (who struck out Carlos Beltran in the 2006 National League Championship Series to end the Mets' season), allowed a hit.

But in the fourth, while Santana remained unscathed, Wainwright was touched up for two runs. The first came on Lucas Duda's sacrifice fly, the second on Daniel Murphy's run-scoring triple.

While Santana's changeup was confusing the Cards, his command was a bit off; he was striking out batters, but walking them, too. He finished the game with eight strikeouts, along with five walks; he also induced 16 fly balls but only three grounders. Afterwards, Cohen observed that Santana "didn't have his best stuff."

Still, the no-hit bid kept rolling along. Rose, who noted on air in the fifth inning that Santana's rising pitch count meant this was unlikely to be "the night," became so nervous about the possibility of a no-hitter that he departed from his standard approach and did not specifically use the term "no-hitter" until after it happened, not wanting to jinx it (an old baseball superstition). He did indicate in other ways that a no-hitter was in progress.

The Mets put together back-to-back three-run innings in the sixth and the seventh to expand their lead to eight, giving Santana a comfort zone in which he could work quickly. Duda drove in all three runs in the sixth with a homer, while a bases-loaded walk to David Wright and a two-run single by Murphy plated three in the seventh.

Most no-hitters require a dollop of luck or a burst of defensive wizardry, and this game had both. In the sixth, Beltran, in his first appearance at Citi Field since being traded by the Mets in 2011, pulled an inside fastball down the left field line that third base umpire Adrian Johnson ruled foul. The

Cards' third base coach Jose Oquendo, a former Met, vociferously protested the call, and for good reason. TV replays showed that the ball actually nicked the edge of the white foul line, and even kicked up some chalk, making it a fair ball. But since this took place before managers could use replays to overturn missed calls, the umpire's ruling stood. Beltran then grounded out to third.

Some say Johnson's mistake on Beltran's liner somehow undermines or even nullifies the no-hitter, but that is simply not true. Since baseball's beginnings, umpires' fallibility has affected the outcome of games, and even today, their calls of balls and strikes—outside the purview of the replay challenge—can spell the difference between victory and defeat. The call was foul, and the no-hit bid remained intact. "That's baseball," said Rose.

A second threat to the no-no took place in the seventh when Yadier Molina, known for the home run that crushed the Mets in Game Seven of the 2006 NLCS, hammered a drive to deep left field, toward the retired Mets numbers. Reserve outfielder Mike Baxter, who grew up a Mets fan in nearby Whitestone, New York, quickly retreated to the warning track and reached out to his left to catch the ball on the run. But he couldn't stop himself from slamming into the left field wall with his left shoulder and crumpling to the ground, where he remained for a few minutes. He suffered a contusion to the shoulder and had to leave the game; he walked off under his own power to a standing ovation. (He subsequently went on the disabled list and missed two months of the season.)

"When Yadier hit that ball, I just saw Baxter going back and running into the warning track," Santana said in his postgame press conference. "And when he made that catch, I didn't even know it was in his glove. It was great, it was amazing."

Santana reached the 107-pitch mark at the end of the seventh inning. In the dugout, Collins asked him how he felt. His response: he felt good. "And then [Collins] told me that I was his hero," Santana said. "It was a great thing. And then I told him that I was not coming out of the game."

In the eighth Santana issued his fifth and final walk, driving up his pitch count and his manager's anxiety. Collins paid a visit to the mound but left him in. Then Beltran hit a blooper that Daniel Murphy caught in front of second base and the inning was over.

Santana started the ninth as the only Mets hurler since Seaver to take a no-hitter this far. The 27,069 fans were on their feet. He retired his first batter, Matt Holliday, on a one-pitch pop fly to shallow center that Andres Torres (who replaced Baxter) caught on the run. The next batter, Alan Craig, required five pitches before he flied out to left. The crowd kept getting louder. Santana had now thrown 128 pitches, the most in his career. He had only one out to go.

Third baseman David Freese, whose postseason heroics in 2011 won him the most valuable player award in the NLCS and the World Series, came to the plate. On deck was Met-killer Molina. Santana's first three offerings were balls, followed by a called strike. Then Freese slapped a slow grounder into foul territory, to the left of the third base line, for strike two. Fans kept up the volume, clapping their hands, some covering their faces. "You don't have anxiety here?" remarked Mets TV broadcaster Ron Darling.

Santana pulled on the bill of his cap, wiped his chin with his jersey, and took a deep breath. Collins was stone-faced, arms crossed, in the dugout. Then Santana threw his 134th pitch, a deadeye circle change that crossed the plate and dropped into the dirt. Freese lunged for it and missed. Strike three.

Santana pounded his glove and pumped his fist, yelling at his catcher Thole. The fans, finally able to exhale, burst into celebration, jumping up and down and hugging, many raising both arms in triumph.

"*It has happened!*" roared Cohen on TV, still a bit stunned. "In their 51st season, Johan Santana has thrown the first no-hitter in New York Mets history!"

"He's done it!" Rose shouted on the radio, sounding tearful, defiant, exultant. "Johan Santana has pitched a no-hitter! In the eight-thousand and twentieth game in the history of the New York Mets, *they finally have a no-hitter!"* And with a play on his signature line, he added, "Put it in the books, in the *history* books." The call still elicits goose bumps. (Rose told me at spring training in 2014 that he kept a running total of the number of games the Mets had gone without a no-hitter in the upper left-hand corner of his scorebook.)

As Santana hugged Thole, several of his teammates surrounded him in a group embrace near the mound. The bullpen pitchers trotted in and soon Santana was embracing each player individually. Then he waved at and saluted the fans, still celebrating to the sounds of "Smooth," by the band Santana, his warm-up song. Before long, his injured teammate, Justin Turner, limped out on the field and rubbed a towel filled with whipped cream in Santana's face during a TV interview. David Wright followed that by dousing him with champagne during a radio interview.

"It is a surreal feeling here at Citi Field," said Rose, who told me that the no-hitter was the game of his broadcasting life.

Finally making it to the Mets clubhouse, Santana was caught on camera addressing his teammates. "Tonight, we all made history!" he shouted. "You guys make it happen. I was just doing my job, having fun, and yeah baby, we did it!" Whoops and cheers came pouring out of the players.

Later, a more subdued Santana, his shoulder heavily wrapped in ice, put his historic evening in perspective for the media. "To be able to accomplish this is an honor," he said. "I know how much this means to New York and to the New York Mets, and it's definitely something that I'm proud of and I'm very happy to be part of it."

In his postgame remarks, Collins was still a bundle of conflicting emotions. "I'm very, very excited for him," he said. "But if, in five days, his arm is bothering him, I'm not going to feel very good. That's what I told him."

The Aftermath

As an individual event, the first Mets no-hitter stands apart from anything else going on with Santana and the team, and will endure as a shining moment in Mets history.

Johan Santana, after his no-hitter.

AP Photo/Kathy Kmonicek

But in the context of the 2012 season, though the no-hitter put their record at 29-23, it did not transform the team into contenders. The Mets would end the 2012 season 74-88, a record they would duplicate the next year. In 2014, they experienced their sixth straight below-.500 season. Santana's gem turned out to be a glorious but brief respite during a period of considerable struggle that began when they missed the playoffs on the final day of the season in both 2007 and 2008.

Then there's the matter of Santana's health. He pushed well beyond his pitch-count constraints—would that hamper his comeback from surgery, as Collins feared? After the no-hitter, he won three of his next five starts, and had good velocity and arm strength, Mets pitching coach Dan Warthen told Adam Rubin of ESPN New York. But he lost his final five starts, with an ERA of 8.27 across the 10 post-no-hitter games.

He suffered injuries in 2012, but not to his shoulder. In July he was placed on the 15-day disabled list with a sprained ankle, and the next month inflammation in his lower back landed him back on the DL, this time ending his season.

His left shoulder remained intact, until early 2013 when he re-tore his anterior capsule, after possibly pushing himself too hard in spring training. He underwent surgery again and, as in 2011, missed the entire 2013 season. In November 2013, the Mets bought out Santana's 2014 option for $5.5 million, making him a free agent.

Santana signed a minor league contract with the Baltimore Orioles in March 2014 and was invited to spring training. But he never made it to the majors. In June he tore his Achilles tendon during an extended spring training game and missed the remainder of the season. Though he had not announced his retirement as of December 2014, his prospects for 2015 appeared dim.

The general consensus is that, while the 134 pitches he threw in the no-hitter did not help, Santana's health had been in decline and he would probably not have enjoyed much more success as a starting pitcher in 2012 and beyond—even if his pitch count that day had been 19 pitches fewer.

"It's impossible to know if the no-hitter hurt him," Rose told me at spring training. "Even if it did, he didn't have much more left."

Santana himself has dismissed the notion that the no-hitter caused him to reinjure his shoulder. But, if it were possible, would he trade that game for two more healthy years?

What's beyond dispute is that Santana left behind a gift for Mets fans, ridding them of the ignominy of rooting for a team without a no-hitter. (NoNoHitters.com now focuses on the Padres' inability to pitch one.) On the other hand, as Rose pointed out, "What are we going to complain about now?"

We'll think of something, Howie.

Chapter 25

TRAVIS D'ARNAUD

Catcher, 2013-present
Throws/Bats: Right

The Game: August 25, 2013 vs. Detroit Tigers, at Citi Field

METS STATS (THROUGH 2014)	
GAMES:	139
AT-BATS:	484
HITS:	113
HOME RUNS:	14
AVERAGE:	.233
ON-BASE %:	.299
SLUGGING %:	.384
RUNS:	52
RBI:	46
STOLEN BASES:	1
FIELDING %:	.992
WAR:	0.0

The Run-up

Teams see a lot in Travis D'Arnaud.

The Philadelphia Phillies certainly did when they drafted him in the first round of the 2007 draft. He later became the centerpiece of two trades in which a club was willing to give up a pitcher with Cy Young credentials in order to receive d'Arnaud, the rare catcher who can hit.

In December 2009, the Toronto Blue Jays traded two-time Cy Young Award winner Roy Halladay and cash to the Phillies in exchange for d'Arnaud, pitcher Kyle Drabek, and outfielder Michael Taylor.

Three years later, the Mets sent their popular knuckleball pitcher R.A. Dickey, fresh from his Cy Young season, along with two catchers (Josh Thole and Mike Nickeas) to Toronto for d'Arnaud, highly touted pitching prospect Noah Syndergaard, and veteran catcher John Buck.

The Mets have fielded many outstanding catchers in their history, from Jerry Grote and John Stearns in the '60s and '70s, to Gary Carter in the '80s, to Todd Hundley and Mike Piazza in the '90s and 2000s. They are hoping d'Arnaud turns out to be the kind of catcher they can add to that list. If he can stay healthy, he just might.

D'Arnaud, whose older brother, Chase, is an infielder/outfielder in the Phillies organization, grew up in Southern California rooting for Mike Piazza and the Dodgers, and playing for a high school championship team. He began establishing his bona fides in the Phillies' system as a nineteen-year-old, hitting .305 with six homers and 30 RBI in 64 games. He kept progressing, making all-star teams and playing on a single-A championship squad in 2009.

After landing in the Toronto system in 2010, he missed half the season with two bulging disks in his back. But in 2011 d'Arnaud had a breakout year with the AA New Hampshire Fisher Cats as he helped them to the Eastern League Championship with 21 homers, 78 RBI, and a .311 average. For that he was named the Eastern League's Most Valuable Player and its No. 2 prospect.

He put together solid numbers (16 HR, 52 RBI, .333) for Toronto's Las Vegas 51s AAA team in 2012, though he missed a large chunk of time after tearing the posterior cruciate ligament in his left knee while trying to break up a double play.

Having acquired him in the offseason, the Mets got their first look at d'Arnaud, now *Baseball America*'s No. 23 prospect, at spring training in 2013. Though they liked what they saw, he started the season back in Las Vegas (the Mets had taken over the 51s from Toronto). His advancement was stymied in April when he fractured a metatarsal in his left foot, which was struck by a foul ball while he was catching. He didn't return to the 51s until August 9.

Eight days later, though he had only played in 19 AAA games in 2013, the Mets brought d'Arnaud to the big leagues, the sixth rookie to join the club that year. He initially filled in for catcher John Buck, who was placed on three-day paternity leave, and then replaced backup catcher Anthony Recker (who returned in late August when Buck was traded to Pittsburgh).

D'Arnaud's first game took place on August 17 in San Diego, not too far from his LA roots; he walked twice in four trips. Despite his pedigree and minor league accomplishments, he was somewhat stunned to be in the major leagues. "The first game, I still can't believe it happened, you know?" he told me behind one of the batting cages at the Mets 2014 spring training camp. "It's still an unbelievable feeling. I still can't believe I'm here."

Carrying the weight of great expectations, he went about learning the Mets pitching staff and settling into life in the big leagues. He struggled with his hitting over the next six weeks, ending the season with just a .202 average in 31 games. But there were several highlights along the way.

He got his first hit—a "ringing double," as TV broadcaster Gary Cohen described it—in his eleventh big-league at-bat on August 20. "That's what I like about this kid, a good line-drive hitter," said Cohen's co-broadcaster and former Mets All-Star Keith Hernandez.

On September 15, d'Arnaud delivered his first walk-off hit, a single, in the bottom of the 12th, giving the Mets a 1-0 win over the Marlins. Eric

Young Jr. burst out of the dugout to hug d'Arnaud, as the rest of the team followed suit.

"It's been a tough go for Travis d'Arnaud offensively, so anytime you have these kind of moments and can share in the win with your teammates, a big moment there for d'Arnaud," said former Mets pitcher Ron Darling, Cohen's other broadcast partner.

But d'Arnaud's biggest moment as a Met came a few weeks earlier, when he hit his first big league home run, his sole round-tripper of 2013.

The Game

By late August, the Mets were well out of contention in the National League East, hewing to a late-season trend that began their first year at Citi Field in 2009. But there was interest in the team's emerging young players, such as d'Arnaud, the gifted center fielder Juan Lagares, and the spectacular young pitcher Matt Harvey (though he would be shut down with a ligament tear and undergo surgery in October).

On August 25, the Mets played an interleague game against the playoffs-bound Detroit Tigers at Citi Field. Triple-Crown winner Miguel Cabrera, in the midst of another prodigious offensive season, blasted a homer in the first off Dillon Gee to give the Tigers a quick 2-0 lead. The Mets countered in the bottom of the third with an RBI single by Daniel Murphy off Tigers starter Rick Porcello.

With the Mets trailing 2-1 in the bottom of the fourth, d'Arnaud, a right-handed batter, came up with Lagares on first. He took ball one, and then squared up Porcello's next delivery, a sinker, down and in ("Not a bad pitch," Hernandez said later) and pummeled it over the wall in deep left-center field, into the Party City Deck. It was the first homer and second hit of his big league career (he had been 1 for 16), and it gave the Mets a 3-2 lead. Citi Field's massive red home-run apple rose from its moorings behind the center field fence, as it did after every Mets dinger.

"I think I sprinted around the bases, I was so pumped up," d'Arnaud said.

On TV, viewers saw a woman in the Party City Deck standing and holding d'Arnaud's home run ball aloft. Wearing a blue shirt with a No. 31 (Piazza's number) in the center, she let out a hoot of delight and smiled. Soon thereafter she was accosted by a green-shirted Citi Field staffer, who negotiated with her over the ball. She shook her head in agreement. It was later revealed that she exchanged the home-run ball for a d'Arnaud autographed bat and ball.

As a smiling d'Arnaud crossed home plate, he high-fived Lagares, the previous arrival. Walking with expressionless aplomb back to the Mets dugout, he removed his batting gloves, the picture of an even-tempered veteran just doing his job. But that belied his actual state of mind. "That was my most exciting moment," he said. "The most exciting, for sure."

In the dugout, he was warmly greeted by a row of teammates and coaches—Ike Davis, Josh Satin, Young Jr., Wilmer Flores, and Buck among them—high-fiving and getting slapped in the rump and patted on the head. Flores lifted his batting helmet off his head and put it away. Buck high-fived him with both hands and then wrapped him in a tight embrace, which was "pretty cool," d'Arnaud said. He got another hug from Lagares.

Meanwhile, the 32,084 Citi Field attendees were standing and applauding, demanding to see d'Arnaud, who was taken by surprise. "I still can't believe that happened," he said on an SNY spot aired during Mets TV broadcasts throughout the 2014 season. "John Buck actually told me, because I didn't know what was going on. I just thought they were cheering for the next guy." He walked up to the top of the dugout steps, faced the crowd, and raised his cap high above his head.

Unfortunately, d'Arnaud's homer was the apex of the game for the Mets, who stopped scoring at that point. They lost their lead in the sixth on a two-run homer by Andy Dirks, and then imploded in the ninth as the Tigers pounded relievers LaTroy Hawkins and Scott Achison for seven runs. Final score: Tigers 11, Mets 3. But two of the three runs were d'Arnaud's.

AP Photo/Seth Wenig

Travis d'Arnaud rounds the bases after hitting his first home run in the major leagues. It was a two-run shot during the fourth inning of a game against the Detroit Tigers in August 2013 at Citi Field.

The Aftermath

Despite his lackluster start, d'Arnaud was given the Mets' starting catcher's job in 2014. But he continued to struggle offensively, going 0 for 15 to start the season. To make matter worse, he suffered a concussion at Yankee Stadium in May after Alfonso Soriano struck him on top of his catcher's mask with his back swing; he missed more than two weeks.

By early June, d'Arnaud was hitting only .180 with three home runs and nine RBI, and the Mets decided to send him to AAA Las Vegas to regain his swing and his confidence.

The strategy worked. D'Arnaud began crushing the ball for the 51s, batting .436 with 14 extra base hits (including six homers) in 55 at-bats, and was back with the Mets after fifteen days. He attributed his resurgence mostly to a change in attitude. "I took a long look in the mirror and had a good conversation with myself and found myself," he told the *New York Times*.

He also figured out how to improve his concentration. "Just focusing in on every at-bat like it's my last at-bat," he told the *Las Vegas Review-Journal*. "Not thinking about a hundred different things. Just focusing on one thing and keeping a solid approach on each and every pitch. I kind of went away from that [in the majors]."

D'Arnaud may have made some mechanical adjustments as well. Las Vegas manager Wally Backman said that hitting coach George Greer moved d'Arnaud's back foot closer to the plate so that he could reach more pitches.

Whatever worked, d'Arnaud brought it with him in his return to the Mets. In his first game back on June 24 at Citi Field against Oakland, he drilled a three-run homer. That trend continued as he showed a penchant for pulling the ball with authority. He finished the season with a .242 average, 13 home runs (the most ever by a Mets catcher in his rookie season) and 41 RBI. D'Arnaud finally demonstrated the offensive talent that made him such a coveted prospect, someone with the potential to hit 15 to 20 home runs annually—a lot for a catcher.

His defense, however, was still a work in progress. In 2014, he led the league in passed balls with 12. (His defense and offense may have been hampered by a bone spur in his right elbow, which was removed after the season.) D'Arnaud's boyhood idol, Mike Piazza, interviewed by SNY at the Empire State Building in June 2014, advised him "to develop defensively and catch a good game for his pitchers, and do the small things."

Added Piazza: "He's a great kid and I know he's going to be fine. You have to be patient with him. People were patient with me when I was young."

SOURCES

The research for this book was based largely on personal interviews I conducted with former and current players on the New York Mets; the time and place for each interview is noted below. I also consulted with a wide variety of Internet sources on each player; in addition to BaseballReference.com (from which I sourced player statistics), Wikipedia, and YouTube, these are detailed below. Other sources, including book references, are noted as well.

Al Jackson

1. Interview with Al Jackson at Mets 2014 Fantasy Camp.
2. Phone interview with Steve Jacobson, August 2014.
3. Studiousmetsimus.com, "The Best on the Worst: Al Jackson," January 13, 2014.
4. Tcpalm.com, "The 1962 expansion New York Mets were losers, but were loved," by Mark Tomasik, January 22, 2012.
5. Retrosheet.org.
6. SABR.org, Bio Project, Al Jackson, by Greg W. Prince.
7. *The Complete Game*, by Ron Darling, Alfred A. Knopf, 2009.

8. Mets360.com, "Pitch counts and Al Jackson's 15-inning game," by Brian Joura, Dec. 26, 2010.
9. *The New York Times*, "Phils Down Mets in 15th, 3-1, Despite Jackson's 6-Hitter," by Robert L. Teague, August, 15, 1962.

Ed Kranepool
1. Phone interview with Ed Kranepool, September 2013.
2. *Total Mets*, by David Ferry, 2012, Triumph Books.
3. *Daily News, The Mets: a 50th Anniversary Celebration*, by Andy Martino and Anthony McCarron, 2011, Stewart, Tabori & Chang.
4. Ira Berkow interview with Ed Kranepool at the Strand bookstore, 2013.
5. SABR BioProject, Ed Kranepool, by Tara Krieger.
6. BaseballAlmanac.com.
7. Jimmy Scott's High & Tight interview with Ed Kranepool, January 2010.

Ed Charles
1. Phone interview with Ed Charles, September 2013
2. *The Philadelphia Inquirer*, "Ex-Met remembers his boyhood idol and hero," April 10, 2007.
3. Bardball.com.
4. *42*, written and directed by Brian Helgeland, distributed by Warner Bros. Pictures.

Ron Swoboda
1. Interview with Ron Swoboda at Mets 2014 Fantasy Camp.
2. *The Last Icon: Tom Seaver and His Times*, by Steven Travers, Taylor Trade, 2011.
3. NBC pregame show, 1969 Word Series, featuring Mickey Mantle and Sandy Koufax.

4. NBC Coverage of the 1969 World Series, with Curt Gowdy and Lindsey Nelson.

Bud Harrelson
1. Interview at Citi Field, September 2013.
2. *Turning Two*, by Bud Harrelson with Phil Pepe, Thomas Dunne Books, 2012.
3. SNY's June 2012 broadcast announcing the Mets All-Time Team.
4. SABR.org, BioProject, Bud Harrelson, by Eric Aron.
5. Video of symposium on the 50th anniversary of the Mets, held at Hofstra University, 2012.

Felix Millan
1. Interview with Felix Millan by phone, 2013, and at Mets 2014 Fantasy Camp.
2. Interview with Mercy Millan at Mets 2014 Fantasy Camp.
3. Interview with Jane Acevedo by phone, 2013.
4. *Tough Guy, Gentle Heart*, by Felix Millan with Jane Allen Quevedo.

John Stearns
1. Interview with John Stearns at Mets 2014 Fantasy Camp.
2. "Former Mets Catcher Stearns Shedding 'Bad' Name," by Kevin Kernan, *New York Post*, January 16, 2010.
3. BaseballCatchers.com, "100 Best Catcher CS% Totals," by Chuck Rosciam, member of SABR.

Tim Teufel
1. Interview with Tim Teufel at Mets 2014 Spring Training.
2. *Imagine a Mets Perfect Season*, by Howie Karpin, 2011, Triumph Books.
3. *The Philadelphia Inquirer*, June 11, 1986, "Mets Rock Phils on Grand Slam in 11th," by Peter Pascarelli.

4. SABR article on Tim Teufel.

5. Ctpost.com, April 28, 2013, "Mets' run in 1986 'like it was yesterday' to Teufel."

6. Centerfieldmaz.com, "Remembering Mets History: Regular Season Walk-Off Grand Slam HRs," April 6, 2014.

7. SNY interview with Tim Teufel, 2014.

Wally Backman

1. Interview with Wally Backman at Mets 2014 Fantasy Camp.

2. MLB Network's "1986: A Postseason to Remember," 2011.

Mookie Wilson

1. *The New York Times*, "Rewound Mets Back in the Chase," by Murray Chass, October 26, 1986.

2. *The New York Times*, "Even Mets Are Amazed," by Malcolm Moran, October 26, 1986.

3. *The New York Times*, "Red Sox Lose Grip on Vision," by Michael Martinez, October 26, 1986.

4. *The New York Times*, "Bloody Ankle Reminder of a Sorry Night in '86," by Murray Chase, October 29, 2004.

5. *The New York Times*, "I Miss Being on the Field Right Now," by Dave Itzkoff, April 27, 2014.

6. *Mookie: Life, Baseball, and the '86 Mets*, by Mookie Wilson with Erik Sherman, 2014.

7. Interview with Mookie Wilson conducted by Heather Quinlan for documentary-in-process about the 1986 Mets.

8. Interview with Kevin Mitchell by Heather Quinlan for documentary-in-process about the 1986 Mets.

9. MLB.com video on the sixth game of the 1986 World Series.

10. Interview with Mookie Wilson by Keith Olbermann on his ESPN2 show in May 2014.

11. ESPN documentary, "Catching Hell," 2011.

SOURCES

Frank Viola
1. Interview with Frank Viola at Mets 2014 Spring Training.
2. Interview with Frank Viola on SNY Insider, 2014.
3. Interview with Frank Viola, *NY Daily News*, April 2014.
4. *The New York Times*, August 29, 1989, "Viola Defeats Hershiser in First Duel of Cy Young Winners."
5. *The New Yorker*, "The Web of the Game," by Roger Angell, 1981.

Anthony Young
1. Interview with Anthony Young at Mets 2014 Fantasy Camp.
2. DeseretNews.com, "Win Puts End To Young's 'Longest' Losing Streak," July 29, 1993.
3. Metsmerizedonline.com, "This Week In Mets History: Forever Young," by John Strubel, May 10, 2013.
4. SABR.org, BioProject: Anthony Young, by Rory Costello.
5. Examiner.com, "Former RHP Young positive role model for youths," by Stephen Goff, May 7, 2009.

Eric Hillman
1. Interview with Eric Hillman at Mets 2014 Fantasy Camp and on the phone, April 2014.
2. AmazinAvenue.com, "1993: The year the Mets broke."
3. Studiousmetsimus.blogspot.com, "Top 3 Lefty Homegrown Starters."
4. *The New York Times*, "Mets' Hillman on Fast Track," Aug. 27, 1992.
5. *The New York Times*, "Dodgers Are Stymied by Mets and Hillman," July 26, 1993.

Edgardo Alfonzo
1. Phone interview with Edgardo Alfonzo, September 2014.
2. Mets360.com.

Turk Wendell

1. Interview with Turk Wendell at Mets 2014 Fantasy Camp.
2. Baseball Almanac, Turk Wendell Trades and Transactions.
3. *New York Post*, "Former Met loves ranch life, hates 'roids," by Kevin Kernan, May 8, 2010.
4. Sportmedia101.com, Mets 101, Seven in Seven Series, Mets Offbeat Personalities, #1 Turk Wendell.
5. Bleacherreport.com, "Turk Wendell: 10 Reasons to Love the Eccentric Pitcher," by Seth Miller, July 17, 2008.
6. SABR, BioProject, Turk Wendell, by Rory Costello.

Todd Pratt

1. Interview with Todd Pratt, at Mets 2014 Fantasy Camp.
2. SNY, Gary Cohen comment on Todd Pratt during 2014 game broadcast.
3. MLB.com broadcast of Todd Pratt home run in 1999 NLDS.

Benny Agbayani

1. Phone interview with Benny Agbayani, September 2013.
2. The Ultimate Mets Database.
3. *Big League Survivor,* by Benny Agbayani, with Shayne Fujii, Watermark Publishing, 2000.
4. SABR BioProject, Benny Agbayani, by Rory Costello.
5. "Former NY Mets OF Benny Agbayani Coming Up Big Once Again," by Anthony McCarron, *NY Daily News,* April 10, 2010.
6. WFAN, Gary Cohen, broadcast of Benny Agbayani handing ball to fan with two outs.

Bobby Jones

1. Phone interview with Bobby Jones, April 2014.
2. Radio call on WFAN, Bob Murphy, October 8, 2000.

3. CNNSI post-game interview with Bobby Jones, October 8, 2000.

4. Associated Press, "One-Hit Wonder," October 9, 2000.

Mike Piazza

1. *The New York Times*, "Mets Magic Heralds Homecoming," by Tyler Kepner, September 22, 2001.

2. *New York Daily News*, "Sept. 11 family will never forget Mets former catcher Mike Piazza," by Peter Botte, September 28, 2013.

3. *The New York Times*, "Piazza Elicits Smiles Early, and Then a Grimace," by David Picker, August 10, 2006.

4. SNY, June 2012, broadcast announcing Mets All-Time Team.

5. Cable TV Broadcast of Mets-Braves Game, September 21, 2001.

6. Video of Mike Piazza Speech at Commemoration of Shea Stadium's 10 Greatest Moments.

7. Interview with Bobby Cox in MLB.com video.

8. *Long Shot*, by Mike Piazza, with Lonnie Wheeler, Simon & Schuster, 2013.

9. SBnation.com, "So about Mike Piazza's defense," by Rob Neyer, Jan. 21, 2013.

10. BillJamesOnline.com, "Should Mike Piazza be in the Hall of Fame?" by John Dewan, Jan. 11, 2013.

David Wright

1. Interview on SNY's broadcast of the Mets All-Time Team, 2012.

2. ESPNNewYork.com, "Wright Gets Biggest Contract in Mets History," by Adam Rubin, November 30, 2012.

3. *The Newark Star-Ledger*, "Mets David Wright acknowledges club faces important winter ahead," by Mike Vorkunov, August 2, 2014.

4. *The New York Times*, "Wright's Innocuous Slide Precedes a Precipitous Tumble," by Jorge Arangure Jr., August 18, 2014.

5. *The New York Times*, "Mets Are Called Out; Cards Head to World Series," by Ben Shpigel, October 20, 2006.

6. *The New York Times*, "Wright Breaks Out of NLCS Doldrums," by Joe LaPointe, October 16, 2006.

7. *The New York Times*, "Delgado's Four Hits Lead Mets Past Dodgers," by the Associated Press, October 4, 2006.

8. *The New York Times*, "Daffy Days of Brooklyn Return for Vin Scully," by Richard Sandomir, October 5, 2006.

9. *New York Post*, "Look back at the Mets NLCS loss to Cardinals with those who were there," by Mark Hale, October 30, 2011.

10. *St. Louis Post-Dispatch*, "What if Beltran had hit Wainwright's curve?" by Derrick Goold, May 31, 2012.

11. MSG Network, Mets announcer Ted Robinson describing David Wright's bare-handed catch, 2005.

12. David Letterman Show, interview with David Wright, 2006.

13. Ultimate Mets Database

Daniel Murphy

1. Interview with Daniel Murphy at Mets 2014 Spring Training.

2. AmazinAve.com, "Mets trade rumors: To trade or not to trade Daniel Murphy," by Kevin Cassidy, July 31, 2014.

3. *The New York Times*, "Mets' Murphy Discusses Fatherhood at White House Meeting," by Tom Rohan, June 9, 2014.

4. *The New York Times*, "A Changeup Keeps the Marlins Guessing and the Mets' Hopes Alive," by Jack Curry, September 27, 2008.

5. *The New York Times*, "With Santana in Role of Ace, Mets Draw Even for Wild Card," by Ben Shpigel, September 27, 2008.

6. *The New York Times*, "Bitter Repeat on Stadium's Final Day," by Ben Shpigel, September 28, 2008.

7. WFAN's Mike Francesca on Murphy's paternity leave, April 2014.

8. SNY interview with Daniel Murphy on paternity leave, April 2014.

SOURCES

Jon Niese

1. Interview with Jon Niese at Mets 2014 Spring Training.
2. AmazinAve.com, "Jon Niese should reconsider having shoulder surgery," by Nicholas Iorio, August 15, 2014.
3. *The New York Times*, "Mets Breathe Easier as Niese Gets His First Win Since a D.L. Stint," by Seth Berkman, August 11, 2014.
4. *The New York Times*, "Exam Finds No Shoulder Problem for Mets' Jon Niese," by Tim Rohan, February 27, 2014.
5. *The New York Times*, "Niese's Injury Is One Step Back for Mets' Staff," by Andrew Keh, June 21, 2013.
6. *The New York Times*, "Mets Set to Extend Niese's Contract," by Andrew Keh, April 4, 2012.
7. *The New York Times*, "Santana Gets Little Support, Then Niese Needs Almost None," by David Waldstein, June 10, 2010.
8. SNY interview with Jon Niese, 2014.
9. SNY program, "Riding Shotgun with Jon Niese," 2012.

Dillon Gee

1. Interview with Dillon Gee at Mets 2014 Spring Training.
2. MLB.com, "Gee spins gem in unforgettable Majors debut," by Anthony DiComo, September 7, 2010.
3. The Associated Press, article on Gee debut, September 8, 2010.
4. *The New York Times*, "Mets Call-Up Pitches Like Ace in Debut," by Thomas Kaplan, September 7, 2010.
5. *The New York Times*, "Where No Mets Have Gone Before," by David Walsdstein, May 30, 2013.

Johan Santana

1. Interview with Howie Rose at Mets 2014 Spring Training.
2. NoNoHitters.com.
3. *The New York Times*, "Santana, Pushing Past Pitch Count, Throws Mets' First No-Hitter," by Tim Rohan, June 1, 2012.

4. *The Wall Street Journal*, "Johan Santana: The Story of 27 Outs," by Brian Costa, June 2, 2012.

5. *The Wall Street Journal*, "The 8,020th Time's a Charm," by Brian Costa, June 2, 2012.

6. HardballTalk.NBCSports.com, "So, Johan Santana's no-hitter was still worth it, right?" by Matthew Pouliot, August 22, 2012.

7. ESPNNewYork.com, "Johan Santana injury questioned," by Adam Rubin, March 29, 2013.

8. Sports-Kings.com, "Johan Santana: 'I don't think the no-hitter caused my injury,'" by Dave Ragazzo, July 31, 2013.

9. SNY broadcast of Mets vs. Cardinals, June 1, 2012.

10. WFAN broadcast of Mets vs. Cardinals, June 1, 2012.

11. WFAN broadcast of Howie Rose-Gary Cohen conversation about no-hitter, June 1, 2012.

12. SNY broadcast of Johan Santana post-game press conference, June 1, 2012.

13. SNY broadcast of Johan Santana locker room speech to teammates, June 1, 2012.

Travis d'Arnaud

1. Interview with Travis d'Arnaud at Mets 2014 Spring Training.

2. AmazinAve.com, "Are we finally seeing the real Travis d'Arnaud," by Michael Avallone, August 26, 2014.

3. *The New York Times*, "Mets Recall d'Arnaud from AAA," by Zach Schonbrun, June 24, 2014.

4. *Las Vegas Review-Journal*, "Mets touted prospect has confidence back in return stint for 51s," by Todd Dewey, June 18, 2014.

5. *The New York Times*, "Mets Limp Away From Tigers With Rookie's Homer as Biggest Highlight," by Zach Schonbrun, August 25, 2013.

6. SNY broadcasts of Travis d'Arnaud's first hit, walk-off-hit and home run.

7. SNY spot on Travis d'Arnaud's first home run aired during broadcasts throughout the 2014 season.

8. SNY interview with Mike Piazza at the Empire State Building, June 2014,